# BROADLAND SPORT

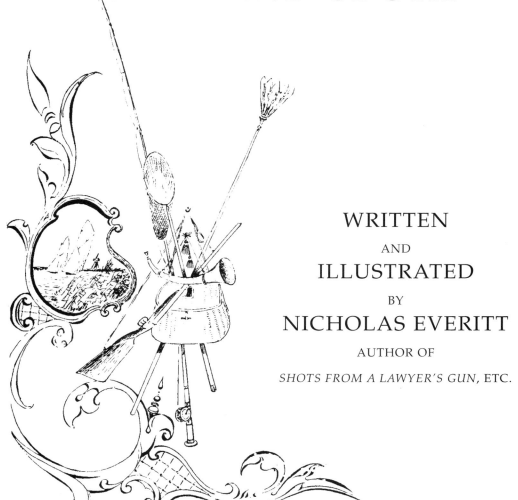

WRITTEN

AND

## ILLUSTRATED

BY

## NICHOLAS EVERITT

AUTHOR OF

*SHOTS FROM A LAWYER'S GUN*, ETC.

First published by R.A Everett & Co 1902
Second facsimile edition  2002

ISBN 1 84114 174 7


**British Library Cataloguing-in-Publication Data**
A CIP record for this title is available from the British Library


**HALSGROVE**
Halsgrove House
Lower Moor Way
Tiverton, Devon EX16 6SS
T: 01884 243242
F: 01884 243325
sales@halsgrove.com
www.halsgrove.com


Printed and bound in Great Britain by
Bookcraft Ltd, Midsomer Norton

TO

# "OUR MASTER"

A SPORTSMAN OF
THE OLD SCHOOL

CURRES AND SHORT-WINGED FOWL.

THIS book has been written with the intention of giving the reader a trustworthy account and description of the sport obtained on and around the lagoons, waterways and marshlands of East Anglia, a district which has been known for many years past by the appropriate name of Broadland.

A great many books have already been published dealing with the Norfolk Broads and the district, but I trust no apology is needed for thus adding to their number, for the present one does not, I venture to affirm, clash with its predecessors in publication—a somewhat bold assertion truly, but one which the title of my book seems to justify, as there has not been, as far as the present writer's knowledge goes, any previous work dealing exclusively with the sports and pastimes in this interesting district, though most, if not all, of the books hitherto published descriptive of this part of the country contain one or two chapters on the subject. Whether the contents of the book justifies its title is a matter which must be left to the kind judgment of its readers.

My facts, I believe, are true to life, and I have endeavoured to the best of my ability to narrate in the following pages the actual experiences of others as well as myself rather than any idle thoughts which might be the outcome of a vivid imagination.

The substance of part of the work has previously seen the light of day in article form which I have contributed from time to time to the pages of *The Field*, *Land and Water*, *The Shooting Times*, *Rod and Gun*, and other periodicals and magazines, and through the kindness and courtesy of the editors of which I am enabled to reproduce them.

Recognising the fact that this is an age of magazine reading, I have here and there introduced short stories founded on fact, in an endeavour to illustrate the better the peculiarities of Broadland sport, which, to many visitors, constitute its greatest charm.

I would thank the many friends who have so kindly assisted me with details and facts not within my own knowledge which especially applies to the chapters on yachting. Amongst them I individualise Colonel H. M. Leathes, Mr T. M. Read, Mr L. E. Bolingbroke, Mr G. H. Lovewell Blake and Mr Richard Fielding Harmer, not forgetting an affectionate parent and a good sportsman of the old school in my father, Mr W. Spencer Everitt.

I owe a debt of gratitude to Mr Russel J. Colman, Mr Edwin Poyser, Mrs A. W. Weldon, Miss M. Pickthall, Mr E. P. Buckworth, Mr R. Lee Barber, Mr G. M. Chamberlin, Mr J. J. Dawson Paul, The Rev. H. Rogers, Mr Ralph Watling, Mr W. S. Parker, Mr H. Johnson, Mr F. Miller, Mr H. Jenkins and Mr Hubert Palmer, for the loan of photographs of yachts or relating to yachting. Also to Mr Herbert Baker for permitting me to reproduce the curious painting in tempora depicted on page 64.

I am extremely obliged to Messrs G. J. and F. W. Skipper, Architects, Norwich, for their kindness in supplying me with the drawing appearing on page 303; also to Messrs

Chamberlin & Smith, Norwich, for allowing me to use an article I wrote specially for them, entitled " Pheasants from Shell to Shot," which is incorporated in Chapter XXV.

I wish to specially mention Mr A. Cecil Taylor as having been a willing and painstaking *collaborateur* in the designing of several of my ornamental illustrations.

To the title of sportsman I rightly or wrongly lay some claim, but to the title of artist-author I can hardly aspire, as my training has been in other channels; should, therefore, the faults and mistakes in my drawings and in my text appear too glaring, I trust some consideration will be shown by my criticisers, when they remember how very few there are who ever attempt the double work of both writer and illustrator combined.

Whilst conscious that the merit of a good deal of the information my book contains is attributable to my friends I cannot forget that on me alone rests the responsibility for its publication, and thus I venture to submit it to the generous consideration of discerning fellow-sportsmen.

NICHOLAS EVERITT.

NORWICH, *May* 1, 1902.

# CONTENTS

## CHAPTER I

### OULTON BROAD AND NEIGHBOURHOOD

## CHAPTER II

### FISHING AT OULTON BROAD

## CHAPTER III

### EELS AND EEL BOBBING

# CHAPTER IV

## SHOOTING AT OULTON BROAD

# CHAPTER V

## DECOYS AND HOW TO USE THEM

# CHAPTER VI

## OULTON BROAD TO GREAT YARMOUTH

# CHAPTER VII

## WILDFOWLING AT SEA

# CHAPTER VIII

## PUNT-GUNNING

# CHAPTER IX

## CURRES AND SHORT-WINGED FOWL

# CHAPTER X

## WILDFOWLING COSTUME

# CHAPTER XI

## SHORE SHOOTING

# CHAPTER XII

## FLIGHTING

## CHAPTER XIII

### GREAT YARMOUTH TO HORNING

## CHAPTER XIV

### A RIVER YACHTING RESORT

## CHAPTER XV

### HORNING TO THE SOURCE OF THE BURE

# CHAPTER XVI
## HICKLING DISTRICT

# CHAPTER XVII
## HORSEY DISTRICT

# CHAPTER XVIII
## THE WAVENEY VALLEY

# CHAPTER XIX
## THE YARE VALLEY

# CHAPTER XX

## YACHTS AND YACHTING DURING THE PAST
### 1800 TO 1880

# CHAPTER XXI

## YACHTS AND YACHTING DURING THE PRESENT
### 1880 TO 1900

## CHAPTER XXV

### PHEASANTS FROM SHELL TO SHOT

## CHAPTER XXVI

### OTTER HUNTING EXTRAORDINARY

## APPENDIX

### THE ORIGIN OF FISH PRESERVATION IN BROADLAND

*CONTENTS*

THE AUTHOR'S DEN

# LIST OF ILLUSTRATIONS

OULTON LOCK AND THE OLD WHERRY INN.

# CHAPTER I

## OULTON BROAD AND NEIGHBOURHOOD

IN these days of progression steam offers such facilities to sportsmen that a trip can be taken to almost any part of the world without an absence of undue length, whilst few are the happy hunting-grounds left unexplored or unvisited. But why is it that those who can often ill afford it travel so far, and incur so much expense for their sport when they have, within a few hours of the great Metropolis, a veritable paradise to the lover of the rod and gun—namely, Broadland. Let us then for the moment imagine that we are worried by the smoke and bustle of the greatest city in the world, that we are sighing for pure air and change of scene, that we wish to leave the cares, the responsibilities, the troubles and anxieties of the daily routine of life far behind, that we wish to enjoy a brief respite which will improve our health, give pleasure and enjoyment, and send us home again with renewed life and energy.

Where shall we go? Where can we humour our wayward fancy within the limits of our purse-strings?

The answer comes as a gentle whisper from the murmuring sea, from the sighing reeds, from the vast expanse of hazy marshes, from the most health-giving resort of the United Kingdom—from " Broadland."

There amusement, pleasure and sport are offered to all. No matter what the hobby may be, or how small a sum at our disposal, Broadland will meet it, and Broadland will provide unlimited interest alike to all comers, rich or poor.

We will then (in imagination) turn our faces towards this promised land, visit its most noted centres, staying for the while where sport can be found, and travelling further afield as the spirit listeth. We will note all we see and hear, chronicling the result of our researches.

There cannot be two opinions as to the best train service to Broadland, so, starting from Liverpool Street with all our paraphernalia and gear enough to stock a small retail sporting establishment, we book a ticket to Carlton Colville, a small station two miles from Lowestoft (the terminus), where we eventually arrive after a three hours' journey and one stop at Ipswich.

Carlton Colville is part of the village of Oulton Broad, and but a hundred yards from the water itself. Should the train not stop and run through to the fashionable watering-place, what matter, it is only a five minutes' run, and a cab or a pony-cart will cover the return distance in twenty minutes for the reasonable sum of 2s. 6d.

The village is well provided with accommodation for visitors. " The Wherry Inn " has almost irresistible charms to offer. The snug little parlour, overlooking the Broad, is a mass of curiosities and trophies of fish, feather and fur; not a spare inch is available; the walls, the tables, the mantelpiece, are all full, and if the day is wet the visitor can amuse himself to his profit and advantage. He will find a facsimile of Pegotty's hut built in miniature from wood taken from the original ; specimens of fish of all species that frequent the neighbouring waters, the like of fowl, and a hundred and one little nicknacks which must be seen to be appreciated.

The best rooms overlook the Broad, and there is no pleasanter spot in the village for the dust-stained traveller than the recesses of a deck chair on the balcony, from which can be seen the ships in Lowestoft Harbour, the shell-fish-gatherer on Lake Lothian flats, and the motley fleet of all sizes, shapes, and rigs of sailing craft that float upon the bosom of Oulton Broad. The sunsets to be seen from this coign of vantage are unrivalled in England. They are quaint and peculiar to themselves, they awaken feelings and instincts in the meditator, they incite the poet and are dangerous to the would-be bachelor in the attractive company of the opposite sex. After sunset, in the cool of the summer's evening, the visitor can take boat and paddle round the yachts, where he will find plenty of life and activity, or he can turn his footsteps to the arcadian bowling - green and participate in the ancient game, or watch its varyings from secluded arbours and leafy bowers.

This word-picture may seem extravagant, but it is not overdrawn.

Then there is " The Commodore Inn," which is also situated on the shores of the Broad. This is not so pretentious an establishment, but it is none the less comfortable. " The Lady of the Lake" also takes in visitors, but " The Waveney " is a more modern inn, with stabling and yachting requisites.

Pleasure boats of all kinds are as numerous as the rowing boats on the waters in the London parks, and one can, at the shortest notice, charter any craft from a sea-going yacht (sail or steam) to the tiniest rowing boat afloat. To all the hotels fishing boats and punts, with professional watermen are attached. Besides these there are many who get their living by letting small craft.

The village, which some facetious wag has nicknamed " Little England," and by which name it is locally known, consists of some three thousand or more inhabitants, and offers much accommodation to choose from. Lodgings, clean, cheap and comfortable, are found in plenty, from well-furnished semi-detached villas to the more humble cottage; from a guinea a room per week to half-a-crown. If this does not suit, the more adventurous and hardier visitor can find quarters on a houseboat or a fishing smack for practically nothing at all, although it may be open to doubt whether there are many who would be so inclined to embrace such opportunities.

The situation of Oulton Broad is unrivalled. The Waveney and the Yare, two of the principal rivers of Norfolk and Suffolk, supply its vast expanse, and the Bohemian tourist has several hundred miles of waterway lying before him, all of ready access. To the north is Oulton Broad Station, on the direct line from Norwich and Great Yarmouth to Lowestoft. To the south Carlton Colville Station as before mentioned. At the easternmost extremity of the Broad is situated Oulton Lock, which separates the fresh water from the salt. Beyond this lock lies Lake Lothian, once part of the Broad itself, but disconnected from it about fifty years ago by a lock. Trains run to and from Lowestoft every half-hour during the season, and almost every hour during the winter. There are several roads and pleasant footpaths to Lowestoft, and the distance can be covered by rail in a few minutes, on foot in half-an-hour, in a pony car in fifteen minutes, and by a rowing boat in twenty minutes. Lowestoft is too well known to need any description, except as regards the sport the town affords, which will be dealt with hereafter.

The fishing on Oulton Broad is distinctly good, and no matter at what season of the year the locality is visited, sport of some kind or other can always be obtained. During January, February and March, pike are on the feed, and good sport is assured unless ice prevents angling. Should this be so there are always large " wakes," or open places, left by the ice-gatherer; the ice-harvest being looked forward to by the poorer inhabitants, who might otherwise go without creature comforts during the winter months. The fish resort to these open places for air, and good baskets are made by those who are enthusiastic enough to brave the cold and try their luck. During April and May little angling is done; at the same time, it is not prohibited, and is free to all. In June, July, August and September, perch, roach, bream and dace bite freely, and can be caught until the angler tires of pulling in the fish. From October to Christmas pike generally claim attention in preference to other fish.

But to return to our imaginary wanderings. We arrive at Carlton Colville Station, where the baggage and kit is left to the care of the obliging stationmaster, whilst temporary lodgings are sought.

We can hardly be called entire strangers to the locality, having visited it before, and profiting by experience we waste no more time than is necessary, but take the road straight to Mutford Bridge, a structure spanning the lock which divides the parish of Oulton from the parish of Carlton Colville. The first bridge built was supposed to have been constructed of timber from Mutford Wood (probably a contraction of Mud-ford), which is one of the largest coverts for miles around, and celebrated for its excellent shooting. This wood lies four or five miles to the south of the lock. As a natural sequence, the hamlet of cottages lying immediately contiguous to the bridge became known as Mutford Bridge, and when the railway was made from Norwich to Lowestoft (by Sir Morton Peto) the station at Oulton was also called "Mutford Bridge," a name which remained unchanged until about 1890, when it was renamed "Oulton Broad."

This bridge is the loafing-ground of the locality, and here all the "know-alls" assemble in great force.

A few minutes' conversation with this interesting group will give us information which would otherwise take a stranger some days to collect by himself, for example:—
What lodgings are to let, what are occupied; who is staying in the village and all about them; the state of the weather, the water, the wind, the tides; the sport, past, present and to come; the boats on the water and the boats that have gone; the new ones built, what they have done and are expected to do; who has been recently married

and who ought to have been; whose family is increased and whose curtailed; in fact, these gentlemen-of-leisure who perambulate the boards of Mutford Bridge seem to know everybody's business and everybody's secrets far better than they do their own, and as they are by no means backward at imparting their information to anyone who consults their opinions with proper respect and a liberal allowance of tobacco and liquid refreshment, a half-hour may be profit-

SOME MEMBERS OF A BROADLAND PARLIAMENT.

ably spent in their company, which is at all times interesting and instructive.

We learn, amongst other things, that a big bungalow has been erected upon the narrow neck of land which juts from the parish of Carlton Colville towards the lock, wherein bunks can be hired, or other accommodation obtained, which a visitor with a sporting turn of mind might wish to know. The rent is low and the conveniences of the residence so elastic that not much time is spent in doubt, and a few moments later we pursue our way southwards, *en route* for the Bungalow.

On the way to the Bungalow "Banker's Shed" is passed, but in vain we seek the familiar faces of the members of the "local Parliament," who, alas! are now no more. They were an interesting batch of old veterans whose pleasure it was to meet regularly every morning in a small tumbled-down harness-maker's shop to discuss local and imperial politics, together with the stirring news of the day.

Seeking the owner of the Bungalow, a bargain is made to the mutual satisfaction of all concerned, and possession is formally taken with a view to a protracted sojourn.

Whilst engaged unpacking the luggage, several chance acquaintances from the bridge drop in to "lend a hand if wanted," which means the dispatch of a messenger to "The Lady of the Lake" for a big stone jar of "mild and sweet" for them to consume whilst they *watch* the unpacking, and at times muster up sufficient energy to handle rods, guns and other paraphernalia as each is exposed to view.

Having completed these preliminaries, arrangements are made with one of the self-invited visitors for a row round the broad in his punt, to which proposition he readily acquiesces, but at the same time shows no inclination to move until the last drop from the stone jar has been drained.

With a natural instinct somewhat akin to the fair narrator of *The Arabian Nights*, he replenishes his glass, relights his pipe, and commences to tell an interesting story concerning a local celebrity, one Jack Sparrow to wit, whose *bonhomie*, deep sporting propensities and dare-devil pranks compelled a liking in spite of contra prejudice, but who has since been called to the happy hunting-grounds beyond the greatest Divide.

As the story may be interesting to the reader it is given *in extenso*.

### JACK SPARROW'S LAST VOYAGE.

Many are the celebrities and heroes of rod and gun that may yet be met with in Norfolk. The subject of the present story was, in his day, numbered, with good reason, amongst them. Jack Sparrow was a born poacher, and, what is more to his credit, a born sportsman. True it is he had a rough-and-ready manner, which was apparent in all his dealings, yet at heart he was good enough, and everything else in life was forgotten by him when real sport could be anticipated.

Jack's great weakness was the bottle; he could not refuse an offer, and thought the best brand of liquids he ever tasted was "other people's." He could not refuse a drink, except, perhaps, it was of water; even then he would hesitate and, maybe, accept it, in the hope that something better would follow—like the dainty dog which eats bread not because he likes it, but from artfulness in attempting to make the feeder believe that he is really hungry.

At the village alehouse Jack was a hero. He could lower a quart without drawing breath; he could thrash anyone within a radius of two miles (a mighty accomplishment in the eyes of other rustics); he could shoot five sparrows out of six from flower-pots at twenty yards, and would bet with confidence upon the result an even bob; he could tickle tench, snare pike, set gins and horsehair snoozes against the best; and last, but by no means least, he could talk politics, tell real genuine lies, and swear any would-be candidate for parliamentary distinction to a standstill.

All Jack's so-called accomplishments have not been enumerated, because to do so would only weary the reader, whilst, on the contrary, this last anecdote concerning him may arouse interest and help to beguile a span of idleness.

Amongst Jack's many patrons was one—a friend of the author's—who had retired from business and desired to lead a secluded life in the precincts of the village green. He purchased, amongst other things, a little house with garden and stabling, a pony-cart, a young retriever, a small yacht, a dinghy, and the necessary equipments of the chase. Then he hired three hundred acres of mixed shooting, and Jack was duly installed as keeper and as general help to the establishment.

To say that Jack was proud of his new position is stating it mildly. He cut many of his former associates—it was well he did so or he might have been dismissed from office sooner than he appreciated—but whether he really cut them, or whether he had come to some secret arrangement was never known. After events seemed to suggest that the ties between them were cemented in private by many and deeper draughts of treble X than his income would admit. Certain it was that Jack's nerves became unsteadier, his face assumed a more bloated appearance as the shooting season advanced, and he seemed to have unlimited cash at his disposal.

Little by little his master became suspicious. Being a man of scrupulous regularity, he always kept everything under lock and key, so Jack's chance of watering the spirits in the cabin of the aforesaid yacht was remote; but he was such a genial and cheery companion that he invariably drew substantial donations from all who were brought into his society, and his master's earliest suspicions were lulled by the opinion that it was from this quarter that Jack obtained his supply of ready money.

Twice a week at least did Jack's master visit some portion of his shoot on which he had a good show of birds in the early part of the season, but very shortly after the opening week the birds seemed to have miraculously disappeared. Several friends, who had begun to get heartily sick of walking the stubbles in the vain hope that the birds had come back again, vowed they would never accept any more invitations, as it was a waste of time, and the ex-poacher-gamekeeper was one day at lunch subjected to a most severe cross-examination by a juvenile aspirant for the Bar. But Jack was such an accomplished prevaricator of the truth that he came out of this ordeal smiling, and quite nonplussed the whole of the party present. He told off on his fingers the wet weather, the drought, the gapes, how some birds had been lost here, others killed there, and in the end quite satisfied his master that he was indeed fortunate to have bagged the miserable five brace and a half that lay before him.

On the way homeward Jack was jubilant. Considering the dressing down he had had his spirits were quite remarkable; he seemed to emulate the immortal Mark Tapley. But the uncertainty of the joys of this life is proverbial, and on opening the evening's letters his master's face assumed a serious expression. One of them was an official communication on blue paper and read as follows:—

> "SUFFOLK CONSTABULARY,
> "FIRTHORPE POLICE STATION,
> "*October*—, 18—.
>
> "SIR,—You will doubtless be surprised to hear that recently several large hampers of game have been sent out by carrier from your village to ——, and taken in by a well-known receiver of poached game. My suspicions were aroused, and I have, after some considerable difficulty, succeeded in tracing the consignments to a man whom I have long suspected of being the associate of poachers. The man is named Jack Sparrow, and I believe you employ him as keeper on the Burnt Hill Farm.
>
> "I shall be glad if you will give me a call and discuss the matter with me.—Yours obediently,        J. B. WIDEAWAKE,
> "*Inspector.*"

Jack's master stared blankly at the letter for some minutes, then he fairly waltzed round the place. To think that he had been thus taken in and his generosity imposed upon drove him nearly mad; and his friends, how they would all laugh at him and say, "Didn't I tell you how it would be when I first heard you had taken on a man like that?" "What could you expect?" "I never heard of an ex-poacher who was any good as a keeper yet." "I don't believe in the old maxim about the best gamekeeper," etc. "Once a poacher always a poacher," and so on. What should he do? At first he thought of a prosecution, but on second thoughts, and as his anger cooled, he determined, for the reasons mentioned, to endeavour to keep it dark if possible, and to drop Mr Sparrow by degrees so as not to arouse people's suspicions.

With this determination he had Jack once more "on the carpet." When he found the game was up and his only

chance of leniency lay in making a clean breast of it, he
threw himself on his knees and implored his master to give
him another chance, explaining the while (with as many lies
as he dared venture on comparatively unknown ground) his
past life, his present sincere repentance and his future
promised good conduct. By this line of action his master's
resolve was strengthened, and on the morrow he visited the
inspector to attempt to hush up the case.

Needless to add that with a little tact with the police
and judicious palm tickling with others he was successful in
preventing the public at large from hearing anything, but it
leaked out among his friends, and sly hints were from time
to time dropped until it was seen how sore the subject was.
Of course Jack was deposed as keeper, but he was employed
as yachtsman, and in other capacities, until his rough-and-
ready trait was brought into conspicuous prominence in a
certain transaction in connection with a pony which brought
about the final *coup de grâce.*

His master's pony died, or rather got so ill that it had
to be killed. Jack knew of another. A beauty, just the
very thing his master required. It belonged to a friend of
his, was quiet, sound, and had no vice. Accordingly, one
bright sunny afternoon in August, the trap was sent away by
train to a station about ten miles distant, the master and Jack
accompanying it.

On arriving at the station they found the pony waiting. It
looked all right, and trotted well up the road in a halter.
After the usual haggle a bargain was struck and the pony
was taken for a week on trial. It was harnessed, and the
pair proceeded to drive home.

After the first mile the pony refused to go any further,
and no amount of persuasion or blows would move it an
inch.

At last Jack hit on a brilliant idea. He would tie a small
bundle of dry grass to its tail with the remains of a box of
fusees in the middle. He would then set light to it. *He had
never known that to fail !* It was done, and both were seated

in the trap in readiness for the start. As soon as the grass began to burn the fusees caught fire. One spluttered on to the pony. Down went its head, up came its heels, and out went the bottom of the trap; then away it dashed at full gallop.

The master let go the reins; Jack tried to get hold of them, and in so doing he was thrown out and left, whilst the master was borne away in a cloud of dust, frightened out of his wits. He continued his wild career for about a mile, when what was left of the trap was upset by a stone heap, and, very much bruised and shaken, he was conveyed home in a milk-cart that luckily happened to be passing. After this, having settled the bill with Jack's friend, he turned his back upon Jack Sparrow for ever. The mere mention of his name was enough to put him in a temper for the rest of the day; more often than otherwise for a longer period.

Jack Sparrow was once more dependent upon his wits for a living, as he was one of those who never did a real day's work in his life.

Now there happened to be living, a few doors from his cottage, an honest, hard-working little widow, whose husband had recently died leaving her to provide for several very young children, and Jack conceived the idea that "he might as well hang up his hat behind her door" as anyone else. He did not consider the matter long, and a fortnight after the above-mentioned episode, Jack was stepfather to the little ones, whilst the ex-widow had another large appetite added to the family board.

For some months Jack passed his time prowling round with a gun, picking up whatever came in his way, and spending all he could lay his hands on at the pot-house of his choice.

One wild and stormy afternoon he went as usual up the Broad for the flight. His fowling punt was at best both small and leaky, and on this, his last trip, the three occupants (himself, friend and dog) were all too large a cargo.

By means of skilful navigation and constant bailing they arrived at the entrance to the river in safety, but as the evening advanced the storm increased in violence, and they would have been wiser had they left their boat at the top of the Broad and walked home. Sportsmen, however, do not know the meaning of the word fear, and Jack was the last to turn back because "white-horses" rolled over the surface of the Broad. He had confidence in his boat, still more confidence in himself, and he ridiculed the bare idea of the suggestions of his companion. Sport having proved a disappointment perhaps made him reckless, or perhaps it was that they had extended their trip as far as Burgh Staithe (two miles up stream), where refreshment was obtainable. Anyhow it was some hours after flighting time before the passage of the Broad was attempted. It was then quite dark and the difficulties of safe navigation considerably increased. The storm lashed the water with fury, and rain descended in torrents. It was all they could do to keep the punt end-on to the rolling billows, any one of which would have instantly swamped her had she been allowed to veer sideways. As fast as they bailed the water out of her more came in from the leaks, the rain and over the bows in the form of spray. They were in the thick of it now, and there was no chance of return, as the fringe of reeds and rands * round the edges of the Broad would hardly admit a landing. "Borrow's Ham" had been safely navigated, Carlton Ham avoided; they had only 300 yards to cover before the welcome shore would be gained. They struggled desperately on with their teeth set and straining every muscle of their bodies to reach the haven of refuge and to beat the elements of nature in the unequal contest. Suddenly, to their horror, the boat gave a violent lurch, and immediately filling with water sank under them. When they rose to the surface they saw a light twinkling from

* Soft, boggy marshland.

the southern shore, and silently swam towards it, encumbered
as they were by thick clothing, heavy boots, and oilies
(waterproofs).

They had not gone far when poor Jack gasped out,
" I'm done for," and the waters he had loved so well, and
all his life defied, closed over his head and claimed him as
their own.

His companion reached the shore, how he never knew :
but numbed with cold, and more dead than alive, he managed
to crawl to the light they had seen, and he frightened the
female occupants of the house almost into a fit when he
presented himself.

A search party was immediately organised but Jack
Sparrow's body was not recovered until two days afterwards.

Poor old Jack ! many is the time the author has been
out with him, and many a yarn he has listened to from
the lips that will move no more. With all his faults he
was a right good sort in his way, but it was a way which
only sportsmen could tolerate ; even to them he was, at times,
a sore trial.

\*        \*        \*        \*        \*        \*        \*        \*

By the time this narrative was concluded the visitors had
been successful in finishing the contents of the stone jar, and
as there seemed no intention of a refill, they made a
move towards the door.

It is evening. The sun is sinking behind the Fishrow
Hills, causing the dark tops of the Scotch fir trees, which
peep over their brow, to give the appearance of a ridge of
rocks. The Broad lies calm and tranquil, except where a
few swans and ducks disturb its bosom, or idlers in boats are
drifting in a listless manner to and fro. The yachts have
laid to and made up for the night. The wherries are unable
to proceed, except with the assistance of the unwieldy quant,
and the wind has died away to a whisper, which is usual in

Broadland at sunset. From one end of the Broad comes the lowing of cows faintly echoed from the marshes beyond Whitecast; from the other the noise of children playing in the street, or bathing in the sheltered bays. We as visitors are enchanted beyond measure—how can we fail to be otherwise?

We drift with other idlers through the fleet of yachts, round the quaint old warehouses with barges and wherries moored to their quays, in and out of silent bays, and past gardens which abut upon the water's edge, noting everything and everybody.

Our oarsman is an interesting specimen of East Anglia. He is a professional yachtsman according to his own description; an unknown quantity according to ours. His age might be anything from forty to eighty years. He tells how he has witnessed more fish caught, more fowl killed, more exciting races with yachts and rowing boats, more hairbreadth escapes from drowning and other accidents, and knows more about everything connected with that neighbourhood than any man living. We are interested listeners, and do not interrupt the flow of his conversation, except now and again to inquire upon the merits of a likely-looking swim, or a corner for wildfowl. He well earned all the beer and baccy given to him, for which the soul of every Broadland waterman (not a Blue Ribbonist) seems to yearn.

Having beguiled several hours of supreme enjoyment in this manner, it behoves us to move a question of inquiry respecting the morrow—What to fish for, and where to fish? The debate is not a long one, and it is soon arranged that we shall try in the early morning for some of the perch, which are reported to exceed 4lb., but in reality rarely reach half that weight. Four a.m. is the hour fixed for the sortie to meet at Banker Gooch's shed, where everything is to be in readiness, including a patent cooking apparatus for early morning coffee.

The Broadland mists, now beginning to rise, add a weirdness to the scene which we feel both loth and glad to leave.

However, it is getting cold, and there is much to be attended
to at the Bungalow, so, directing a course towards the land-
ing-place, we are soon threading our way up the moonlit
street of the village towards our temporary home. One last
pipe, one last nightcap, then in dreams we struggle with
Leviathan perch, the like of which Broadland waters have
never seen, and the whirr-r-r of the small alarum clock seems
to call us from our slumbers before we have begun their
enjoyment. It is four o'clock, but we turn over in bed for
another half-hour, and do not reach the quay until nearly
5 a.m.

EVENTIDE.

# CHAPTER II

PERCH. Perch. Perch.

These are the magic words which tingle in our ears as we emerge from the Bungalow.

What a lovely morning it is! The air is fresh and invigorating; there is a gentle ripple on the water such as anglers love, and the wind is in the right quarter.

The rods are stowed on board, baskets, bait cans and paraphernalia. Then a hitch occurs. Shrimps are scarce, and on this water shrimps are considered the best bait for perch.

Whilst in the very act of grumbling on the quay the fresh-water shrimper is hard at work, with a large landing net, shrimping round the edge of a stone embankment, and we hasten to see if his early morning efforts are productive of success.

On joining him he smiles a knowing smile and points to the fish kettle, saying he has more than we shall want for that day, at least, which fact a hasty inspection confirms. There, under a spray of green weed, are dozens of the small crustaceans; our hearts rejoice, and blessings are invoked upon the head of him who but a few moments before we were prepared to verbally consign to a period of torture.

These shrimps are a peculiar race in themselves. They emanate apparently from Lake Lothian, coming through the lock and thriving in the brackish waters of the easternmost end of the Broad, where they breed in myriads, and appear to do well. Perch are very fond of them, and prefer them to almost any other kind of food. They are easily caught in a small-meshed landing net, or in old baskets filled with weeds and stones, and sunk, in which baskets they readily take up their quarters.

Having transferred the fish kettle to the boat, a course is steered past the ice-house towards the abandoned fishing vessels, of which there are all too many lying in the Ham or bay ensconced by the Great Eastern Railway Company's embankment near to Oulton Broad Station. In rowing there we have to thread our way through a fleet of craft of all dimensions, lying moored to promiscuous buoys and anchorages, put down haphazard, without any regard to law, order or navigation.

Arriving opposite to the ice-house we make for the nearest smack. The *Saucy Jane* belies her name; she is neither gay, pretty, nor enchanting; nevertheless we board her and put the rods together upon her roomy and dismantled decks. During the winter she is loaded with ice, which indignity may have dispelled all her present claims to sauciness. It matters little, we do not give the subject a second thought, we are busy impaling a lively shrimp upon the perch hook, and a moment later drop him quietly over the starboard quarter into the dark and silent water passage which ebbs and flows between her grass-grown planks and those which similarly adorn the *Blue Belle*. A mental note of the number and direction of the rusty chains lying out aft has been made, and should we get a bite, we know within a little how to play the fish for the clear water.

One of the party wanders further afield. The *Saucy Jane* has no charms for him, and later he perches himself high on the rotten bulwarks of a broken-masted coal ketch.

Half an hour passes and no sign of fish. One angler becomes disheartened and adjourns for coffee, but no sooner do the inviting fumes arise from the cooking apparatus than suddenly his rod, which has been left balanced on the bulwarks, gives an animated jump. In the excitement the stove, coffee and condensed milk can is upset, and an election becomes compulsory—not between the devil and the deep, but between a $\frac{3}{4}$-lb. perch and an action for damages for the destruction by fire of other people's property. The ship is saved but the fish is lost, as well as a new gut trace by *Farlow*.

But another scriggling shrimp is softly dropped into the swim, and almost before the dainty morsel has touched the surface of the water a perch has snapped it, whilst the green and white float disappears into the uninviting depths with a vicious dive which thrills the nerves and, at the same time, tells us that the fish is a heavy one. In a few minutes the struggle is over and a beautifully-marked perch (which subsequently pulled the scale at $2\frac{1}{4}$ lbs.) is jumping in vain upon the grimy deck. Such a beginning is encouraging, and for half an hour the sport is as good as the heart of angler can desire. During this time twelve fish are landed, the smallest 6 oz., the largest the one first mentioned, whilst their average weight is about $\frac{3}{4}$ lb. Besides these, several others are lost, as well as three traces on the chains and ropes which run out in all directions around. But anglers' joys are fleeting and the shoal of fish leaves as suddenly as it came. When perch stop biting like this it is little use continuing on at the same swim, but success generally causes one to linger, and for another hour we fished and hoped in vain.

We have, however, no cause to regret the early rising, and can crow over less energetic anglers whom we observe commencing business long after the sun is high in the heavens, generally, as in this instance, with less success. At 10 a.m. a return is made for breakfast, and by twelve we are anchored about twenty yards from the reed beds, just outside the fringe of white-flowered weed on the point of what is known as Carlton Ham. Here will be found at low water almost a seven-foot plumb, with a long stretch of hard gravel bottom, and one of the best perch swims between the Horseshoe Point and Mutford Lock; but although we fished continuously until five o'clock in the afternoon, little was added to the take of the early morning.

Perch fishing is at all times precarious—even on Oulton Broad one cannot always command success—but, taking one day with another, and given favourable circumstances, better bags are made here than on many other public waters, whilst there is always the satisfaction of knowing that the fish are there in quality as well as in quantity and in size—if one can only get amongst them.

Referring to the plan the reader must understand that "J" represents jack and pike; "P," perch; "B," bream. The places of note and landmarks are named. The dotted lines show shallow water and mudbanks, whilst the whole map is compiled from memory with a view to assist the intending visitor rather than to accurately represent the district. With this map, and the directions to be obtained on the spot, it will be the visitor's own fault if sport is not obtained.

The best swims for roach, perch and bream are from A to B, which includes the southern shores of Carlton Ham from the entrance to Oulton Dyke (on the west) to "The Point," from C to D at the south-eastern corner of the Broad, and from E to F running round Borrow's Ham and the northern shores to the fleet of dismantled fishing craft near the Great Eastern Railway Company's embankment.

In fishing, the boat should be moored, fore and aft, about twenty yards from the shore, just outside the fringe of weeds which are conspicuous during the summer and

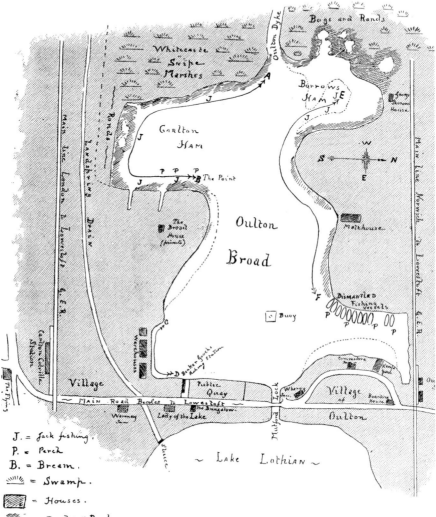

J. = Jack fishing.
P. = Perch
B. = Bream.
= Swamp.
= Houses.
= Reeds & Rushes

autumn months. In the spring and winter, when the weeds
have died down, a position can be taken up nearer to the shore.

Like a church, the Broad lies east and west ; the sea-water from the German Ocean washes one side of the lock, which in summer is open and shut so often that the water at the end of the Broad is decidedly brackish.    When the water is at flood in the Broad it is at ebb in Lake Lothian, and *vice versa.*

In fishing for pike and jack in winter, the nearer one fishes to the yellow reed stems, in reason, the better are the chances of success.    Roach, bream and perch fishing are carried on in almost the same manner, with slight local peculiarities, in all parts of England, therefore it is not necessary to describe the fishing in detail, beyond the fact that in Norfolk the " takes " are estimated at so many stone, not in exact weights as elsewhere.

In fishing for pike the fishing of other counties is differed from in that the dodges utilised are so numerous and ingenious that it is a wonder there are any fish left to be caught, whilst it seems incredulous that they are proved to be on a decided increase (rather than a decrease) as every year goes round.    Borrow's Ham and Carlton Ham are the most celebrated places in the locality for pike fishing.    Many is the twenty pounder that has tested the angler's skill in days gone by, and many there are still left exceeding that weight which lurk in the reedy nooks ready to do battle again.

We were one day attracted by the movements of a small boy who was wading up-stream in the spring drain which flowed from the freshwater marshes of the Carlton level in the Waveney Valley through a sluice gate into Lake Lothian.

It was a fine evening, there was nothing better to do, so we leant at ease upon the boundary wall of the street over the archway, by means of which the drain runs under the high road, and watched the youthful angler, in company with the large crowd there assembled, with considerable interest.    Whilst thus intent in following his movements several inhabitants of the village joined the crowd, and from them we gleaned plenty of information on the subject.

The youth was " butt spearing," and during the twenty minutes he operated near the archway, he took no less than thirteen good-sized fish as well as three small eels.

## BUTT SPEARING

is a sport that is obtained on saltings and tidal estuaries, and is very good fun whilst it lasts. Breydon Water and Lake Lothian afford good facilities if the visitor will trouble himself to find out the ways and means.

Butts are flat fish which also go by the name of flounders and dabs. Flounder is possibly the correct name, but in Broadland they are called butts. Almost all the year round the sport is in vogue, varying, of course, according to the time of tide, the weather, and other circumstances.

When the tide is ebbing and the flats are bared, the overflow from the backwaters finds access to the main channel through countless runs which everywhere dissect the ooze. It is in these runs the butts are found, and the spearer works his punt up them, covering all the likely banks and well-known haunts in a similar manner to that in which the eel spearer goes to work. A butt spear is, however, dissimilar

BUTT SPEARS

in shape to, and considerably lighter in make than an eel spear ; the prongs are wider apart, and each is capable of securing a fish, instead of catching them wedged in between two of the prongs, as eels are caught.

Spearing from a boat is not the only way in which butts are speared. In some places a landspring drain runs into the saltings through sluice gates, which work automatically. They open as the tide on the salting ebbs, and the force and weight of the fresh water (accumulated in the drains beyond)

proves greater than the salt water on the outer side; closing
in a reverse manner when the flood rushes up from the sea.

Often these landspring drains have a hard bottom, and
the butts love to make their way up against the strong-
running stream. This affords the spearer a favourable opportunity. At about half-ebb the depth of the stream will
probably not exceed a few inches, and it is then easily
waded.

The spear on these landspring drains is generally discarded in favour of a common kitchen steel fork, for reasons
which the reader will soon discover. With pail, fish-can,
or bag (having a prepared mouth) slung on his side, or on the
back, the fisher enters the stream as near to the sluice gate
as he can.

He generally wades barefooted, as butts are at all times
difficult to see, lying on the bottom of the stream slightly
embedded in sand or mud, the colour of which their upper
surface or back most closely resembles, and by wading barefooted the fisher can feel with his feet quite as many as he
will see; if he treads on a butt and then stands quite still
he can with his fork feel the centre of the fish and drive
the fork through it. By putting one or more fingers on
the under side of the fish, he raises it from the water without fear of losing it. It is then deposited in the carrier, and
he proceeds on his way up stream.

As he wades along the running stream takes away all
the discoloured water which is disturbed by his feet, which
would otherwise obscure his view, thus giving him a clear
field for operations. Zigzagging his course, he does not pass
a bunch of weeds or a mass of *débris* which may be caught
by an overhanging briar or bough, but he carefully dissects
it with his fork, and spears any fish lying under it which he
thinks worthy of capture.

In this manner eels of good size, butts, small jack and other
fish are taken; in a couple of hours (the turning of the tide
rarely permitting a much longer fishing) the author has
caught nearly a pailful of good-sized fish of several varieties

In wading like this the spear is not of much use, the handle is somewhat long, eels cannot be taken with it, and a fork will be found more wieldy and more advantageous all round. There is one drawback to wading. Thorns are in almost every stream of this kind, whilst glass bottles, broken crockery and flints are apt to lacerate the feet, and a butt coming down stream at full speed gives a blow to the naked shin which would upset any nigger and severely punishes a white man.

Taking it all round, butt spearing, whether by wading or from a boat, is an interesting sport, and to those who have never indulged in it there is the extra attraction of its novelty.

BROADLAND TALISMANS

# CHAPTER III

### EELS AND EEL BOBBING

In Broadland the natives use the provincialism "bab" and "to go a babbing," but as the sport is generally known by the name of "bobbing" the author has used that term in preference.

Bobbing is practised by almost every native of East Anglia living near to any of her waterways. The spring is the most favourable time, and it is a fishing which is conducted generally by night. When a bobbing excursion is contemplated, the bobs are the first requisite, and these must be used fresh if success is to be assured. A large quantity of lob worms are necessary to make a good bob. They (the worms) are kept in an ordinary flower-pot or similar utensil, with some damp moss and a little earth in which they can burrow. Worsted yarn is used, and the

26

worms are threaded with a needle from end to end upon
the yarn in a continuous string until long enough to bunch
up sufficiently for the purpose required. This string of
worms is about two yards in length and is bunched up and
tied so that each loop which hangs downward is equal in
length from the top. A lead of pyramid shape, about six
ounces in weight, is used as a sinker, and is fixed to the
bobbing line, immediately above the worms. This forms the
bob, which as a whole much resembles an ordinary tassel in
shape. The line consists of good stout cord, its length being
regulated by the depth of water in which it is to be used.
The length of the bobbing pole (generally a straight rod)
is about four or six feet. Should the line be found too long
when bobbing, the bobber simply turns the pole round and
round in his hand until a sufficient quantity of the line is
rolled at the far end of the pole, which shortens it to the
required length.

The way in which lob worms are procured is interesting
if not amusing to those who participate in it. On a dark
night the worm catcher sets forth with a lantern, throwing a
strong light in one particular direction—the pattern known
as the bull's eye lantern is best fitted for this purpose. With
the lantern and a small can in his left hand, in which to place
the worms, he goes to the nearest pasture or lawn where
lob worms are supposed to frequent. Walking with stealthy
steps, he casts the full glare of the lantern upon the ground,
which enables him to see the worms lying on the surface of the
pasture amongst the roots of the grass. When he sees one he
must be exceptionally sharp in catching it before it manages
to wriggle back to its hole. Lob worms are very much
quicker at this than one at first would imagine, and unless
the catcher proceeds in a thoroughly business-like manner he
will have to work several hours before he obtains a sufficient
number to form an ordinary-sized bob. On the other hand,
to the onlooker it appears extraordinary how easily the
worms are taken by anyone who is expert at the business. In
a very short space of time far more worms are caught than

are required, should circumstances and weather be favourable. Although it is difficult to dig them from the soil, there is another plan which at times proves successful. It consists in a simple expedient. Mix a pailful of mustard and water, or weak lime and water, and pour it, with the assistance of a watering-pot with a rose spout, over the lawn or grass where lob worms are known to abound; such a dressing will often bring them to the surface in a few minutes.

Having now briefly turned to bobs and how they are made, we will describe the evening's bobbing.

Some two hours after the sun has sunk to rest, and the mist is covering the reed tops and rising from the marshes, we proceed to the edge of the Broad, where a boat is lying in readiness. The old Suffolk marshman is sitting there in waiting, his short black pipe between his lips, from which he silently draws his peaceful puffs, and rests content with all the world. Our overcoats and other belongings having been taken on board, not forgetting the stone jar and the whisky bottle, we push off from land and punt down a muddy creek *en route* for the open water. Rowing across the Broad many others may be noticed bent on a similar errand. They, like ourselves, are heading for the river's mouth, which is looked upon as one of the best swims in the neighbourhood for the purpose in question. Before we arrive at the place where it is agreed to make the first attempt, we are enshrouded in a dense marsh mist, through which it is difficult to find a way, but, with the instinct of his race, the old marshman makes his destination, and, planting two poles firmly in the mud, secures the boat fore and aft in readiness to commence operations. We are moored on the outskirts of a reed bed at the entrance to the river, and notice that down-stream several other boats are already engaged seeking to lure the eels to destruction by the fascinating temptation of a fresh bunch of worms.

An inquiry from them as to what sport they have had elicits a reply that " the eels are biting freely, though they *don't fare to hang well "*— the meaning of which expression will soon become apparent to the reader.

Having sampled the stone jar and lit pipes, we unroll the bobs. The depth of the water is not more than four feet, the bottom seeming to consist of hard mud. Clearing the rowlocks and all impedimenta from the gunwale of the boat, we take up our positions fore and aft, and, dropping the bobs overboard, as near to the side as they will conveniently go, commence proceedings. The bobs sink to the bottom immediately, and, rolling up the slack of the line, we bob with the end of the poles within a few inches of the surface of the water. At first the bob is allowed to rest on the bottom, but this is simply in order that the exact depth may be conveniently gauged. Having done this, the bob is raised two inches from the bottom and kept in constant activity by a smooth, regular, up-and-down movement. This causes the bunch of worms which forms the bob to dilate and expand by reason of the resistance of the water, and when there is any doubt as to the depth we are fishing, we bring the bob in contact with the bottom.

It is not long before a vigorous tug tells us that an eel is at work. As soon as this is felt the bob is brought to the surface of the water with a steady, even pull, at the same time keeping a regular pace upon the movement, which is continued until the bob is brought over the boat, and a scriggling eel, whose teeth have stuck in the worsted yarn, and who fails to let go until he finds himself dangling in mid-air over the bottom boards of our boat, is brought to bag.

The bob is reinserted into the water, and as time goes on we get many more bites, our bob being as often in the water as it is out, but, as our friend remarked in the early part of the morning, "they do not fare" (*Anglicè*—seem) "to hang well this evening," and we find we do not land more than one eel for every five or six bites. Besides, those caught are so small in size that we decide to try our luck in fresh waters.

Pulling out the mooring stakes we row down the river some half-mile or more, to a place where the stream divides, and the entrance to a backwater gives us hopes of better sport. Moving some five or six yards from the rand, fortune

BOBBING AT NIGHT.

is once more tempted in a similar manner to that before described, and on this occasion with more success.

For ten minutes we sit with very poor luck, and are discussing the advisability of leaving for another quarter, when the eels commence to bite. Not only do they bite, but they seem to hang with a pertinacity which is astonishing. Often we have to drop the bobs several times upon the bottom boards before they can be induced to let go, and two at a time is by no means uncommon. On several occasions three eels are pulled up together, although we do not always land them in the boat.

Having enjoyed excellent sport for upwards of three-quarters of an hour the eels seem to leave as suddenly as they came, and although we remain in the same place for another half-hour, we do not secure sufficient to tempt us to linger any longer.

Returning to the Broad, we lay-to near a reed bed, which is dissected by a broad dyke leading up to an over-grown pulk hole,* where we obtain very fair sport, although nothing like so good as that obtained near the entrance to the backwater. But one eel captured here amply repays our patience, and subsequently pulls down the scale at nearly a pound weight. When hauling him on board we could not help thinking our bob had caught in some large bed of weeds, of which there were a quantity in the immediate neighbourhood, as the pull seemed so inanimate.

As it was now well past midnight, we thought it advisable to make tracks for home to tumble in between the sheets.

Was it the night air or the liberal potations from the stone jar and whisky bottle that made us so sleepy? In our belief we incline to the former, but in any event we lean back in the comfortable stern-sheets, listening to the regular measure of the oars as they disturb the surface of the Broad, and to the weird cries of the waterfowl from the reed beds and swamps beyond, where they were now revelling in the full enjoyment of perfect security from their many enemies. In this position we almost fall asleep, and dream that we are miles away in other latitudes.

Suddenly a crash arouses us and we start to our feet, under the impression we have struck a stake and may have the enforced indulgence of a cold swim before coming to the shore; but our old friend assures us there is no occasion for alarm—that we have merely bumped against a yacht's moor-ing, which proved us to be not far from our destination. He is right in his prophecies, and a few minutes later we are

* A small pond in the swampy reed margin of a broad.

once more following the dyke to the landing-stage. The
short tramp home awakens us too much to our liking, and
when we do get between the sheets we have some difficulty
in obtaining the sleep we so much desire.

Next morning, after a substantial breakfast, we go to the
landing stage to view the catch of last night. Two or three
bucketfuls of water had been thrown into the boat, the bottom
of which now looked alive with slimy, scriggling eels varying
from the size of a lead pencil to the one a pound in weight
before mentioned. In all there were some five or six stone—
no unworthy catch, my masters, considering the time spent in
bobbing.

Having taken sufficient eels to suffice for home consumption we presented the rest to the old marshman, who informed
us that he stored them in trunks until he had a sufficient
quantity to send to the London markets, where they brought
him from 3d. to 6d. per pound.

Such is a description of bobbing in Norfolk and Suffolk
waters. The sport varies in accordance with the district, the
time of year and the state of the weather. Almost anywhere
in Norfolk bobbing may be indulged in, and at almost any
time, except when the eels are embedded in the mud during
the winter months.

Not much skill is required to take some eels by the process
of bobbing, but the more one sees of the sport the better is one
likely to appreciate it and become a strong advocate in its
favour. On saltings good bobbing can be obtained, and the
eels form an excellent dish—the discussion of which some
consider by no means the least enjoyable part of the business.

Although there are several kinds of eels, the two species
most abundant in Broadland are the Sharp-nosed Eel
(*Anguilla Acutorostris*) and the Broad-nosed Eel. The
former is much appreciated for table, but it is not so
voracious, nor does it attain so large a size as the other
species. It is mostly taken by the eelmen in nets, which
are stretched across the river in various parts of Broadland,
and are called " eel setts." At certain periods of the year,

when eels migrate to the sea, many of them are thus taken. Breydon Water is a favourite place for eels, especially during the winter, when they hibernate in the mud. The largest specimen recorded was taken in May 1839, and was upwards of 20lb. in weight. Another was recorded from the fens of Cambridge, which bore down the scale at 25lb.

The other species of eel referred to is the Broad-nosed Eel (*Anguilla Laterostris*), which is more voracious than the Sharp-nosed Eel, but is not anything like so good for eating purposes. These eels are also taken in the eel setts during migration, but are not so regular in their habits as the sharp-nosed variety, and they are more often taken on eel lines and in osier traps, which are both freely used for the purposes of their capture.

It is wonderful how eels will travel over land from one water to another, and how they will surmount obstacles which would be thought most difficult to climb, unless weeds, grass or moss growing thereon assisted them to wriggle upwards. It has been said that they will surmount sluice gates three or four feet high if there is any quantity of grass on them.

EEL SPEARS.

Eel spearing is much in vogue upon the rivers and Broads of East Anglia. During the winter months, when the eels are lying asleep in the mud banks, the watermen and marshmen, using a spear made especially for the purpose, diligently probe all likely spots, capturing a large quantity of eels, which at that time of the year are in good demand at most of our large markets.

On Oulton Broad, Breydon Water, Lake Lothian, and many other places, a number of eel-spearers may be seen at work almost any day throughout the winter. Standing at one end of their small boats, they thrust their long spears (the hafts of which are about twelve or fifteen feet in length) again and again into the mud, constantly drawing them to the surface to see whether they have been successful in securing a prize. The boat is kept in position by the spear so constantly coming in contact with the ground, and in this manner they work along the mud banks where the eels are thought to be lying

When ice covers the water so that spearing from a boat is impossible, the eel spearers often cut holes in the ice over the favourite mud banks, through which openings they use their spears to their advantage and profit. Selling the eels for about 4d. per pound, many men are thus enabled to earn from 10s. to £1 per week, which is very acceptable when other work fails; but the majority of eel spearers are watermen and marshmen, who gain most of their money during the summer months, and during the winter—the off season—they are only too glad to obtain what money they can by eel spearing, wild-fowl shooting, or at the ice harvest.

AN EEL-SPEARER AT WORK.

# CHAPTER IV

## SHOOTING AT OULTON BROAD

A COCKNEY WILDFOWLER.
("Any duck abart?")

XCELLENT sport was to be obtained in the precincts of Oulton Broad with dog, boat and gun. In days gone by there were several inhabitants in the quaint little waterway village who gained their sole means of livelihood from fish and fowl. That was before the railway came and before steam drainage mills were heard of, and a Cockney would have been considered daft had he then thought fit to appear in the regions of Broadland in the costume and general rig-out which is now no longer strange to the quiet dwellers in this out-of-the-way corner of old England.

Drainage was the first great blow to sport, steam and railways the next, then the breechloader, and finally the invading host of would-be sportsmen all eager to kill something. Year by year the water-birds have diminished in number, and by degrees they desert the more frequented rivers, streams and broads, until on many of the more public waterways there is hardly an edible wild water-bird per hundred acres. Oulton has suffered most in this respect.

35

We do not suppose there is a public shooting water in Norfolk or Suffolk which has been so harassed.

Often are seen pictures in the London illustrated papers entitled " Wildfowling on Oulton Broad," wherein the artist depicts a shooter sitting on the bottom of a punt, in the reeds, with his waterman holding an anxious-looking retriever by the collar. Overhead are flying streams of mallard and wild duck, and the envious looker-on anticipates that at least a score will grace the bag before the shooter returns to breakfast.

What a myth! What a snare and delusion! Years gone by such a picture would not have been an exaggeration, but now things are sadly altered, and if the shooter killed one couple of mallard during the month of August on Oulton Broad, he would be considered fortunate. In the first fortnight of November a good many fowl drop into the water whilst migrating towards other less-disturbed haunts, and during the grey, cold mornings of that month, especially when the wind is high, several are shot over decoys and by other means. Borrow's Ham and the reed beds all round the entrance to the river Waveney, or Oulton Dyke, are the favourite stands to take, and the pulk holes and rands are worth carefully searching and beating with the first streak of dawn. Teal used to frequent Borrow's Ham about ten or fifteen years ago ; now they are rarely, if ever, seen anywhere on the Broad. In August there are a few redshanks, sandpipers, turtle-doves, moorhens and snipe to be met with, but the owners of private property round the shores of the Broad have a strongly-rooted aversion to seeing the sandpipers and turtle-doves (which come every year from Africa) shot or taken, as the presence of these birds adds greatly to the enjoyment of everybody. Snipe are found in November round the rands of the Broad (in Carlton Ham especially), and heavy bags are sometimes made. When such is the case great secrecy is observed, otherwise the next morning sees a gunner to every bird. Punt guns are not used on this water ; they would be very dangerous, and the most energetic gunner would not average six shots a season of six birds each.

Between Lowestoft and Oulton Broad lies Lake Lothian, once part of the Broad itself, now a tidal estuary with mud flats and what the gunner loves, except marshes and scope. But there is rarely anything here, and it is hardly worth a visit, except, perhaps, in November, when plenty of wind is blowing, or during a hard frost.

The snipe marshes of " Whitecaste," marked on the rough map before referred to, are quite historic in the annals of the East Anglian hunting-grounds. They belong to the parish, and are let to one person for the litter which grows on them, to another for the shooting. Many years ago the snipe shooting to be obtained here was indeed extraordinary. Twenty years ago it was something to be remembered, and the author can recollect having more than once seen from 500 to 1000 snipe on the wing at the same time. During the migration they visited these marshes in hundreds, and wisps of snipe were a common occurrence.

The rent then was not more than two or three sovereigns, if anything at all was charged, but as the reputation of the ground spread the rent rose accordingly, until no one living in the neighbourhood thought it worth their while to try and hire it. The marsh is not more than forty acres in extent, and it is said " a bet was once made that one could not dig up a square foot of soil without it contained an ounce of shot." We should say this yarn must be taken *cum grano salis.*

The rands, bogs and pulk holes to the north of the river and due west from Borrows Ham are now more or less private, but they always were disappointing, rarely yielding anything beyond rails and moorhens. To the west of White-caste lie the poor's marshes, which everyone shoots over, yet snipe are always found there if there are any in the neighbourhood.

A visitor staying in Oulton Broad who hires a little shooting and is a genial sort of fellow and a keen sportsman, will find he will get more sport than he requires, as every inch of land that can be hired is snapped up and preserved, whilst good guns are exceedingly scarce and much in request.

Before the Wild Birds' Protection Act of 1880 was passed, which has been such a boon and a blessing to all lovers of nature and sport, a good time was obtained round Whitecaste, from about the 4th to the 14th of July, shooting young redshanks, or redlegs, as they are provincially called.

The mode of pursuit was as follows :—Having previously noted the most-frequented and favoured marshes by watching the movements of the older birds, a day was appointed and the guns apportioned, some for walking up, others for placing in fixed stands to shoot the wilder birds. These stands were made from reed hurdles, temporary screens, a convenient bush, clump of reeds or coarse marsh litter, whichever came most handy and convenient for the purpose.

The walking-up division carefully beat the ground with dogs towards the guns concealed in the stands, shooting what young birds rose or circled within range ; the old birds they spared as a rule, because at that period of the year they are comparatively worthless. The guns who were posted forward got the best of the fun, as all their shots were more or less sporting ones, and generally at birds which flew past them at a high rate of speed, having been considerably frightened by the remainder of the party.

One drawback to the sport was the flies and midges which swarmed around (once experienced, never forgotten), with the excessive heat generally to be endured. To counteract this as much as possible old boots with plenty of holes in them were worn instead of the heavy and cumbersome long marsh boots, and to fall into a dyke or bog-hole was not objected to, except for the nastiness of the mud ; but this could easily be got rid of by a swim in the river after the beat was over, which indulgence the author has frequently treated himself to in days gone by without troubling to divest himself of one inch of clothing.

Large bags of redshanks were seldom procured, but the practical knowledge of the ground and habits of the birds, coupled with the hard work, which are all essential to success, lends an attraction to the sport without which it might have been dull and uninteresting.

Redshanks are interesting birds at all times, and if properly cooked are considered savoury morsels for an epicure's table, more especially if the birds are young.

In March, or early in April, they leave the saltings, arriving at the breeding grounds, where they pair off and distribute themselves over the face of the fens and the marshes. They commence to lay their eggs about the middle of May, and, unlike the lapwing, they select (in preference to more open ground) a thick tuff of rushes in which to conceal their nest, contiguous to swampy and more rotten places. The young as soon as hatched emerge from the nest, and the downy active little birds form a most interesting subject to those who are enabled to obtain a position commanding a view of their movements. This, however, is seldom the case, as the parent birds are most vigilant, being always on the alert, and so soon as an intruder appears within their domain they circle round and round overhead, uttering shrill, piercing cries, warning the whole neighbourhood of danger.

Should the intruder appear in the form of a dog, cat or fox, they feign and counterfeit maimedness and inability, fluttering away almost touching the ground, to lure the intruder from the vicinity of their young; sometimes actually placing themselves in danger through over-zeal in their parental duties.

The young of the redshank grow rapidly, but they are not able to fly until fully fledged and quite fit for table. The progress of their growth at this period is so rapid that within a few days of their using their wings for the first time the old birds lead them off to the saltings. Therefore, unless the fenman can take his chance at the exact time (which a judicious law now forbids) he has no other opportunity until a subsequent year.

There is another branch of sport to be mentioned before quitting the hospitable shores of Oulton Broad for other fields

—namely, shooting over decoys, which at one time was practised somewhat extensively.

One young fellow in particular could be named who lived on the shores of this water, and who gained (until recently) a fat livelihood from sporting in the winter and yachting in the summer. Being well versed in the geography of the waterways of Broadland and all the branches of sport they were capable of, his services were in great demand by amateur yachtsmen and sportsmen who visited the neighbourhood. After the reeds had turned from their summer green into yellow brittle stems, and the visitors, like the swallows, had departed for more congenial climes, the products of his shooting and fishing supported him through the winter and spring.

He worked his decoys from a promontory of the Broad with great skill, and rarely returned home empty-handed; but now these days are past and the quantity of fowl which visit this particular water is so limited that it is not worth anybody's while to attempt decoying from a professional, or even from an amateur, point of view.

It was the custom of the youth alluded to to be up long before daybreak and take up a position on a prominence of thick reed-beds which jutted out into the Broad, affording a secure retreat to his boat and to himself. The position was well chosen, as all fowl entering the Broad would pass close by this particular point, and they seldom failed to pitch near to his imitation birds.

The decoys, or stales, were made of wood painted by himself, and excellent imitations.

In some of the districts of Broadland decoys are still successfully used, and a fair number of fowl are shot with their assistance. But, like most other inventions, they are not always to be worked either easily or propitiously; everything depends upon the minor details, which, although trivial in themselves, are only mastered by a thorough course of study and training with many years of practical experience.

The subject of decoying is such that it must be allotted a special chapter.

# CHAPTER V

## DECOYS AND HOW TO USE THEM

And as a skilful fowler birds employs,
Which by their well-known form or treach'rous noise
Allure their fellows and invite to share
Their fate, sealed from a hidden lair.

*Vaniere Revised.*

DECOYS are, without doubt, of great assistance to the wild-fowler, under certain circumstances, but they are now much more used in America—where sportsmen assert that nothing goes so far towards making an expert duck-shooter as a full knowledge and the proper use of decoys—than in the British Isles. In fact, one rarely hears of decoys being used at all, except in Broadland and a few other out-of-the-way fen-lands.

The ways of utilising decoys to advantage are many, and they vary according to the districts and localities in which they are worked.

In the numerous books on wildfowl-shooting already published, most of these methods have been more or less explained, and in some dilated upon at length. Therefore, it is best to confine present remarks as much as possible to personal practical experience.

First, let us review decoys when used in connection with punt-shooting. In this branch of sport they are less used than in any other, and only when it is almost impossible to move about on account of ice or stress of weather. Yet we have known the time when their assistance was in no wise to be despised, more particularly in "wakes," or, rather, the open sheets of water which, either from artificial means, tidal eddies, springs, or sheltering trees, have not been grasped by the iron clutches of Jack Frost until long after other more exposed places are securely locked in ice. The appellation "wake" is certainly peculiar, and in the sense here referred to cannot be found in the dictionary; but, nevertheless, it is in constant use amongst punt-gunners, marshmen and wildfowl-shooters in general, who, when once in the sole, undisputed possession of a good "wake," situated in a prominent and well-frequented district, have, in their estimation, attained a long-coveted empyrean of blissful contentment.

"Wakes" formed on saltings and mud flats are caused by the rising and falling of the tide, which, on the ebb, leaves ice resting on uneven hillocks of mud, or over runs and drains, and if the ice is insufficiently strong it falls in; then, on the tide rising again, the wind blows all detached pieces to leeward, clearing an open "wake" of varying dimensions. On inland lakes and waters "wakes" are often formed through springs or tame birds.

If you do not have the luck to come across a naturally-formed "wake," one can be made. Select the ground, or rather water, in a part well open to the wind, because, so long as waves roll across the water it will remain open, and this in still, frosty weather is always a great difficulty. Again, remember always to commence breaking ice from extreme leeward, working to windward. If you begin to windward, and work to leeward, you will be surrounded by so much floating ice all the time, that far greater difficulty will be experienced in working. Whereas, in the former case, as soon as the ice is detached the wind carries it away to leeward, and you are not further encumbered or annoyed by it.

The "wake" made in a suitable position, attention should be turned to the channel by which the punt is to enter, and this must be regulated according to circumstances.

The decoys are placed, some in the water, others on the ice, the shooter being guided more or less by fancy, selecting what he considers the most desirable positions. It will be found best (if you expect your "wake" will not be open) to arrive on the scene of action an hour or so before daybreak, in order to re-break the ice, place the decoys, and put all straight before retiring to the retreat, to watch and wait like a spider over his web. Provided there are any fowl at all in the neighbourhood, we do not think your patience will be very much tried before the melodious whistling of wings startles your reveries and causes that keen excitement which the sight of mallard in the grey dawn invariably stirs up in the breast of a true wildfowler.

If the "wake" is small and the surroundings suitable, an ambush can be made and splendid sport with shoulder-guns obtained, answering to all intents and purposes the French *huttier* system.

The main reason why decoys are used in "wakes" is obvious, for, as there are usually many more "wakes" than one in any large sheet of water, the wildfowl would assuredly prefer selecting those furthest from the shore, unless lured by counter attractions.

Again, decoys can be used when punt-shooting under the following circumstances. Where one is gunning on an estuary frequented by a large number of shooters, it is usual to divide the ground into berths, and the maxims of "first come," etc, and "possession nine-tenths of the law" prevail. Then it will be found an advantage to lay out several decoys opposite your berth, as, when skilfully placed, it is marvellous how the wild birds are deceived.

In " tubbing " decoys are frequently used with great success, not only when shooting from tubs sunken in the ooze, but also by means of the floating tub raft. This consists of a float, or raft, of rough planks, encircled round a large and spacious waterbutt, about 1½ft. from its top, which is garnished with grasses, weeds and mud, in order to make it resemble a drifting island. In this bulky craft our sportsman launches out into the estuary, lagoon, lake, or wherever his happy hunting-grounds may be, propelling his float by means of small oars, from semi-circular sculling holes which are cut in the edge on each side of the tub to take the place of row-locks. Having paddled to a good position, the gunner either anchors himself, or drifts promiscuously about, his decoys also being either anchored or attached to his craft in such a way that in drifting they go also. Some are actually placed on the raft itself, and when all is arranged to his satisfaction he can make himself at home in the interior of his tub, which, as a rule, has ample room to carry many desirable little comforts.

Very often, on spotting a goodly bunch of short-winged fowl, the gunner will quietly and stealthily scull well to windward of them, and then allow himself to drift down into their midst. Ducks, more especially mallard, are naturally of a very inquisitive turn of mind, and when they see this curious craft, which at first appears to them only a detached portion of floating-rand,* with some of their feathered brethren bobbing round it, they generally swim straight towards it and fall victims to their own temerity.

In this method of wildfowling we strongly advise the shooter to carry a little peat in his tub with him, so he can burn some of it when in the act of drifting towards the birds, otherwise the exquisite sense of smell possessed by most wildfowl will soon put an end to his manoeuvres.

In boisterous weather the tubman often lays an anchor to windward with a free length of cable, by means of which he can regulate himself to the desired distance from the shore without emerging from his hide, and circumvent the danger

* Spongy masses of aquatic vegetation peculiar to Norfolk.

of his craft overcoming him and carrying him away to leeward into the rough water.

Another killing dodge on some waters is to select a favoured prominence of reeds, rushes or other aquatic vegetation, which juts out into the water, affording a secure retreat to your boat and self. The decoys are anchored some little distance away, and, if the position has been well chosen, the incoming birds cannot fail to notice them, when the customary toll is taken from their numbers.

This latter method is almost the same as using screens, but with this difference : in the former one is enabled to move about and alter his position according to wind, weather or other circumstances ; in the latter he can only go where his screens are placed. These screens are built in reed-beds and made to assimilate their surroundings as much as possible, consisting of four stout piles driven firmly into the deceptive subsoil, to which is attached a rough platform ; four reed-hurdles form its wings, a seat is added, and the screen is complete. Not only are these screens used for decoying, but also for diurnal and nocturnal shooting (flighting at dawn and dusk) and for drives.

On land we have often used decoys, but with indifferent success. Here the live birds are decidedly the better of the two, and on corn or pea stubbles, near corn stacks and such like, they are usually made use of in preference to the artificial birds. As lures for geese, however, they are indeed a godsend, and splendid sport may be obtained with their assistance. The shooter can either lie upon the ground, having, of course, first provided against dampness, or he can dig out a pit in which to secrete himself, or, more comfortable still, he can sink a barrel or tub ; in each case assimilating himself and his hide as much as possible to the surroundings. The depth of these stands varies according to the whim of the shooter, but ours have always been four feet, with a diameter of three or thereabouts. Above all things be very careful to either cart away the excavated soil, or break it up and distribute it evenly over the adjoining acres, leaving everything with as natural an appearance as possible. Further, carry a cover for the dug-outs, so that when leaving them you can not only exclude the dust and elements, but also, by sprinkling a little soil over the cover, you leave the ground with no ostensible appearance of disturbance.

The position of the decoy birds, again, varies in accordance with the sportsman's fancy. Some prefer them all on one side, others in a line, some only two or three in number, and some, on the other hand, in enormous quantities. But we have always found that a dozen posted in natural positions is amply sufficient.

The best all-round gun for this class of decoying, in our humble opinion, is a double 8-bore, full choke, with No. 3 chilled shot right barrel, and No. 1 left. Weight is not so much a serious consideration, as you have not to carry the gun about very much; whereas, if you wish to combine flighting, decoying and marsh work, the best plan is to go in for a double 10-bore, 30 in. barrel, full choke, substituting No. 2 for No. 1, and No. 4 for No. 3 shot.

The actual artificial decoys with which we are acquainted are as multitudinous as they are various in design. We will comment briefly upon a few of them.

First, there are the stuffed birds. If these are intended to be used on uplands or marsh, they are either set up on small boards (fastened by pegs), or upon wooden or iron supports, which can easily be stuck into the ground, good care being taken that, in placing them, their natural attitude, appearance and altitude are made as natural looking as possible.

The position of the decoy birds, according to the varying circumstances under which they are used, will be found of the utmost importance.

Take, for example, wood-pigeons on trees. If, as is too often the case, they are shaped with head erect and wide-awake appearance, their posture would convey the impression to the real birds arriving that they had just alighted or saw danger near, thereby at once exciting suspicion. Whereas, if made with heads down, all snug, and properly fixed, facing the wind, the wild birds would drop to the apparent harbour of refuge without fear or mistrust. Or if placed on a stubble or clover field, some should be picking, others looking up, and their positions varied. If, on the other hand, all are sitting up, alarm is indicated.

The above remarks apply equally to all decoying with stales ; * and although they may appear at first sight to be minor details, it is just these trivial points which make all the difference between partial and complete success.

A device for constructing temporary decoys may, perhaps, be worthy of attention. Before departure for the happy hunting-grounds the sportsman provides himself with some stoutish wire netting and a pair of nippers. On killing his first bird he fashions a simple framework from a small portion of the netting, fitting the neck, head and breast, and, with the aid of a few props, has as life-like a decoy as heart could desire. Upon another kill the same performance can be repeated, until the requisite number has been procured.

FIG. 1.

A similar plan is the wire-stake trident, with the central tine convex, the latter being firmly fixed into the under bill of the bird, with one of the side prongs under each wing ; the position being varied by the different curve of the central tine.

When stales are intended for use on water, it is entirely different, and "floats" constitute the main consideration.

In Fig. I. will be noticed a good overlap, and an absence of lead on the keel, the balance being effected through a weighted dead-line. This one is drawn from a model which we saw in use in the southern part of Sweden, and it took some time learning the whys and wherefores from the Scandinavian duck hunter, who spoke in the broadest *patois* imaginable. The object of the overlap seems to be for the protection of the bird, which it effected in some measure, both in transportation and otherwise.

* Artificial decoys.

Here let it be stated once and for all, that when using the genuine stuffed bird great care must be taken, otherwise a fresh batch will soon be needed. The attaching hole, it will also be observed, is differently placed, and must be varied according to circumstances. To the dead-line, however, we must

take exception, as in fleet water it would be a great nuisance having to alter it, and a lead or iron keel answers quite as well, without the bother of extra strings.

Figs. II. and III. are the shapes we invariably make and use, the former appearing to answer best. Sometimes we have fixed solid three-cornered blocks of wood, as shown

FIG. II.

by the *dotted lines* in Fig. IV., the more in order to assimilate the lines of a boat, but find that so doing adds considerably to the weight, and is really no advantage. Therefore, we recommend the would-be user, who thinks of turning out, or superintending the manufacture of, his own decoys, to adopt the patterns given in Figs. II., III. and IV. (without the addition indicated by the dotted lines). Of course, the size of the float-board equals the duck's measurement round the water-line, and the depth of the keel can be made to fancy, but six to ten inches will be found ample; the amount of lead on the keel being regulated in a great measure by the species and weight of the wood used, otherwise the bird will appear heavy and unnatural. The desire being to liken each decoy to the genuine bird as much as possible, weight it accordingly, so that it will ride buoyantly and lightly over the wavelets, neither ploughing through them nor allowing them to dash over its head, neck and shoulders. In

FIG. III.

carrying it is as well to have a separate bag, case or covering for each bird, with a slit in the bottom for the keel to come through; for, as before mentioned, these stuffed decoys rarely last long. In anchoring, some people attach a separate line and weight to each bird used; others place three in a line, all three being kept in their respective positions by a fore-and-aft anchor attached to the rear and leading birds. But we do not believe in so large a number as the Americans seem partial to.

Perhaps many will wonder at the notches cut under the support-board, or just above the keel, therefore we will explain their use. Many shooters, on picking up their decoy birds, or "stales" as they are more often called, wind the wet anchoring and connecting lines round the necks. This may be all very well for a time, but it soon destroys and injures their appearance; so to remedy it we wind our lines round the keel, with the assistance of these notches, where they are securely held without detriment to the birds.

Under this division might also be included the canvas-made decoys, which are to all intents and purposes the same as stuffed birds. The pattern is taken from a live bird, and the canvas cut out to measure, sewn up and stuffed (body with cork, head and neck with tow), the exterior being painted to complete the deception. We have made these, and used them, finding they answer well—in fact, if anything, better than the wooden ones, the balancing arrangements of the latter being the only thing that makes them the better of the twain.

FIG. IV.

With regard to the shape of your dummies, of course it is best to get it as near to perfection as possible; yet, at the same time, you will not find the wild birds so very exacting in this respect as you would suppose. They see the dummies bobbing about, and on fine or calm days, after wheeling and hovering round awhile, drop to them. On finding out their mistake they do not at once fly away, but often remain some time unless suspicions raise an alarm.

And now a word as to the species best to be represented. Golden eyes do very well for short-winged fowl, which

D

include pochards, tufted ducks, rattlers, *et hoc genus omne.* But for mallard, teal, widgeon and all long-winged fowl—in fact, short-winged and all-round general duck shooting—there is nothing to equal good representations of duck and mallard.

Secondly, there are the wooden imitations, These can be bought at almost any gunsmith's or naturalist's, and, in our opinion, are far away the best for wear, efficiency and economy. No fresh figures are necessary to illustrate their manufacture, as they are almost identical to Figs. V., III. and IV., with, of course, the exception of the water-line or floating-board. One thing is very important, and that is not to have them too shiny and bright, with which the uninitiated are so fascinated. On the other hand, the wood had better be prepared with size, or something of that kind, prior to painting, for unless this be attended to the wood will absorb the paint without being rendered water-resisting or showing the colours to advantage.

Thirdly, there is another species of wooden decoys which we remember once to have seen, but as it is some time ago, and our memory not of the best, we are afraid our explanation will not be so lucid as we should like. It was fashioned somewhat after the style of the American silhouette decoy, which, we presume, is known to be the outline or profile only, and painted as the others. Those intended for use on *terra firma* were pivoted on a stake, whilst those for the water were pivoted on a "float-board." Each was in two pieces, and thus easily packed, carried and stowed away. We have never shot over them or seen them in actual use, so we cannot speak as to their efficiency, but we should consider that a duck, looking from an angle of 45 deg. (about the average elevation when dropping to a decoy), would hesitate before placing implicit confidence in so meagre, skinny and gaunt an object.

Fourthly, we have the indiarubber substitute, either with or without an inflation tube, its object, of course, being to facilitate stowage and transit. But they are easily disposed of, for a single shot striking them (by no means an unusual occurrence) brings about ruination. Besides, unless weighted, the generality of them behave as one returning home in the early hours of morn, having passed the evening with such-like companions as Priapus, Silenus and Bacchus. In other words, they roll over at the slightest draught of wind or ripple of the waters.

Fifthly, may be included the collapsible, reversible tin, copper and other metal decoys, etc.; but when the simpler ones answer so successfully what need is there of all these gimcracks?

Sixthly, there is an invention which we have never had time to put to a practical test, yet it seems so ingenious a device we have taken the liberty of again placing it before the public.

It was described in an American book on *Wildfowl Shooting,* * by Mr Long, one well conversant in the art, therefore we cannot do better than use his own words:—" A few years ago a Mr T. H. Snow took out a patent for a flapping decoy. A board, which served as a floater, had a hole cut through it the size of the decoy, and in this the decoy (which was made like any common wooden one) was placed and fastened to the board by pins running into its sides, and serving as hinges, upon which the decoy tilted easily. Wings, formed of wire, and covered with cloth or other similar substance, were hinged in position, and the decoy anchored in the usual manner. A line leading to the blind was so fastened to the decoy that, upon its being pulled, the forward end was raised upon the hinges to a nearly erect position, similar to that of the live duck when flapping its wings, and the wings were elevated at right angles with the body. It was quite an ingenious contrivance, and helped considerably to attract attention to the decoys, especially on dark, calm days."

Seventhly, and finally, there are the real decoy birds in the flesh and blood. Whether the little white call ducks that one often sees in small flighting ponds, etc., are really conspicuous in attracting wildfowl is a question very much open

* Published by the Orange Judd Company, 245 Broadway, New York.

to comment, but a semicross between the wild duck and our domesticated species is always a good draw, when properly managed, although it goes against the grain to fasten them to the stake or anchor, at which they are so often wounded, and perhaps killed, when dummies answer almost equally as well. The following anecdote, which was told to the author by a native wildfowler on the banks of the Tagus, better exemplifies the existence of live decoy birds, doomed to temporary and involuntary martyrdom :—

In the sunny land of Spain, one auspicious wildfowling morning, a sportsman, evidently meaning business, proceeded up the Esteira Furado Creek, near Moita, with craft wisely and yet too well provisioned and found. Not only was he provided with shot and shell, but also enticing lures in the form of live decoy ducks, with the assistance of which he hoped to secure better results than had ever fallen to the lot of sportsman before. Arrived at his destination, he inserted in the mud a long pole, about thirty yards distant from his proposed ambush, to the top of which a swivelled slip was attached. From this, with not more than two feet play-line between each bird, were secured by the leg his unfortunate victims, the top of the aforesaid pole being level with high-water mark ; the tide, it must be added, being then on the turn. Having arranged everything to his satisfaction, with a smile of approval at his own cuteness, he pushed his craft into ambush to await events. Now, whether this well-intending sportsman was so much engrossed in the anticipated fruits of his stratagem, or whether it was the soothing influence of the native grape that made him oblivious to the fact of the magnitude of the rise and fall of tide in these parts, tradition relates not, but he fell asleep. What his dreams may have been are best known to himself; suffice it to say that, hearing the cries of ducks in his immediate vicinity, he awoke with a start and grasped his gun, thinking that the supreme moment was at hand. Imagine the gunner's feelings on finding his boat high and dry, whilst from the top of his too well-fixed pole depended the fluttering decoy birds, clamouring loudly at their uncomfortable position aloft.

In Holland, we have been told, they use trained drakes, which fly up to the wild ones and lure them down to an ignominious death, although, when there, we have never had the pleasure, if so we may term it, of being initiated into the secrets of this particular device.

The *huttier* system of the French, with their decoy birds staked down in lines, is so well-known, and has been before so admirably described by far abler pens, that there is no need to touch upon it.

Having shortly commented upon the decoys more generally in use, the next point is how to lay them out.

On land this is easy enough, as the only thing of any importance to be remembered is (and this applies equally as much to the water) to place all your birds head to wind. If the reader requires a reason for this, let him visit the nearest farmyard and watch any ducks that may be in a place exposed to the wind.

The whole tribe has a great dislike to have their feathers ruffled, which an aft wind invariably does. Stales therefore must not all be sitting up nor all lying down, but grouped as natural-looking as the shooter can place them.

On the water there are numerous other things to think about besides the actual grouping. Position selected convenient to the ambushed sportsman ; the wind, whether lee or weather shore; attachment-lines; prevention of possible fouling of the anchoring lines; with a hundred and one other little things which experience and practice can alone teach.

The ordinary way of anchoring a single decoy is merely to attach a line to the fore hole shown in either Figs. I., II. or III., and allowing extra length or depth according to how deep the water is, with a stone, or other suitable object, as an anchor. A random string of decoys may be used, and is brought about by anchoring the first in the usual way ; to its eyehole aft is attached the connecting line of the second bird, which runs, of course, from the fore float-board eyehole ; the third is attached in a similar way, with the exception of an anchor-line running from its after eyehole, keeping all three at regular intervals, and in the required position. An anchor is hardly required in a high wind or good breeze.

Another method for securing three decoys, which is equally good, if not better than the former mentioned, is, with the assistance of the four-in-hand cross-bar arrangement, or diminutive square sail yard, shown in Fig. V. The pole is somewhere about five feet in length, and cut from green wood, sallow, or osier, so that it barely floats ; not too large, but just large enough, that is, sufficient to bear the necessary strain. The middle bird is tied to the stick

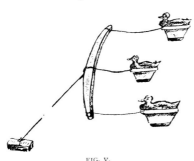

FIG. V.

by kyah (Indian grass rope), which floats, and is half as short again in length as the two other lines of hemp or manilla, which sink, besides being double the length of the middle ones. The reason is obvious, as, by so doing, fouling is almost impossible. The main anchor runs from the very centre of the pole.

Here also, as well as in the anchoring of single birds, a slight, simple and effective plan is often resorted to, which is as follows:—If you wish your birds to be sedate and steady, fasten the anchor-line exactly to the middle of their cutwater. But if (as is mostly practised) you wish them to swim about in a restless and animated manner, fasten the line slightly lower down, when the desired result will be arrived at. It is wonderful how natural they appear when laid out by a cute hand.

The hoop is of great assistance in likening the dummy to a live bird, and is an ingenious device. A wooden hoop with a diameter of about three feet is procured, its edge being most carefully smoothed to allow a wire ring to run round it with ease—allowance being made for the swelling of the wood when sodden with water. Two rings are placed on the hoop, and a wire stretched from one to the other; from each of them is a line to the anchor weight, and connected to each ring is a dummy bird. Thus it will be seen that these two birds can chase each other round and round the hoop, but never overtake or come any nearer than they are originally set. It can be tried with four, but they look unnatural, and two will be found to answer best; yet, at the same time, four rings can be used to advantage without the addition of more birds. See Fig. VI. Perchance some may say, "this is practising against the preaching, for one of them must be tail to wind," but *exceptio probat regulam*, and it does not matter so much here, as these birds are constantly on the move. In the drawing will be noticed a four-ringed hoop by dotted lines, and also an additional anchor, which can be used if so desired; but it is not a necessity, although it may be preferred by a few people. To the length of the lines from the rings to the anchor there is no defined limit, and they can be regulated according to depth.

FIG. VI.

Another addendum to the already long list of artificial decoy ducks has been patented by Mr William H. Jencks, Clinton, Iowa, and was filed February 5, 1889, serial No. 298,723.

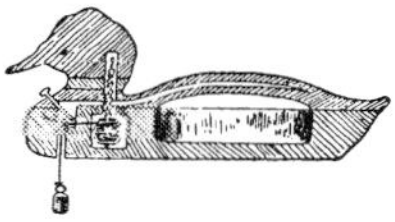

From the appended sketch (Fig. VII.) the reader will gather a good idea of the invention.

FIG. VII.

The following claims cast sufficient light to give a fair idea of any advantages or general utility which it may possess :—

"1. A decoy-duck provided with an internal anchor cord-winding reel, in combination with a set-screw, adapted to bear upon the reel and lock the same in position.

" 2. A decoy-duck with forward and rearward internal recesses, in combination with a shaft mounted in the forward recess, and provided with a spool or reel, a decoy-head mounted on the shaft and adapted to revolve the same, and an anchor cord, one end of which is made fast to and adapted to be wound upon the spool."

Dogs, too, are often useful as decoys. To be an attractive draw, the dog's colour should be brownish, with corporeal dimensions not too large; in a word, the nearer it resembles a fox the more effective will it be. Its training need be neither long nor tedious; all that is required is that it will gambol about in an eccentric fashion, implicitly obeying every gesture of its master's hand. Instances are not rare where black-coated retrievers have decoyed birds within range, but then their antics must be carefully superintended, and the dogs must be extra intelligent if the practice is to be repeated.

Another way in which to decoy birds within range of the gun by the assistance of dogs is as follows :—" Wypes," or, as they are more commonly called, lapwings, are very fond of mobbing an intruder, more especially a fox, or its near ally, the dog, and they have been known to pay the same attention to cats when prowling upon their domain. Taking advantage of this you must train your dog accordingly, and on discovering a field or suitable marsh which the lapwings frequent, conceal yourself close by, and either send the dog (carefully trained in this branch of sport) round, or in company with an attendant who, upon arriving at the opposite side of the birds, loosens the dog, directing it the course to take. It instantly starts off at top speed through the very midst of the birds, they, upon recovering from their first shock of alarm, and upon seeing their disturber running away, follow screaming, in some cases, swooping down to within a few feet of its head, until their temporary boldness is suddenly dispelled by the ambushed sportsman, who should secure a good recompense for his cunning. It must not be supposed that the first efforts of the inexperienced will be crowned with brilliant success, but then he ought to be consoled by the recollection that the more difficult the obstacles the sweeter will eventually become the fruits of victory.

In this method train your dog to run straight into your ambush, and upon his arrival to instantly crouch motionless to the ground, as these birds, when one of their number is struck down, almost invariably follow it, and many times several couple can be secured. In this instance, if they neither see you, your attendant, nor the dog, and one or more are shot, they are almost certain to swoop to them, and it rests with the shooter whether he takes good advantage of this their peculiarity.

Another plan is confined almo.t exclusively to decoying wild ducks. It is extremely simple, and generally effective, but requires the aid of an intelligent dog, otherwise failure is certain.

Upon seeing some wildfowl upon a small lake or other sheet of water, and within reasonable distance, you conceal yourself from their sight, then direct your faithful canine attendant to go through his part of the performance. He jumps suddenly into view upon the shore or bank, and madly chases his tail round and round, then as suddenly disappears. Out again, and back instantly, with many variations of antic. The ducks act almost precisely as they do at the entrance to a decoy pipe. First, they are a little disturbed, then fear gives way to curiosity, and with outstretched necks they swim for the shore, collecting closer and closer the nearer they approach it. Biding your opportunity, and covering them the while, in case their suspicions turn into genuine alarm (in which case, of course, the best offer must be turned to account), you quietly wait until they arrive within easy distance, when the well-directed contents of both barrels rudely cuts short their suppositions, and leaves few cripples to try the patience and endurance of your gay deceiver.

It should be taken for granted that both these deceptions must not be overdone. That is, you must not too often repeat them upon the same ground, and with the same birds, within a short time, but rather look out for fresh arrivals, migratory or otherwise, and not harass constant frequenters more than is absolutely necessary. The importance of this advice cannot be impressed too strongly, and it is only by observation and bitter experience that the gunner finds out the truth of it, and the unfathomable value of having obtained the confidence of his every-day attendants.

For hardiness and endurance, especially in such a trying neighbourhood as the Fen Country, there is nothing to equal a good cross-bred dog. A cross between a water spaniel and retriever produced the author one of the cleverest and neatest little workers it was ever his good fortune to shoot over. That dog, however, had its peculiarities. If you went out with it after cock pheasants and it constantly flushed hens, which you allowed to go away without a shot, it would put up with it for a while, but if it continued it would take itself off home in disgust. Again, it would never run home after work on a dirty night, but insisted upon being driven; and if it was refused, it trotted, with head and tail erect, to the nearest farmhouse, where it would seek quarters for the night. On wildfowl it was splendid, and never gave up a cripple unless compelled to. You might trust it in any covert to persevere for hours, once having touched the scent of a wounded bird; and to mark down two or three birds in succession, retrieving each at a gallop on receiving the longed-for word of release, was with it a common occurrence. Its manner was most eccentric, and you could not lose it if you tried; but it abominated music, which its teeth marks to this day testify— because in an inopportune hour it was once serenaded by the author with a concertina when he thought he was safely sitting in a hammock, the supporting rope unfortunately giving way when least expected.

The dogs mostly in use for decoying purposes, and pre-ferred, are retrievers, both liver-coloured and black, curly and wavy, with no distinct preference for one in particular, but selecting a sort of happy medium between the two.

A great deal has at different times been said about artificial and natural calls for wildfowl and other shooting.

By artificial are meant the wooden and other instruments used for producing the sounds required; by natural imitations those emitted from the mouth with which Nature has provided every one. The former are all very well in their way, yet they take up much time and trouble to learn; but no artificial arrangement can equal a good imitator who has arrived at a fair stage of perfection, which is not half so difficult as most people imagine. It is a little difficult at first, perhaps, but the acquirement of one call invariably leads up to others, and when once two or three have been mastered the remainder are easy. To be efficient, however, the mimicking of one sound only for each bird is not what is required; you must habituate yourself to invariably listen and notice the different sounds emitted at the different times, which you will soon find conveys to you their intentions; every species of birds having a separate language, that of the widgeon and curlew, perhaps, being the most commonly known. Study and endeavour to learn the meaning of each cry and whistle, and then attempt to mimic the correct note; as, of course, if you give vent to the wrong note, say, for instance, the note of alarm, what result can you expect? That veteran and thoroughly practical sportsman, Mr H. C. Folkard, gives good advice upon this subject, which applies equally to shooting over decoys as it does to punt and other shooting.

"A good ear for ornithological sounds is as necessary to the midnight sportsman as the natural musical ear is to the most accomplished harpist. He must be familiar with the different calls and confabulations of the various species of wildfowl, as is the fair warbler alluded to with the most popular airs of the day; and but little success can be expected unless he is so gifted. The language of wildfowl is instinctive and pleasing alike to the ears of both sportsman and naturalist—to the one for the advice it gives him as to the species, as well as the whereabouts, of their talkative assemblages; and to the other for the opportunity afforded of contemplating, from lessons of life, the beautiful perfections of Nature, so exquisitely revealed even in the simple and apparently unmeaning voices of the feathered tribe; but which, in reality, express to their species the unmistakable language of the heart—its love, hatred, wants, sympathies, doubts and alarms—and all by sounds so short and feeble, yet too distinct and expressive to be misunderstood by those for whom they are intended, though to human ear a jumble of inexpressive similarities. With these and many others the wildfowler becomes so easily acquainted that a mistake of species cannot well be made; but it is with other signs of their language that the master of the art has to do before he can become an adept at evening and midnight sport, for whilst these sounds reveal the species, others less vociferous betray their action, their movements and suspicions."

As previously stated, it is an acknowledged fact that birds possess a language of their own, and one can soon convert a disbeliever by placing him in a position where he can both see and hear a flock of curlews; or, nearer home, let him listen to and observe on old hen with her brood of chickens.

The use of artificial calls need not be disparaged as, when in proper hands, they are often made good use of; but the best advice to give to anyone who has fowl approaching his stales or decoy-birds is not to attempt to emit any note unless certain that the imitation is perfect, besides being in the right note and in the right key.

When fifteen years of age the author could lean against a gate-post at evening flight (the easiest period for calling) and time after time call peewits to within ten or fifteen yards. The bag generally astonished flighting companions, and often places were changed with them, but with the same result.

No definite rules or advice can be given for "calling," as its utility at seasonable times will only become apparent after practical experience and observation.

As to boats, the sportsman had best choose that craft most suitable for the particular branch of decoy shooting he is about to practise. An ordinary gunning-punt will be found best all round, if it is available, but almost any boat answers, if the other extreme is not taken by selecting one excessively clumsy and incapable of concealment. The only essential requirement necessary to your selected craft is "stability," in order thereby to secure a steady aim, which the oscillations of an ordinary light skiff would certainly destroy.

Guns are things which depend in a great measure upon what a man has been accustomed to. Some can shoot and handle any weapon with a proficiency which is remarkable, and bend appears of little consequence to them; but then these are men who have spent the whole of their lives in shooting. Yet it has been long ago decided that when once you find a gun really suits you, it is very unwise to exchange it for another. The worst shots one meets with are those who are constantly changing their guns and trying new bends and such-like experiments. Strength of trigger is also of importance, and you should not have a weapon on board pulling under 3 lbs. or 4 lbs., otherwise accidents are likely to arise—perhaps fatal.

How many are there who have not fallen into the error of taking a too heavy gun with them for this branch of sport, and having in consequence missed half a dozen good shots, four out of which they would at least have killed with their ordinary weapon? They seem thoroughly satisfied because they kill one long shot, and they do not pay any regard to the many pricked and wounded birds which they never ought to have fired at.

It is the most pernicious practice possible to plume one's self over long shots, as one cannot fail to comprehend, who considers for a moment, the subsequent misery and lingering deaths thereby brought about; much rather pride one's self and relieve one's conscience in having killed clean such birds as are within easy range.

In shooting over decoys, weight of weapons, so long as they can be easily handled, is not a very material consideration, for you must remember that you are stationed in one position most of the time, and moving about is adverse to success; more specially when on the water, place your gun in the rack and do not handle it until required. Bearing this in mind, one should choose a heavyish weapon (if you can swing it with equal dexterity) in preference to the one you would select with thoughts of marsh perambulation. For all-round shooting over decoys, a double 10-bore, half and full choke, is most advantageous. And if you like to have in reserve a mower-down for flocks and longer ranges, why, a single 4-bore with india-rubber heel-pad will be found of great assistance. The charges rest more with the boldness of the sportsman ; but heavy loads are' more often a mistake than otherwise. You might however recollect that the more metal and the tighter you nip the stock of your gun the less recoil will be felt, and a substantial breech is an advantage rather than a fault.

In shooting do not attempt snap or wild shots, if you can possibly obtain any other, as in the long run they decidedly do not pay. The most telling and deadly method to adopt is the cool, deliberate and calculating shot, which is a noteworthy peculiarity of the expert, who is always a first-rate judge of velocity, height, distance and the resistance of the wind. Also bear in mind that shots drop considerably, especially the heavier pellets. And when birds jump, or are flying from your decoys, they are rising with more or less velocity, according to the species—another item for study, so therefore do not fear to shoot well over them, *vice versa* when going away straight over your head.

Never neglect to clean your guns both before and after usage, especially if on saltings, as the air alone is amply sufficient to do serious injury if the cleaning is neglected. The names of the different receipts for this are legion, and amongst them vaseline will be found by no means a despicable one.

A few words more as to the actions of wildfowl upon observing decoys. Wildfowl, upon entering the boundaries of a strange water, generally take many sweeps round, high up, gradually lowering in order to obtain a fair idea of where they are settling themselves, and also the general surround-

ings. If they do not like the look of affairs, they lead round
to windward and make off in another direction; but if, on the
contrary, they entertain intentions of sojourning awhile, they
lead round to leeward, lowering on the lee side and mounting
again on the windward. Several circuitous reconnoitres of
this description are, as a rule, quite sufficient to settle all
doubts; yet, if it be very mild weather, or there is hardly any
wind blowing, they usually fly round much more and at a
higher elevation.

During these gyrations they are almost certain to spot
your decoys, and the greatest caution must be taken that
they do not catch sight of you at the same time. On seeing
the lures they invariably lower, and eventually, finding
nothing of a more attractive nature, drop to them with
extended pinions. If it is a single bird or a pair, do not wait,
but give it them as they are alighting, for there is far more
satisfaction in killing your quarry in mid-air than taking
the pot-shot. Neither be too sparing with an odd cartridge
if you have the slightest reason to suspect that a shot bird
is only a cripple, for many a fowl is lost through this absurdity.
Well does the author recollect one August evening, when he
dropped a mallard in full view of an army of peaceful
piscators, whose amusement knew no bounds, because the
instant it touched the water the left barrel was also discharged, but previous bitter experience had taught the value of
prudential forethought, and having been successful so far, he
had no intention of being baffled in the end by the well-
known subaqueous skill and cunning of a slightly-tipped
wildfowl. If three or four patronise you, wait and watch
until two or three are crossing, or until they settle and mass,
or get into line, then fire. To a larger flock the same
tactics apply. But in all cases never shoot unless absolutely
certain that your birds are within range; rather let them go
altogether than fire a random and wild shot, as it only
frightens them thoroughly, or slightly pricks them. Rest
assured that if they do not pitch or lower to your decoys at
the first, second or third round, they eventually will do so

if everything is in order and as it should be. They will often disappear entirely from sight for an hour or more, and yet come back, affording an easy chance. Their memories are far better than the majority of people give them credit for. Do they not return year after year to the same nesting haunts? and do they not well remember and avoid those places where they have been persecuted? Veteran, experienced decoy-piping men can narrate many instructive, amusing and interesting yarns to support this theory, and will often go so far as to point out certain birds which are known to them by sight, in order to more effectively illustrate a particular narrative.

Bearing all this in mind, the natural reasoning will ensue that your decoy birds looking and behaving as though real, and yourself well concealed, the wildfowl are almost certain to return, sooner or later, bringing, perhaps, others with them, when your patience will be amply and substantially rewarded.

WATER FOWL
*From a painting in tempora by Jan Weenix, 1640-1719*

# CHAPTER VI

## OULTON BROAD TO GREAT YARMOUTH

SUNSET.

STAYING for any length of time round the shores of Oulton Broad instils the desire into one's mind to seek other quarters in Broadland of which so much is heard, and to experience the quaint, water-gipsy life which the guide-books eulogise so extravagantly.

Many are the craft of various tonnage and rig that may be hired, suffice it therefore, for present purposes, if one or two of the leading classes are described.

The *Warrior,* one of the numerous comfortable letting wherries, fitted for pleasure cruising, is a craft of a class which is a peculiarity to Broadland. In no part of the world, except Norfolk, are these wherries to be met with, where the more they are used, the more useful and convenient to the waterways are they found to be.

In order to convey a clearer idea a plan is appended showing the amount of accommodation afforded on board.

On the *Warrior* (a vessel of thirty tons registered burthen) six or more have plenty of elbow-room and to spare. She only draws three feet of water, her mast lowers with great ease, and she is capable of going anywhere it may be desired to take her. Besides, there is a 14-foot dinghy with a lug-sail of about 140 square feet area, and dagger plate centre-board, as tender ; also a small gunning-punt for fishing and shooting purposes. There is a dark room for photography, a yacht's piano for the muse, warming apparatus for cold

F.                                         65

evenings, w.c., and every other luxury that heart can desire
on a house-boat. No wonder in Norfolk these craft are so
much appreciated and in such great request, especially during
the summer months.

Norfolk wherries, which were until recent years used only
for trading purposes, range from fifteen to sixty tons burden,
and to contend against the roughness of the intending usage
they are clinker built, well tarred and pitched. A narrow
deck, or quanting path, runs all round the vessel; there are
no bulwarks, and the navigators' cabin is situated aft. The
fore deck makes a good size platform, under which is a
store-room for spare gear; the hold is capacious, and
the hatches are raised three or four feet above the deck,
which in a wherry fitted for pleasure cruising allow windows

to run all round the ship, so there is no want of light: and,
when lying to, these hatches form a magnificent promenade
deck. Wherries have but a single sail, of enormous size, held
in place by one spar only. This sail is hoisted by a winch,
and can be lowered at a minute's notice with the greatest
ease. Sometimes it is enlarged by lacing a strip of canvas
along its base, which is termed a bonnet.

The mast is stepped well forward and held by a single
fore-stay, and is easily balanced with lead (averaging over
a ton in weight), and a boy can lower or raise it to its proper
position with the assistance of the aforesaid stay.

There are hundreds of trading wherries in Norfolk, and
of late years a large number have been temporarily or
permanently converted into pleasure-going craft. Amongst
the latter are many magnificently fitted, with every conceivable convenience, luxury and *bric-à-brac*, which would
rival many of the best house-boats on the Thames.

In sailing, wherries are safe but slow, yet it is astonishing the ground they can cover in a short space of time, forty to fifty miles a day not being uncommon. In price of hire, pleasure wherries vary from £8 to £20 per week, according to their accommodation and size. This includes two men, the tender before mentioned, and everything requisite for a cruise, excepting food and drink. There is plenty of room for eight

THE WHERRY "WARRIOR."

persons on board, so the expenses do not come very heavy when divided.

For those who do not feel inclined to hire a wherry, there are many other craft to select from. Cutters, schooners, Lateen, Una, and yachts of other rig may be hired at Oulton Broad, as well as elsewhere. The yachts vary in tonnage from two to fifty tons, and in price accordingly, but they are so numerous and varied in design it would be tedious to minutely describe them. Then there are the open boats with awnings, as well as canoes and other boats which carry tents for camping on shore; the latter are the least to be recommended. Of late house-boats have come more into use, and it is not an altogether unusual sight to see a gentleman of a sporting turn of mind coming up the river in a steam launch, drawing behind him a comfortable house-boat for living purposes, a half-rater, and a 14-foot racing dinghy.

In order that the reader may gain the desired information as to sport and locality in the most interesting and readable form, an imaginary cruise had perhaps best be organised.

The preliminary details as to requisites for creature comforts, varying so much in accordance with the tastes of the individual, need not be commented on. Therefore let us start.

Everything having been stored on board in accordance with our liking, we hoist the sail at Oulton Lock and shape a course towards Great Yarmouth and Breydon Water. Passing over the Broad the water foams at the bows, and excellent headway is made under a stiff south-easterly breeze. On crossing Borrow's Ham many anglers may be noticed at work, still more of them further westward occupying favourite swims. One of our party, whose sympathies are solely with the gun, is sitting disconsolate on the forehatch, hoping against hope that he may obtain the first mallard of the season, but Fortune does not smile on him. Although several ducks are seen hovering over the Whitecaste Marshes, they know far too much to come within 200 yards of the river when so many boats are in evidence. Quitting the Broad, Oulton Dyke is entered (or as this part of it is perhaps more commonly called "Fishrow"), with Whitecaste and the Poors Marshes on the left, and che pine-clad gravel hills of Fishrow on the right.

What an excellent rabbit warren these hills would make. But, as our waterman says, and he is a practical man, who goes more by rule of thumb than theory, "No doubt the situation would do, perhaps it is one of the best you could get in the county, but the cost of protecting the rabbits against poachers would prevent the job paying; bounded as it is on the north by the railway, on the west and east by country lanes, and on the south by public water, the temptation to the wayside and professional poacher would be too great."

Leaving Fishrow, the Horse-shoe Point is rounded, giving a straight run of over a mile up Oulton Dyke. On the right-hand side are the remnants of the Old Skeleton Mill—a landmark for good bream swims; at the end of the reach, on our left hand, is the entrance of the Beccles River, and a hundred yards further on the right is the picturesque station of the water-bailiff, who is the servant of the Yare and Bure Fish Preservation Society. An intending visitor cannot do better than consult him as to the ways of the fish and fowl in his immediate neighbourhood. Within a few hundred yards of the house-boat are many good swims for bream, and five or six stone a day is a long way short of the record.

The bailiff's quarters are well chosen at the junction of the two rivers, whilst his temporary home is anchored in an indent to the entrance creek of Flixton Broad, and well screened by a clump of willows.

As this most picturesque nook of Broadland fades in the distance, the White House Reach, at one time notorious for flight shooting, is entered. Fowl from Flixton Broad and Fritton decoy are accustomed to pass over this reach to and from their feeding-grounds, but it is not worth while to stop on the off chance of a shot, the North River being far superior in this respect to anything to be obtained hereabouts. Flixton Broad is an ornamental piece of water, well-stocked with fish notable for their size. The Broad is very prettily situated, and although private and strictly preserved, it is not difficult to obtain the necessary permit.

On rounding the bend of White House Reach, Somerleyton comes in view, and our companion with the gun has his patience rewarded by several long shots at peewits, although the birds are too far off for his shot to take effect.

At Somerleyton Bridge one often has to wait for the train to pass over before they will open it to allow one to proceed on the way. Between Somerleyton and Haddiscoe Bridges, a distance of over a mile, there is little to interest the sportsman. Peewits are at all times plentiful, although they seldom come within gun-shot of boats on the river. A few years back this reach was a breeding-ground of a considerable number of moorhens, but now they all seem to have been shot or driven away. Emerging from Haddiscoe Bridge, the New Cut lies directly in front; it is a canal some three miles in length, built by Sir Morton Peto when the ruinous project was in vogue of attempting to make Norwich a port. There is no fishing to be obtained in this Cut, and as the train runs beside it all the way, the shooting is equally profitless. Yarmouth being our destination, and having a fair wind for the old river, we leave the Cut on our left, and immediately arrive at St Olaves Suspension Bridge. In order to pass under it the mast must be lowered, which occupies some little time, and a trip along the banks of the river, to the ruins of the old priory, on the right-hand bank, is worth taking.

The remains of the once famous and grand old abbey, from which the village of St Olaves takes its name, are more interesting than is at first anticipated; the crumbling walls run quite to the water's edge, and in many places they have been desecrated to common and base uses, as barns, cow-sheds, pigstyes and cottages.

Headquarters for sportsmen will be found at St Olaves Bell, a house much frequented by tourists during the summer season. It is an old-fashioned inn, with bowling-greens and tea-gardens beside the river bank. Living as well as boat hire will be found exceedingly cheap, and good fishing can be obtained in the neighbourhood.

A stoppage should be made here in order to pay a visit to the far-famed Fritton Lake which in shape is like the letter S, it is two miles in length and wonderfully picturesque, whilst many are the pictures of this Switzerland of Suffolk that have been hung in the Royal Academy. The fishing is excellent, and, at the same time, free to all, and more bream may be taken in one day with a rod than can be carried home alone. Several abandoned decoy pipes are to be found in the secluded nooks round the water, and at the easternmost extremity is one in full working order. During hard weather thousands of wild ducks are taken in this decoy and sent to the London markets. The average season produces about 1500 to 2000, but as many as 180 have been taken in a single haul. There are many other decoys in Broadland, but they are gradually being abandoned owing to the great seclusion they require. At Somerton, on the sand dunes, between the Broads and the sea, was the smallest and most successful decoy in the whole of Broadland, but some thirty years ago it fell into disuse and has now quite grown up. Norfolk decoys have of late years been more often worked as a hobby than from a mercenary view, therefore the records of their victims cannot be compared with elsewhere, as, for instance, the old Ashby decoy in Lincolnshire, where the bag from September 1833 to April 1868 totalled 99,052 fowl; including 47,764 mallard, 44,658 teal, 2119 widgeon, 285 shovellers, 275 pintail and 11 gadwall.

The property round Fritton Lake is owned by several persons, chief among them being Sir Saville Crossley, who strictly preserves the shooting, which, it is needless to say, is excellent. Boats may be obtained on the water at Fritton Old Hall. The grounds surrounding the house are prettily laid out, well kept up, and this is a good place for a picnic.

Returning to St Olaves, we find all in readiness to proceed on our voyage. In sailing away from the old grey ruins of the abbey, an expanse of heath on the right-hand bank of the river cannot fail to attract attention; it is very good shooting ground, but private. Away to the left stretches nothing but marsh and water. On a fine afternoon, with the sun haze rising over the marshes causing distant objects to be indistinct, one is reminded of Holland so strongly that it is difficult to realise one is not again in that interesting country. Whilst the number of watermills that can be counted upon the horizon is astonishing.

As the course of the winding river is pursued, unmistakable signs of salt water are encountered, and as the river widens more and more so do the mud banks show themselves, until, rounding a low point, a glimpse of Breydon Flats, left almost bare by the fast-ebbing tide, presents itself. To the right, two or three miles distant, are the ivy-clad ruins of Burgh Castle, or all that now remains of it. Its walls stand out bright against a background of dark-foliaged trees, which show up more prominently against a blue sky, and with the lime-kilns at the foot of the hills, and the green flat marshes in the foreground well studded with the yellow marigold, form a picture long to be remembered.

At this junction of the three waters—Breydon, the Waveney and the Yare—is situated the Berney Arms, a marsh tavern, unlike any other inn, because of its peculiar situation and its uninteresting surroundings. Queer company one meets with within its smoke-begrimed walls, and many a good punting yarn the old benches could tell if they had but tongue. The quarters are not to be recommended, although the wildfowler may be glad at times to avail himself of whatever poor hospitality the inn can afford. In the "good old days" many a cargo of contraband goods found a temporary resting-place here; the situation being most auspicious for its distribution.

A little further into Breydon, on the left-hand bank, is a breakwater of wooden piles, locally called the Dicky Works, and further on, in a small harbour leading to a sluice-gate, a fleet of house-boats of the poorest kind, used by the fishers and gunners of Breydon Water. This bleak and exposed part of the flats is the most sought by the professional gunner, and it is capable of affording more sport than at first would be anticipated. At due season of the year smelts are to be obtained in large quantities, which many consider the finest fish that come to table from inland waters. Codling, coal fish

and whiting may also be taken. The deep water here is
more frequented than many other parts of Breydon by fowl,
and heavy shots are made, either at early dawn or dewy eve,
and being so far away from the town of Yarmouth (some
three or four miles), the shore shooters are not so likely to
disturb the punter when laying-to fowl.

Those visiting the neighbourhood for the purpose of shooting on Breydon Water will do well to pass some of their time
moored to the
Dicky Works, or in
the above - men-
tioned creek.

ON THE PUTTY.

Breydon Water
is one of the largest
lagoons in the
Broadland district,
and when the
weather is at all
foggy or hazy one
cannot see across it.
It is about five
miles long and one
mile broad. The
channel by which
vessels cross and
re-cross is marked
out by posts set a
hundred yards or
more apart, but the
shallows extend some way beyond the posts, and a local
knowledge is required to navigate a yacht successfully
against wind and tide, unless one does not object to occasionally "touching the putty," as the yachtsmen say, or, in
other words, running aground.

At high water the mud flats are entirely covered, at low
water they are bare, with channels or creeks dissecting them
in every direction ; whilst being but a mile from the sea, the

estuary is a favourite haunt for fowl and waterbirds of all descriptions, and sportsmen and ornithologists come many miles to visit this locality in the hope of sport and specimens.

When a party cruising in Broadland contains one or more sportsmen on board, a council meeting is generally held on arrival at the Dicky Works.

The question to be considered is, whether to lay-to for the night, or proceed to the quay at Great Yarmouth? We compromise matters, arranging to stay one night at each place. Next morning our gunner is up before dawn and out in the punt with one of the watermen. He was fortunate, as he secured a duck and mallard, a reeve, two May birds (whimbrel), a young curlew, and a nice bunch of oxbirds. He informed us he might have shot several herons had he been of a mind to do so, but he refrained—with which course we all heartily concurred. At twelve o'clock we once more proceeded on our way, making Yarmouth in time for lunch. Great Yarmouth is so well-known that there is no need to describe it, beyond the few words which may be useful to sportsmen.

Yachts, boats, punts, steam-launches, and almost every kind of craft may be bought or hired at Yarmouth from many agents, but it is not as good a centre to start from for a sporting cruise as either Oulton Broad, Norwich or Wroxham.

On the North Quay and in the hamlet of Cobham Island reside many professional gunners and watermen. Punts can be hired by the day or week, with or without a swivel gun, and either breech or muzzle-loading. There are many hotels in Great Yarmouth, but those who go for the shooting only will do well to take up their quarters as near to Breydon Water as possible. If they are working for the early morning they had better secure a berth on one of the house-boats lying in the creek before mentioned, otherwise they may have to row a couple of miles or more before the first streak of dawn appears. During a hard winter, when the feathered tribe is frozen and starved out from inland waters, birds of all kinds congregate in vast numbers on Breydon Water, which, but for the number of gunners and shore shooters that abound, would be an excellent gunning ground. It is and always has been celebrated for the rare birds to be obtained there.

At certain times of the year good rod and line fishing may be obtained off the Knole Point, situated about 100 yards from the Suspension Bridge, due west. Fishing in the sea from the piers is much practised in the spring and summer months, and casting from the beach in the spring and autumn.

To obtain sport at wildfowl in the Roads out at sea off Caistor or Gorleston it will be found best to hire a shrimp boat, in the bows of which a swivel gun can be mounted. The man who handles the swivel must be an extremely smart hand, or most of the shots will be discharged into the briny within a few feet of the bows of the boat. The shooting to be had in this manner is often very good, but the fowl are so wary that approach is difficult, and only those who are experienced and old hands at the game make heavy bags. Fowl which frequent the sea are accustomed to see the shrimp boats daily, and do not pay so much regard to that class as to other craft.

When one is unable to obtain a shot by sailing, it will often be found advantageous to success to lay-to, riding at anchor upon a long cable, with one hand at watch on the rope, who can sheer the boat when he observes a bunch of fowl coming within apparent range, so that the man at the swivel can get a pull down at them as they pass by.

Sometimes a large party hire a fleet of shrimpers and anchor in the Roads about eighty yards apart, in a line at right angles to the beach, and well out. They are armed with heavy shoulder guns, and have in attendance one or more small boats with which to pick up the dead and wounded, which are soon washed beyond all hope of recovery by the fast-running tide, unless some precautions are taken to guard against it. Other boats sail about north and south of the line and stir up the fowl, which lead up and down the sea-covered sandbanks. Good fun, with plenty of difficult shots at all angles, may be obtained in this manner, but it takes a large party to ensure anything like success.

When the sea is smooth enough a punt, with or without a sail, may be used, and gunners often bring home fifty to a hundred fowl shooting in this style.

Sometimes enthusiastic shooters hire a tug and go out in her, but it is not a course to be recommended, and the sport must be indifferent unless the shooters are murderous enough to choose seagulls as their quarry.

The shooting on the beach is at all times poor and indifferent, although a collector often picks up good specimens of a valuable nature. Not so long ago an Asiatic plover was killed near the Yarmouth jetty, which was sold to the Norwich Museum for £10 or £12.

Sailing from Lowestoft in the direction of Southwold is a better hunting-ground for sea-shooting than Great Yarmouth. If anyone is desirous of trying their luck they could not do better than hire a sea-going cutter during September or October, so they can lie at anchor all night off Cove Hythe in order to catch the mallard, widgeon and pochard, which use Easton and Benacre Broads as well as the sandbanks in the Roads. Later on in the season Brent geese are migrating as well as many kinds of long-winged fowl, and sport is almost a certainty. During October the duck in this locality can be numbered in their thousands. The trip can also be extended up the Ryburgh and Aldeborough rivers; the Blackwater and other good punting grounds can also be visited. The cost of yachts at this season of the year is about half what it is in the summer, and with food would not cost each member of the party above £5 per head per week, whilst the fowl shot, if sold, go some way towards paying expenses.

PUNTSMEN'S HOUSEBOATS ON BREYDON.

WORKING BEES.

## CHAPTER VII

### WILDFOWLING AT SEA

THE first morning at Great Yarmouth the rain poured down incessantly, and the time was passed smoking and studying the few books that were on board. From one of them it was discovered that the then present father of scientific puntsmen, Mr Fielding Harmer, resided in the Borough, and as he was known to one of the party it was determined to send a note inviting him to an "At Home" during the afternoon, *R.S.V.P. en personne.*

Graciously he accepted the invitation, and as it was our wish to have a debate upon the question of estuary shooting both with shoulder and punt guns, he gave the names of several professional gunners living near the North Quay (to which we were moored), who were also invited to the "At Home." These guests were most entertaining. Some were rough, uncouth specimens of humanity, whose exterior appearance would have prejudiced the minds of many, but the knowledge that genuine sporting instincts lay hid beneath their furrowed and weather-beaten skin cemented a kindred fellowship of which there was no reason to be ashamed.

At first the majority of these visitors were reticent and uncommunicative, but after a few yarns had been spun and the whisky bottle freely circulated, tongues became loosened,

77

and anecdote after anecdote, with quaint experiences and most interesting personal reminiscences, followed one another in quick succession. All branches of estuary shooting were freely discussed and debated from most points of view. The company included men who had had opportunities of wildfowling on nearly every nook and corner of the coastline of England, Ireland and Holland, consequently much valuable information was imparted as the outcome of the gathering, and its termination could not have been regretted more than by those who had been the organisers of it.

Mr Fielding Harmer, of course, was looked up to as an authority few would dare venture to contradict, and he gave many minute details of the habits of fowl on estuaries, gleaned from personal observation, which, with his consent, found place in our capacious note-book. For over forty years he has made wildfowling his hobby and study, and although seventy years had passed over his head he still punted up the creeks of Breydon Water before the first flush of rosy dawn showed itself upon a wintry sky.

The experiences of this oldtime gunner assisted more than anything else to extract the opinions of the others, and our roughly-scribbled notes of the views expressed soon assumed bulky proportions.

After the company had dissolved we sat far into the night arranging, classifying and editing the salient points.

To dissect a mass of hurriedly-taken notes and place them before a reader in an interesting form is a task which is big in itself, and at the same time puzzles the editor not a little. Therefore, in order that this difficulty may in a measure be overcome, we have divided the discussion into branches of the various phases of sport to be obtained from the estuaries and roadsteads on the East Coast, which in reality form the borders of Broadland.

### Preliminary.

Few persons have any clear conception of the amount of

skill and knowledge of the habits of birds which one must possess in order to become a successful wildfowler.

" Unwearied patience, persevering toil
Alone can crown the fowler's eager hopes,
Whate'er the season or whate'er the sport."

But beyond these there are a thousand and one other little incidentals which books and instruction can never teach, however useful they both may be ; these can alone be acquired by practical experience.

The habits of wildfowl will be found to vary considerably according to the locality they are frequenting, whether it be a tidal estuary, an inland morass or a fresh-water Broad.

On a tidal estuary, for instance, certain species feed on the ebb and rest during the flood (regardless of night or day) ; whilst, in contravention to this, freshwater fowl, consisting chiefly of long-winged fowl and surface feeders, when at home in open weather, take their rest during the daytime and commence feeding as nightfall approaches, their habits being regulated by weather, daylight, or their own convenience ; whilst others adapt themselves to the ever-changing phases of the moon. And it is only by a careful study and knowledge of their habits that one can tell where they are eventually to be found. Generally on estuaries the great quarry is widgeon, which keep their feeding-time strictly in accordance with the rise and fall of the tide, so if the birds have arrived one invariably knows where and when they should be sought. The most extraordinary peculiarity of widgeon is their own peculiar language, concerning which a great deal has been previously written and discussed; and the manner in which experienced punters understand what the birds are doing and thinking about by their cries is certainly nothing short of marvellous, and not to be believed until put to a practical test. Yet the habits of wildfowl on estuaries, except in frosty weather, are fairly consistent. The birds frequent the sea and open water for a quiet siesta, and uninterrupted toilet after dining, and return inshore immediately the banks of ooze and edible grass

commence to become uncovered, remaining there until the
rising tide again drives them to sea ; whilst, if persistently
persecuted and hunted, they will leave the district entirely,
seeking elsewhere more favourable and secluded shores.

There is nothing more harmful to a " ground," and alarming to birds, than the continuous firing of shoulder guns
(either from a boat or the shore) if it is wished to preserve the
district for punt-gunning. Of course, public waters well
stocked with gunners are not thus referred to, nor are estuaries
where there is an eager shooter for every fowl in the place, as
in that case it would be an utter impossibility to restrain them
from their endeavours, the argument being that if they don't
shoot the birds somebody else will. This, therefore, accounts
for the diminished stock on our large public shooting grounds,
and the various devices and plans for the destruction of wildfowl now carried on, regardless whether they come under
the lawful denomination of sport, or the injury inflicted on
the district, so long as the shooters have the satisfaction of
being able to say that they have shot *at* a duck. Again,
in some localities it is only possible to carry out one class of
shooting. Where this is the case it should not be too often
resorted to, but carried out in a systematic, skilful manner ;
thus a good day once a week may become almost certain,
where otherwise all the labour, patience and skill in the
world would produce but little result.

### WILDFOWLING AFLOAT.

This branch of sport should on no consideration be chosen
for a "gunning" district, which is a broad principle that all
alike should strictly follow.

The reasons for this ought to be apparent to anyone possessing the crudest rudiments of wildfowling without further comment. Fowl, after feeding on the ebb (or at night), resort to
the open water for rest and sleep, and if they find no security
there, and are unduly harassed, they will desert the coast
altogether ; indeed, in some parts of England it is to be

feared that wildfowl shooting has become a matter of history on account of the enormous number of craft of all kinds (steam, manual and sailing) which have incessantly pursued them in their once much-frequented haunts. Not only do these inexperienced harassers expend a maximum of ammunition for a minimum of birds, but they bring about far more mischief in destroying their confidence more in one day than a skilled punt-gunner would do in a season; for rare are the occasions upon which a puntsman leaves his favourite shallows to venture into the deep water, since, when he does so, the result usually proves unsatisfactory, wind, weather, swell and fifty other things impeding his working, to say nothing of the other risks to which he is subject.

Birds whose *habitat* is deep water are generally of the short-winged and hard species, which are little esteemed by the epicure; they invariably sit scattered, rarely being packed, as on the feeding grounds, thus adding considerably to the difficulty encountered when trying for a shot a little above the average, which bright pages in the record of one's sporting career are, alas! so very few and far between.

But to the floating armada of boats, what matters it whether they sit loosely or otherwise? Their ambition, at most, does not aspire beyond two or three birds for one discharge; and if approach is rendered difficult, rifle, shrapnel shells or some other devices are brought into play, utterly disregardful of the great danger attendant on their usage. Their fleet possesses quantity, quality, also variety, and through its medium is conducted a special branch of warfare against the feathered tribe. Let us investigate the different methods of procedure which they employ. We will take an imaginary trip in a steam-launch, such as is often met with cruising about the mouth of Harwich Harbour, the Thames, the Medway, or, in fact, on almost all waters near large towns capable of affording refuge to even a gull or loon. Our craft is well suited for her purpose, has smokeless and silent engines, is freighted with provisions, plenty of good liquor and tobacco, a punt-gun mounted on her bows, and a jovial party inside, armed to the teeth with 4-bores, 8-bores, double and single rifles, and every imaginable device calculated to slay or drive away any living thing in or out of range. A fitful wind off the land, with occasional snow squalls, is most favourable to the project, so let us have it so. Such conditions of weather cause an uneasiness in the birds, and plenty of small "trips" to constantly lead about, gladdening the hearts of the blood-thirsty crew.

Presently the man in the bows, with binoculars, sights a bunch of fowl, and a chorus of excited exclamations ensue. Our captain, however, asserts command, and silences all by issuing his directions. One takes his position at the big gun, another in the stern, while the remainder, grasping their weapons in eager expectancy, crowd under cover of the gunwale, reminding one of pirates preparing to board an unsuspecting merchant vessel. "We must be near enough now," whispers No. 1. "No, we're not," replies No. 2. "But the swivel, surely" (which he thinks can kill anything within sight), "will easily reach them," chimes in No. 3, and so on, until at last the birds settle further dispute by "jumping" prematurely. No. 1 cannot restrain himself longer, and lets off both barrels of his double 8-bore at quite 200 yards' range (which, over the water, does not look one-third the distance), then No. 3 and No. 2 respectively join in, whilst, perhaps, the man at the big gun (who ought to know better), overcome with the general excitement, adds its dull boom to the already deafening serenade. Thus the party proceeds, obtaining shots now and again with little variation and less result, until at last an unfortunate duck, receiving a stray pellet, is pinioned, then—oh, joy!—up starts the whole piratical crew, eager to claim and prove that to his own individual prowess fell the prize, and, amidst the general confusion, irregular volleys are discharged haphazard at the victim, which, at length, half-drowned with constant and prolonged diving, is secured by the assistance of boat-hook and landing-net.

Or, to vary proceedings, perhaps, after several unsuccessful attempts at approaching some "hard fowl," a volley of pellets and rifle bullets is discharged at the artful curres, when, lo! and behold, peaceful (too often otherwise disposed) fishermen may be discerned in the distance, expostulating with frantic signals at what they evidently consider a direct attempt at murder on the high seas, and on coming within earshot are discovered to be remonstrating, in language more forcible than refined, against shooters in general and our party in particular. These manœuvres are repeated until many miles from home, when the boat bears up and retraces her course, discovering that great success has been achieved in one respect at all events, viz., in thoroughly frightening every bird from the neighbourhood; for now there remains only an odd cripple or two, with a solitary "sprat-boy," * where in the morning hundreds of birds had been visible. Even that solitary and usually so tame old loon * will not have the politeness to gratify the desires of the gentleman with the Martini-Henry who thinks perhaps that, fisherman or no fisherman, he would otherwise have distinguished himself.

This trip may be a day's outing, but it cannot be called sport, and its participators, in mitigation of the harm they have done, argue that they will not be likely to revisit the district for some time to come, when more birds will be sure to have found their way back again.

Assuming a party, such as described, chance upon a fairly good gunning estuary for their so-called sport, the poor gunner who may have been for days nursing for a shot will find his ground so thoroughly upset that he will be compelled to wait patiently for weeks before he can continue his shooting.

The steam-launch party, after having scared away all the fowl from the open water, are rarely contented to remain there, but skirt the shore and poke up every creek capable of receiving their draught of water, blazing at oxbirds, sandpipers, and every bag of bones encased in a feathered skin.

* Speckled diver.

This is a true sketch taken from one of many suchlike excursions, where the shooters know little or nothing of fowling, but, having gleaned a few hints from some work on the subject, their purse provides the remainder.  Yet, on the other hand, when the right men go in a properly-adapted launch, managing her judiciously, with a thought for the morrow, good sport is sometimes obtained, where by other means it would be impossible, although on fairly private water it is always to be deprecated.

Turn to another and, on the face of it, perhaps more feasible method of fowling afloat, viz., under sail ; though this method likewise, when improperly carried out, is almost as injurious in its results as wildfowling from a steam launch.

After mentioning that campaigns similar to the one just described are also organised in shrimpers and small sailing craft, with a big gun mounted in the bow, we will take another imaginary flight with the crew of one of the small coasting yachts so often seen anchored at the mouths of our estuaries, for a day or two's fowling, and not being provided with swivel or punt guns, make shift with what sport can be obtained from her deck with ordinary large-bore shoulder guns.  As sailing craft are more or less dependent upon tides and weather for their progress, they cannot possibly cover half the "ground," nor bring about one tithe of the injury that a steam vessel invariably accomplishes.  Nevertheless, in "gunning" districts, every other manner of shooting is obnoxious and hurtful to the punter's interests except legitimate punting.

We are on board a small yacht (or, best of all, fishing boat of that class mostly used in the neighbourhood one happens to be in), with a good sportive old salt as gubernator, anchored under the lee of the shore, our party having turned in to bunk earlier than usual to obtain the requisite sleep prior to rising before the dawn, which is by far the best time for duck shooting.  We turn out an hour before Aurora shows her first glimmer above the eastern horizon, and, full of expectancy and hope, get under weigh, gliding noiselessly from our moorings, with binoculars and ears in full action. As previously, let us suppose the circumstances to be favourable, with every man at his place, for it is often at this hour one finds himself suddenly and unexpectedly at close quarters with the birds. But see! the preconcerted signal; arm dropped and finger telegraph denoting the presence of fowl, whilst strained eyes detect several indistinct movable dots on the surface of the briny, not a hundred yards distant. All three guns are levelled in readiness; nearer, yet a little nearer, and then they rise; bang—bang! bang! bang! The welcome smell of powder, a flapping on the water, the inveterate cripple making off to windward, and the helm is put down intercepting his course, which the 12-bore effectively finishes. Then the craft is shot into the eye of the wind in the midst of the struggling victims, the cripple net is eagerly called for in two or three places at once, and by its aid the dead birds are gathered in. But over zeal has caused too much way to be given to our boat, leaving a third cripple astern, necessitating intricate nautical manœuvres, deftly carried out under the direction of the skipper, accompanied by much hauling on ropes. After some difficulty in "re-spotting," all the cripples are secured, whilst, of course, a vain search is made for the imaginary remainder. Congratulations and the inevitable dram follow, when observance of bearings shows that a considerable advance has been made into the open water, whilst daylight has rapidly developed from its glimmering glow into full clearness. Another bunch of fowl is shortly announced, and we sail directly for it, but overconfidence from former success leads our party to misjudge distance and fire prematurely.

Judging distance when shooting over water is the greatest difficulty which a gunner has to surmount, and to what extent this is the case only those who have experienced it are able to realise; but here it acts as a wholesome steadier to one's intrepidity, causing the old salt to seriously shake his head, take a fresh quid of twist, and mutter, " Warts

t' use o' waisten powder an shart loike that there ? better
sheut t' bleuming moon," etc., whilst the fowl begin to
awaken to the fact that that seemingly innocent-looking
exterior must contain rather more dangerous inmates than
they at first supposed, and they apparently determine to
give it a wide berth in future. Their quiet domestic circles
are filled with suspicion and fear. The last volley in the
open confirmed their worst apprehensions, besides alarming
the whole neighbourhood, for as soon as our bow is turned
towards any of the birds, they rise, leading off in all
directions, and leave our small boat alone on the billowy
wave. So we ease her sheet and take a run to leeward,
where fortune intervenes in the shape of a small skein of
geese, sighted from the starboard quarter.

Now, fowl at sea, or in the open water, and more
especially geese, where they have not been harassed too
much, will often allow a sailing boat to approach within a
short distance, in comparison to what they will in the case
of a rowing-boat, gun-punt or steam launch. The reason can
only be assumed to be, and most probably is, because, firstly
—they are accustomed to see sailing ships and fishing vessels
in their immediate proximity, and rarely being molested by
them do not attach one half the suspicion or importance that
they would to any other class of craft which they observe
cautiously sneaking down upon them ; and secondly—a small
sail may appear to them little different to a larger one, which
happens to be further off; whilst the great speed at which
a shrimper or gunning-punt (she must not have too much
freeboard for this work), with strong tide under her, and
fair wind, travels, enable such to approach within a hundred
yards before the birds can decide in their minds whether she
really is near or afar off.

Knowing this, our crew adopt these tactics for the geese,
and with a flowing sheet, under the fast-freshening wind,
" romp " into their midst, dealing death and destruction by
a sudden volley from all the artillery on board, resulting in
five killed and two wounded. Bringing up head to wind

the dead are secured, followed by luffing up on a real wild-goose chase after the cripples. In the general excitement to secure them, however, we make much farther seaward than "old Salubrious" likes, and we are obliged to take in a couple of reefs before his cautious old soul is satisfied. But his "larnin' and prorfecy 'o trorshin to win'ard in a 'ead wind as bein' a trifle damp," is fully justified, and one and all are greatly relieved to find themselves safely ensconced in a small creek under shelter of the land. All the fowl have long ago been driven away by the noise of firing, and nothing beyond the plaintive shriek from a solitary "whaup" * greets our re-appearance, so, letting go the anchor, we make up for the night, clean our guns, lay the cloth, and complete all arrangements in providing comfort for the inner as well as the outer man.

Then we have trips made by would-be sportsmen in rowing boats and such like, but these are too common and well-known to need touching upon.

But to describe what is known to be a novelty to most people, whether they be ooze-trotters, wild-fowlers, professional gunners, amateurs, or casual readers, is a method only in vogue on the east coast of England (where curres, short-winged or hard fowl abound), which is brought into practical use either at the mouth of a large estuary or in a comparatively open roadstead with good rise and fall of tide. It may aptly be designated "a wildfowl battue."

For the purpose of describing it we will start on another imaginary expedition. Hearing from the fishermen on the coast that immense quantities of fowl are in the roads, we form a party, and charter ten to fifteen shrimpers, yawls, or, as before mentioned, boats of that kind which are used and suited to the neighbourhood; apportioning a couple of shooters to each boat, besides her usual crew, we sail, row, or are towed to the intended scene of action, where we anchor at equal distances apart, at intervals of about sixty yards, with a very long line for cable, and to enable us to

* Curlew

sheer about, impelled by the tide, as may prove desirable. Loading the heavy shoulder guns, also our soothing pipes, we lie low and await the issue of events. Some, perhaps, indulge in the gentle art of fishing to while away the time between the flights of the fowl, for, similar to partridge driving in a sparsely-stocked country, there are not only certain periodical intervals of waiting, but there is also the glorious uncertainty of their coming over your stand as the fortunate gun. Our men placed in position, the driving launches or other craft used for a similar purpose commence their part of the work; making a big circuit, they get on the far side of the birds, and then commence such eccentric movements as to raise suspicion, causing the birds to rise in detachments and work over the line of boats, who take their toll accordingly. These tactics are repeated again and again, until the birds become too knowing for their persevering would-be destroyers.

If the fickle goddess Fortune turns her countenance upon the sportsmen, good fun sometimes results, the bag, however, consisting mostly of hard fowl and scoters, the latter worthless for consumption and the former not so very tempting, which rather mars one's enjoyment of the sport; for where is the pleasure in killing that which is harmless and unfit for food? or what sport can one find in killing for the sake of killing only? But then, on the other hand, although a refined palate objects to the fishy and oleaginous flavour of a tough old "mussel duck," there are many people in the great Metropolis who by no means turn up their noses thereat, and finding that that great vortex for the receipt of game—namely, Leadenhall Market—will always dispose of them, the objection grounded on killing for killing's sake is overcome, and on reconsideration the fun does not seem "so dusty" after all. Again, the birds are by no means easy to "double up," especially if one is unaccustomed to shoot from a boat, and that boat on the sea, and when they are "doubled up" it is far from being the last of them; they must be gathered, and if one succeeds in bagging three only from every five knocked down it is indeed fortunate.

This reference to the difficulty encountered when gathering the birds brings to memory an amusing incident which happened many years since, and runs as follows:—All arrangements for a scoter battue had been completed, and the party was on the point of starting from Musseldom beach, in the county of Curreshire, no less than eleven boats strong, not including the drivers, when a young enthusiast begged very hard to be allowed to take part in the expedition. He had lent a helping hand in former fowling exploits, on more occasions than one, whilst his pleading, upturned countenance, and eyes aglow with all the fire of overpowering excitement, which he could ill conceal, was so entreating that one's fellow-feelings of sporting instinct softened towards him, and he was granted a berth in one of the boats. Not much notice was taken of this extraordinary shore-loafer until the line was fairly anchored, and the first batch or two of black duck had passed over. He fired, although the birds were at least eighty yards off, and then attention was drawn to the peculiar appendages produced for extracting his loading requisites. First came the powder, taken from an old medicine bottle, and carefully measured in an ordinary clay pipe bowl: on the top of this a ball of brown paper, rammed home, followed by a handful of shot from his left-hand breeches-pocket; another paper wad, and barrel No. 1 was charged to the full satisfaction and evident pride of its owner. Barrel No. 2 he did not interfere with, because, as he explained, it had long since burst, and was now *corked up* to prevent mistakes. The lock (kept in position by a piece of string) was next cocked, primed and capped, and is it to be wondered at that, after this display, he was generously allotted the whole of the bows of the boat for his absolute disposal during the remainder of the day? One last remark on his prowess. He actually drew first blood by winging a " black " duck, and his joy thereat was far greater than can be described in words. Jumping on to the boom, he was just in time to see his bird dive, and turning to us a piteous face, the very picture of despair and disappointment, he exclaimed, in a voice of anguish, "Why, I'll be blowed if my duck ain't gone and sunk."

But, taking it all round, this, together with all other methods of wildfowl-shooting, is poor indeed in comparison to punt-shooting proper, for besides being injurious to the "ground," the bag is invariably small, the birds are not half so palatable, and the expenses attendant thereon are far greater. Further, if the practices mentioned under this heading are continually resorted to on good gunning estuaries, the better species of fowl are apt to be irretrievably driven away for the remainder of the season. Whereas, on the other hand, by judicious punt-shooting on the flats, as will be hereafter shown, a large quantity of birds are usually obtainable without perceptibly breaking up or injuring their haunts, whilst the sport is a thousand times more scientific, satisfactory and enjoyable. But that want of skill and endurance, which so few possess, and still fewer exercise sufficient perseverance to attain, prejudices the many against the few who are capable of successfully carrying it out. It is, however, to be sincerely hoped that common sense and good judgment will weigh the balance in favour of the much-abused and so little-known art, namely, "Legitimate Punt Gunning."

THE OLD SHIP RUN ON BREYDON.

# CHAPTER VIII

## PUNT-GUNNING

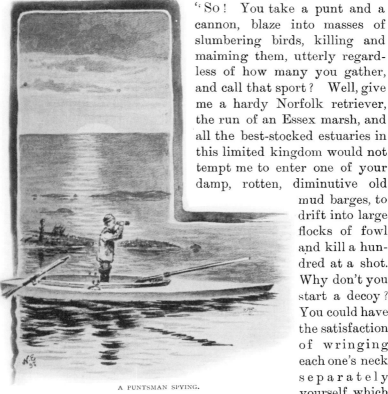

A PUNTSMAN SPYING.

"So! You take a punt and a cannon, blaze into masses of slumbering birds, killing and maiming them, utterly regardless of how many you gather, and call that sport? Well, give me a hardy Norfolk retriever, the run of an Essex marsh, and all the best-stocked estuaries in this limited kingdom would not tempt me to enter one of your damp, rotten, diminutive old mud barges, to drift into large flocks of fowl and kill a hundred at a shot. Why don't you start a decoy? You could have the satisfaction of wringing each one's neck separately yourself, which would give you far more gratification than killing them all at once, I'm sure."

Thus ventured to speak an almost anti-shooting member of our party, who actually had the audacity to express his personal opinion in the face of our thoroughly practical company of visitors on board the *Warrior*. Whether he did so by way of a show, or to see what they would say, we do not know, anyhow, it had the effect of instantly rousing every man into action and words. They gesticulated and argued on all sides, several leaving their seats to get closer to the heretic of their faith, and they almost climbed on to his lap in their eagerness to convert him.

"You may have had plenty of experience in most sports, but you clearly know nothing of punt-gunning, or you would never thus expose your ignorance by repeating such absurd notions; light your cigar and give us your attention for half an hour only, and we will try to convert your very erroneous ideas into a reasonable shape."

. Eventually they brought our friend round to vouchsafe that perhaps it was "not so bad after all," etc. The arguments that were used included the following :—

A good and successful puntsman may in some respects be compared to a good general; the latter must be well up in the geography of the place, and the tactics of managing and manœuvring an army of men; whilst the former must also be well acquainted with the handling of a large army of wildfowl, and the skill he requires for such is quite on a par with that of his bellicose compatriot. When he attacks, single-handed, a large company of several hundreds—maybe, thousands—of wildfowl in the open, with perhaps no better shelter than a small cloud to back him, it is next to impossible to get within range of the main body; for the number of ears, eyes, and quantity of outposts, sentries and stragglers are always the more numerous the larger the flock. The extraordinary amount of skill, perseverance and judgment required in outwitting their instinctive wariness is incredible. First, the gunner ventures a semi-approach from the right, then from the left, now in the centre, until the birds are worked into a favourable position, and gradually, little by little, ground is gained. Yet he must in no way alarm the sentries beyond bare suspicion, but play with their susceptibilities to such an extent that they retire

LAYING-TO GEESE.

nearer to the congregated mass without sounding an alarm. He may be hours, sometimes days, before he has the satisfaction of relinquishing his scull for the trigger; but patience is a virtue, and success, in the long run, will inevitably attend those who persistently persevere. It is not unusual to be several hours in traversing one hundred yards across flooded marshes, but such patience is generally rewarded in the end. And oh! the excitement experienced when laying-to a large number of wildfowl; it far exceeds anything that can be described. It savours of the kind of excitement that is felt when all depends upon the issue of a single cast; like the feelings of a man whose whole fortune hangs upon the result of a horse race and who is watching the panting quadrupeds tear up the straight for home locked neck and neck. Then, perhaps, after an hour or more breathless excitement, and severe trial to the nerves, your cup of pleasure remains untasted on account of a miss-fire, or even more trifling mishap, followed by the roaring of many pinions, like the waters of a cataract, as all rise in a moment and are gone, lost to sight with none left to make their memory dear; you alone remain.

How often does one make a shot such as that mentioned? Not more than once or twice in a lifetime. Perhaps the gunner may be indefatigably working the whole winter in an estuary crowded with birds, and scarcely obtain half a dozen good chances during the whole season. And further, a gunner has other things to learn besides the management of a boat under oar or canvas, and the handling of a staunchion gun; he must be a good judge of weather, a man of indomitable courage and perseverance, well conversant with tides and winds, a thorough ornithologist, so that he can at once recognise every species by sound or sight, besides understanding the different actions and habits peculiar to each section of the tribe, as they all require different handling accordingly. When he turns out in the early morning, long before daybreak, he should know by the elements and barometer where to find his quarry, and how, in all probability, they will be engaged as soon as he arrives within earshot of their haunts.

These facts should be established to a certainty, so that he need not approach and disturb them until the right time arrives. Thus good gunners, who have the "ground" more or less to themselves, nurse, rather than harass their birds. On the other hand, an ignorant one attacks, regardless of circumstances or future results, so long as he bags more birds at the time, whilst comparatively small entries are afterwards noted in his diary to those of his more skilful brother sportsmen.

Again, by knowledge of the weather a puntsman knows that certain conditions are favourable for certain parts of the "ground," therefore he will work at most favourable times, and in the most auspicious locality, leaving the birds at absolute rest during all other periods; neither will he worry his fowl before they have fed, except in stormy or hard weather, when liberties may sometimes be taken.

The actual working hours of our friend on the flats may well be divided into four distinct periods, namely, early morning, midday, evening and night. By far the best time is that period from when the earliest glimmer of light appears flickering above the eastern horizon till sunrise. With that first flush of dawn the gunner is enabled to ascertain whether the day will be fine or not. If it is to be fine, it invariably comes low and streaky; on the other hand, when wind and wet may be expected, it breaks high up, often right overhead. At least an hour before daybreak (earlier still if a long distance from his punt) the gunner rises, and having fortified himself with a substantial breakfast, proceeds to put his craft into perfect order, as, unless there be a place for everything and everything in its place, one cannot get on with any degree of comfort in the dark. One should be able to lay one's hand on whatever is wanted at a moment's notice, and not be fiddling everywhere, or striking matches to find it, as a great many do who ought, by this time, to know better.

To take another imaginary trip. Presuming the punt launched, swivel shipped into its knee, and all stores on board, we take a careful observation of wind and weather; wind north-east by east, moderate breeze, and flowing tide— very good. Our course is immediately decided upon, and we head for " Devil's Bank," well known to our skilful companion as the widgeon's favourite haunt, which, with these auspicious omens in the weather, should surely be found there now, or else not at all. Half an hour's hard rowing and then our oars are rested upon, and our auricular organs resorted to. Nothing ahead yet; on we go, cautiously listening the while; another stop with perfect silence. Yes, there they are, sure enough. " Weoh!—we-o-oh!"—those, to us, sweet notes, come faintly over the water and touch the right string in our hearts; our oars are carefully and deliberately unshipped, one being placed in the sculling crutch, the other stowed away. Our scientific man takes possession of the scull and directs his other hand to lay the gun. Then, getting daylight sky behind the fowl, with wind on the port bow, we glide slowly and stealthily nearer and nearer to the unsuspecting birds, listen-ing every few minutes to ascertain that their suspicions are not aroused. Large bunches often, when they have the slightest cause for alarm, are as silent as the grave for as much as five minutes at a time; or, perhaps, they break into a " charm "—when an entire flock, guided only by the whistle of one old cock, accompanied by the clucking of the hens, burst into music all at once, which sudden outburst is called the " charm."

We are now within 150 yards, but the bank is not sufficiently covered to mass our birds, so we relinquish the scull and wait for what is in reality only half an hour longer, yet, seemingly, ages. But the daylight is rapidly developing; we dare not remain much longer for fear of detection, so, with one last look to the gun and boat, we make for where that greedy, squabbling crowd seems thickest. One hundred yards —eighty yards—sixty yards—up goes a forest of heads, and as part jump, a pound and a half of single " B " is nicely landed into their very midst. In an instant the sculls are out and the cripple-stopper in the hand; one rows whilst the other sits athwart the staunchion gun forward and directs the course. The dead are discarded in preference to the livelier cripples, and after all are collected, nicely and cleanly packed away, the big gun is reloaded and we are again in readiness for further action.

But, presuming a duffer had been in our place, how different it all would have been; ten to one he would have crossed the birds' wind and jumped them before being aware

THE CRIPPLE-STOPPER IN ACTION

of their close proximity, or if he had got a shot he most probably would have rushed in prematurely — misjudged distance—or shot too high or too low. In any case he could not possibly have bagged more than half the number that we have here depicted.

Sometimes a single cock widgeon will get into the middle of a flock of gulls, and many instances are on record when, in the uncertain light of early morning, a shot has been made into a large flock of such, killing many, including, perhaps, the deceptive smee.

Very often, too, when a shot is made in the dawn, another flock from a distance, disturbed by the flash from a gun, rise and re-pitch quite close by, enabling you to obtain a second shot, or even a third shot being fired before a single cripple has been gathered, which, as one is favoured by the fast-increasing daylight, flowing tide, and certain assistance as to their whereabouts by cannibalistic seagulls, few are seldom lost.

The daylight shoot here described clearly indicates the advantages of an experienced over an inexperienced hand. To quote an example. Two amateurs started single-handed from the same place, on the same estuary, three consecutive mornings, with equal opportunities, one securing 115 fowl and about 140 waders, whilst the other got three fowl and a score of waders. The unsuccessful one created more noise and disturbance than his more experienced brother gunner, as the latter, would refuse to lay at an indifferent chance, whilst the latter, in an excited manner, blazed away at everything that offered.

Mid-day hours are generally employed when mornings have, from various causes, proved impracticable or ineffective, and one has then to be satisfied with the smaller "trips," it being quite out of the question to disturb a big flock, for, unless they are fresh arrivals, or have been punished by stress of weather, they will not allow your punt, or any other craft, to approach within a quarter of a mile, the main body always being timely warned by their videttes. In the early morn, widgeon (smee, as the professionals call them) are the chief birds for the gunner, but in the daytime all kinds of fowl that seem quietly disposed may receive your attentions, and these failing, you have recourse to whaup, whimbrel, plover, or whatever offers.

Thirdly, there is the evening shoot, which is nearly always unsatisfactory, and seldom indulged in unless the preceding day has been unfortunate in bringing sport; but one is now and again tempted out by exceptional circumstances, or by the close of the season being near at hand. It is more particularly to be deprecated because the waning light necessarily causes great loss and waste in cripples, but an occasional good shot at that hour is made after rough weather, at a bunch of fowl in a favourable position for re-covering the killed or maimed.

Fourthly and finally, gunning under the moon is con-sidered far from satisfactory; it is highly injurious to the shooting grounds, and it is very seldom that the gunner makes any really good results from this latter method of shooting, except by launching—a very laborious and dirty pursuit at any time; in fact, as Buffon would have said, " *Le jeu ne vaut pas la chandelle.*"

A successful shot under the stars, judging entirely by sound, is possible, but it is more than probable that under those conditions the shooter would have to feel for the dead with an oar, not bagging half what he had killed. What can be more unsatisfactory than this? The same remark applies also to a very great extent to the former manner of shooting, and birds in moonlight are shyer and more difficult to handle than in broad daylight, although occasionally telling shots are pulled off when a friendly cloud temporarily obscures the light of the moon. But, unfortunately, these said nebulæ have an obstinate plan of always uncovering at the wrong moment, showing you up to the birds as a brightly-reflected star of rather unpleasant magnitude. Another drawback to gunning by night is the great danger attendant thereon from icefloes, especially on an ebb tide, as one some-times gets caught in a great ice-field, and can neither see its ex-tent nor find out how to circumvent it or force a way through, to say nothing of the chance of being nipped, which may occur at the least expected moment, whilst all the time the punts-man is rapidly drifting far out to sea in a perfectly helpless condition ; or, to make matters worse, sudden squalls of snow may arise, which either swamp him then and there, or chafe his punt against the edge of the ice until her planks are cut through.

It must be borne in mind that during frosty and hard weather, or preparatory to some great atmospherical change, the habits of fowl are completely revolutionised; one must therefore work according to the locality, time, weather and season.

There are men who coast all round a country, staying but a short period in each wildfowling district. This is, on the face of it, all against large bags, as one so doing can have but an indifferent knowledge of the ground he works, and local knowledge is one of the most essential points to success. Then, on the other hand, it is "rough" on the resident shooters of the visited neighbourhood, for the visitor is usually totally indifferent to how much alarm he creates—he bags what he can. The only advantage of the system is the following of the migrating birds as they work southwards; even that is open to serious doubts.

Some atmospherically-learned people erroneously believe that shooting on estuaries in a fog is very auspicious towards the gun, but practical experience proves that little or nothing can be done under these circumstances. Now and again geese can be "got in" at when it is not too thick, but fowl rarely if ever, for they almost invariably detect the punt, which can best be accounted for by a simple lesson drawn from Nature herself. By way of example, if a clamorous Brent goose looms out some twenty times its natural size, when seen through a fog, what an enormous apparition must the punt represent to the birds being approached.

Referring to forbearance in shooting on preserved waters until a good opportunity offers, the author one season restrained from firing a shot for three weeks on a small estuary where the birds had been previously harassed with shoulder guns, in order to allow them to regain confidence, although punting about in the midst of hundreds. The reward came in due course, for the first shot was a good one, and was rapidly followed by others. Had a favourable opportunity offered itself before it would of course have been taken, but not being able to obtain a really good " home thrust," and the weather being unfavourable for new arrivals, it was thought best to watch and wait, knowing full well that the day was not far distant when the chuckle would be inside instead of outside the punt.

THE OLD GUNNER.

SCAUP.

## CHAPTER IX

### CURRES AND SHORT-WINGED FOWL

THE word "curre" specifies a class of ducks which is not covered by any scientific or ornithological term, and therefore it should not be allowed to lapse.

The word seems to have been handed down by the gunners of the old school, and it embraces that species of wildfowl which obtains its food from the bottom of fairly deep water by diving: whereas the more commonly-known and generally-termed "surface feeders" include "long-winged fowl," or such as do not feed in deeper water but where they can reach the bottom by (what is called) standing on their heads, or by very short dives.

Nature has provided "curres" with shorter wings, greater paddling power, and different corporeal formation; perhaps it is on this account that they seldom visit the land, but obtain their requisite amount of sleep, and perform their toilet, always afloat. It is not therefore a very difficult task to prove that their habits are quite distinct from the long-winged species, which are more esteemed for the table, by reason of their vegetarian diet, whereas, on the other hand, the food of most of the "curre" species consists chiefly of shell fish and other molusca.

Again, " curres " comprise several distinct varieties, which had best be subdivided into those keeping strictly to the open sea, and those which sometimes come inland.

The former revel in the waves, and when on wing seldom rise any height above them, riding out the heaviest storm or roughest water, which their more active *confrères* do not at all relish, seeming to prefer the smoother water, and on any violent atmospheric disturbance they at once make off to the inland lakes or larger stretches of open water near the coast. In speaking of them (the latter) as the more active it is in allusion to their strength of wing, because, although they scuffle up, rising heavily and obliquely, when once they are fairly under way they fly with extraordinary rapidity, often at great heights and distances, making at the time a rushing, peculiar sound with their pinions, which is at variance with the more musical whistle of long-winged fowl.

The habitual method employed by " curres " in obtaining their food is another peculiarity. They float on the tide over their favourite feeding grounds, and when there happens to be a very large " mob " of them, they make such a tremendous noise diving and splashing after their food that it resembles the noise produced by a cataract, and may be heard during a calm, or in still weather, at incredible distances. As soon as they have reached the utmost limits of the mollusc bed they rise in batches, flying back again to the utmost extremity of it, in order that they may once more be carried down by the friendly tide.

One of the largest, and perhaps best-known, resorts is off the coast of Belgium and France, where " curres " may be seen in thousands upon thousands nearly all the year round. They may be observed when crossing the Channel, more particularly on the routes to Ostend, Calais or Dunkirk. In some seasons vast packs visit the Suffolk and Norfolk coast, apparently revelling in the fleet water and on the much-dreaded outlying sandbanks.

Another peculiarity in certain varieties of " curres " is that they do not obtain their full plumage until they are

two or three years old, nor, in some cases, do they breed until
then, which may account for their presence amongst us during
the summer months, as some of them may always be found
in the roadsteads off Broadland, in small flocks, accompanied
by very old birds, who have no object in migrating to the
breeding countries. This peculiarity is also common to
certain waders, gulls, and last, but not least, swans.

Between true "curres" and "surface feeders" there
exists an intermediate variety, which partake of the habits
of each, such as tufted ducks, etc. Golden eyes form
another link in the chain connecting tufters and scaups,
but the fear of being tedious prevents further minute
details being given here.

The little tufter embodies high edible qualities, although
often seen and shot in company with his oleaginous,
mollusc-feeding brethren, which shows that he does not
cultivate their piscivorous tastes, although he may freely
mix with them. All "curres" are not unpalatable, for their
is yet another variety in the fresh-water-loving "curre,"
namely pochards (commonly known in Broadland as
" pokers "), which never feed in salt water unless forced there
by unavoidable circumstances. These fowl are strict vegetarians, delighting in a weed called pochard grass, of which
the greatest beds in Broadland exist on Hickling Broad and
Heigham Sounds, whither they flight in from the surrounding
country with great regularity at sundown, leaving early
for their resting-places in the morning. This shows that they
have a flighting disposition similar to the long-winged species,
of which true "curres" possess no spark; yet they are
similar in one respect, in that they always keep to the open
water, and, when disturbed, invariably remain *over* the
water, avoiding the land as much as possible. " Curres "
afford little or no sport to the shoulder gunner, and are
only fit quarry for a punt gun; in fact, they can be secured
in no quantities by any other method, as with "curre" in-
stinctiveness they are immovable to the blandishments of
the decoy-man.

Sometimes they are captured in small quantities by snares placed along their grass-beds, under water, and in another manner by the assistance of a net stretched on lofty poles, which is made to rise suddenly and take the pochards in their flight. This method of fowling was formerly practised in Essex, and is referred to in Daniel's *Rural Sports* article, " Pochard," also in the *Moor and Marsh* shooting volume of the Badminton Library, p. 186. Although perhaps effective, it seems almost as unsportsmanlike a proceeding as the pegging of nets at the bottom of the sea, a usual practice in the tidal waters on the other side of "the silver streak."

Some years a few pochards stay in Broadland to breed, which can be verified at Lord Walsingham's estate ; and the author once shot a young one at the evening flight on the 1st of August 1878, some ten miles inland near Barnby Broad in the Waveney Valley.

Most wildfowlers know the taste of pochards when in good condition. The Rev. R. Lubbock (in his *Fauna of Norfolk*, page 111) says : " This is the best wildfowl for the table of all the *Anatidæ*; it has the honour of a near relationship to the celebrated canvasback of America, which has its name, *Valisneria*, from a particular grass on which it feeds, besides being there found in its company."

As to the reference to the canvasback duck, it is believed that it derives its flavour from feeding on wild celery.

Another habit distinct from the long-winged species is, that " curres " pack whilst resting and spread out when feeding, room being necessary for their diving operations, whereas it is just the contrary with long-winged fowl, which on a flowing tide gather greedily round the choicest spots. Therefore, in punting to them with a swivel entirely different tactics are adopted to those exercised when punting to " surface feeders."

Scaups are similar in their habits to pochards, excepting the latter are chiefly fresh water frequenters and vegetarians, whereas the former are not strictly so, preferring salt water, and being typical "curres."

It is an invariable rule amongst wildfowl in general, and "curres" in particular, to sit head to wind, and in punting to "curres" an exception to the rule, "to always punt up-wind," must be made and these fowl approached more or less down wind, as they do not object to one's crossing to windward of them so strongly as the more sensitive long-winged fowl (widgeon or mallard), although, in most other respects, they are, if anything, a good deal more shy. At first they swim away from the suspicious-looking punt, but finding their headway by no means so fast as that of their pursuer they huddle together, and as he draws nearer to them they open a bit and rise to windward, offering a good cross shot ; whereas, if punted to up-wind, they will deploy into a long straggling line (similar to the historical thin red line which will ever be proudly remembered by all in connection with the glorious 93rd Highlanders at the battle of Balaclava), swimming away as fast as one can scull the punt, and when they eventually do rise they scatter so that it is seldom more than a couple, or at most half-a-dozen, are within range of the shot circle.

All "curres" are very hard indeed to kill. They carry away an incredible amount of shot, and are even more tenacious of life than the proverbial cat ; actually when in the hand, unless one is conversant with the decoy-man's art of neck-breaking, it is most difficult to effectually extinguish the vital spark of life. To quote instances. On one occasion nine scaups were knocked down by a long shot from a parcel leading past on the open sea, in a dead calm, and although a prolonged cripple chase followed and several rounds of small ammunition were expended not one was bagged.

On another occasion seven velvet scoters were shot at on the water, and the punter believed he had stopped the whole, whereas, as a matter of fact, he did not materially injure one ; they all "ducked to the flash" and came up at various points considerable distances away from the punt, flying off singly and in different directions.

Like the much-abused French partridges, "curres" may be made to produce a fair amount of sport in one way and another (when and where there is nothing better to be had), if deftly handled and worked ; what is more, they will bear rough-and-tumbling handling, which does not require the immense amount of knowledge, skill or perseverance that is essential to properly secure "surface-feeders," and which is a great factor in the mind of the embryo gunner who contemplates an initiatory attempt.

READY FOR LAUNCHING.

NOT SUCH AN ASS AS HE LOOKS.

# CHAPTER X

## WILDFOWLING COSTUME

IT is, or should be, patent to all that, before entering on the long course of practical experience requisite to attain any high degree of scientific skill in punt shooting it is absolutely necessary to be furnished with all appliances, and to pay due regard to the important question of clothing required for the purpose. For it must be borne in mind that winter, and not summer, is the period for wildfowling, and the coarser the weather the better at intervals will be the sport. Again, a start should be effected long before dawn, and the one hour before daylight is always the coldest of the twenty-four.

The particular dress about to be described is by no means the only one in vogue. But how many really possess a proper outfit? Very few will acknowledge the faults of their own pattern, yet on inquiry there is sure to be a weak point somewhere—some little defect which they invariably make out to be of no consequence. One cannot scull comfortably; another's circulation is impeded if he lies in a certain position; whilst a third is unable to get his cripple-stopper up, or some other difficulty. Without any feeling of egotism Mr Fielding Harmer may well say, " *Rem acu tetigisti.*"

His dress is the outcome of some forty years' experience, and has only lately been regarded by him as perfected. At one time or other he has given almost every possible method a fair trial—adding, removing, improving—until at length a costume was arrived at, which he has worn and adopted with success in every way. Could he, at the age of seventy, be up morning after morning before daybreak, alone and unassisted, if he had not thoroughly protected himself with proper clothing during his earlier days? No; far from it. The mere thought of such a thing causes visions of rheumatism, ague and other diabolical complaints that flesh is heir to, to float uncomfortably through the mind. For, all things said and done, robust health is an essential factor in the successful pursuit of wildfowl, even more so perhaps than in any other form of sport.

The following is a short description of Mr Harmer's dress, omitting the minuter details. The underclothing is all flannel, as recommended by most authorities on gunning; but trousers of Bedford cord, with seat extra strengthened, roomy, and lined with washleather. Fisherman's guernsey and coat or waistcoat, according to fancy. For the feet—the most important part to keep the blood in good circulation—the usual pair of hand-knitted socks, and a long, thick, coarse pair of overall boot stockings. The boots reach well nigh to the top of the hip, and are properly fastened with the usual garters below the knee, the lower parts being made of very stiff leather; but the uppers require a vast amount of skilful paring by the currier to obtain the requisite thinness, so as to enable one to kneel or bend the knee in any position without incurring discomfort of any kind. Some uppers are from a different class of leather altogether, and are sewn on; but the ones used by Mr Harmer consists of whole pieces, which will be found preferable. An admonition against indiarubber boots and clothing in general cannot be too often repeated, for its non-porousness lays open a death-trap to be avoided.

The most important feature in this costume consists of a peculiar loose pair of dressed waterproof knickerbockers, or rather breeches, fastened round the waist by means of a strap and buckle, and falling almost below the knees, followed by a slop of similar material extending from the neck to the hip, and overlapping the aforesaid breeches. The former of these overalls has a leather-lined seat, with extra strengthenings in the crutch, besides being cut after an eccentric pattern, with view neither to beauty nor fashion, but solely and simply for warmth and comfort. A wrapper round the neck, and cap, sou'-wester, or other head-gear, "according to fancy."

Thus it must be obvious that in such a complete suit of armour one can bid defiance to the whole of the aqueous elements. Standing or wading in water in such a costume does not affect future comfort. Nor, on the other hand, can the heaviest downpour penetrate its folds. Just as rain on a slate roof drips from one slab to another, and finally falls to the ground, so in this case it descends first upon the head and shoulders, from whence it runs on to the breeches, thence to the boots and bottom boards. Besides, in this one can lie for any time, if desirable, upon damp flooring, or in slush, etc., with impunity. How many wild-fowlers' costumes at the present day can be subjected to such a crucial test?

With regard to head covering, this is a subject open to endless controversy. Mr Harmer affirms his small cap, exemplified in the illustration, to be better than all others, but an east-coast "sou'-wester" with a stiff back seems to be by far the best all round. In this you are enabled to listen more intently, for on slightly elevating your face to leeward the ears are completely protected from the blast. When worn in the ordinary fashion it protects the back of the neck and ears; when reversed, it shields them from the glare of the sun; and, on emergency, if turned inside out, it can be used as a drinking-bowl, bailer, or basin. The headgear, as well as the slop, is painted the same colour as the punt—that is, like a gull's back—so as not to attract notice. The painting is done in the spring of the year in order to allow time to take off its glossiness.

The hands, as will be noticed in the sketch, are incased in rough woollen mittens with one stall only (for the thumb), and are made to fit so that, by a sudden, dexterous flip, they fly off, allowing a cripple-stopper to be more easily handled. The fingers being together keeps them warmer than would otherwise be the case; and a dry pair or two of these mittens should always be carried.

The dress depicted and described is of course for hard, rough-weather shooting. When much bodily exercise has to be endured the slop may be discarded, and a thinner one of bluish-grey linen substituted. If the hands become perished with cold, a good plan is to dip a pair of mittens overboard, and, having wrung them out, put them on, and, like rubbing one's nose with snow in Russia, it will bring about reaction.

One would hardly credit the complete disguise which such a wildfowl costume affords. Mr Harmer tells many amusing anecdotes of mistakes of which he has been the subject during his punting career, two of which are worth

MR RICHARD FIELDING HARMER IN PUNT-GUNNING COSTUME.

repeating. He had on one occasion during a heavy squall punted up a creek to get a berth under the lee of a weather sea-wall

on Breydon Water when a shore shooter walking past had his
hat blown well out into the water.   Mr Harmer, ever obliging, pushed off and fetched it, returning it to its owner, who
upon receipt thereof fumbled in his pocket and handed him a
penny, saying, "Here, old chap, is a half-pint for you."    On
the other occasion referred to, when going down Channel, he
passed a "brig" at anchor waiting for the tide, from whose
deck one of the hands hailed him with, "What cheer, old
bloke!  Do you git many on 'em in that there coffin o' yours?"

Although the costume here described may not be regarded
by most people as "a thing of beauty," it will undoubtedly
prove to those who try it "a joy for ever."

### STALKING-HORSES.

When speaking of appliances used by wildfowlers it may
not be thought altogether out of place to include a short discussion on stalking-horses, which are never to be despised by
those who have large tracts of shooting ground at their disposal, and who find the birds shy and difficult to approach.

No matter how rough and uncouth the apparatus may be,
if it is only shaped somewhat like a horse, a cow, or an ass,
the birds are deceived by it and good bags secured until dearly-
bought experience teaches them caution.

Geese may be circumvented by the aid of a tumbril, or an
ordinary cart used in the neighbourhood, the shooter concealing himself inside.    The real or artificial stalking-horse
answers equally well for geese as for ducks and other wildfowl: it was Drayton who wrote—

> "One underneath his horse, to get a shoot, doth stalk ;
>   Another over dykes upon his stilts doth walk."

First in the rank of stalking-horses should come the real
live animal in the genuine flesh and blood, and, if it is trained as
it should be, great execution may be accomplished at times with
its valuable assistance.    But it requires a quadruped of no
mean training to stand unflinchingly the deafening and awe-

inspiring discharge of a large-bored gun, often under its very nose, or, at least, within a few feet of its ears. It requires great care, forbearance and patience to thoroughly accustom it to the report alone, which is only done by gradually increasing the charge and decreasing the distance from it until it shows itself utterly indifferent thereto. And the whole is a matter of time in establishing a firm belief and confidence in its trainer, who must do all by kindness, and prove himself to be, besides an instructor, a benefactor and a friend.

Secondly, there is the artificial stalking-horse, which is now, comparatively speaking, a rarity. To make one of these one must obtain either a horse or bullock skin (readily procured from any butcher, knacker or slaughterer); otherwise one will have to make one by cutting out and painting as good an imitation in canvas as possible; the latter, if done really well, answers to all intents and

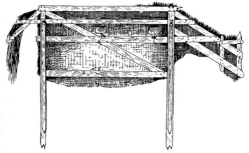

FIG. VIII.

purposes as well as a genuine skin. If the real skin be utilised it will be found an advantage to thoroughly cure it before proceeding to mount it, as it will then last much longer, and its obnoxious odour is removed.

The preparations for accomplishing this task are many; but the best plan is to send it to the nearest fellmonger, who, for a few shillings, will return it perfectly cured and in a soft condition.

The skin complete, the next move is to knock together a rough wooden framework (as defined in the accompanying sketch, see Fig. VIII.), and after the skin has been firmly nailed, or otherwise secured to it, your animal is quite ready for business; and the cost of its keep is far less than that of a living one!

The height from the shoulder to the hoof should not exceed

H

5ft. 6in.; also, on closer observation of the sketch it will be noticed that the main props, or legs, are made double, the reason for this being that the duplicates are light splines, and attached only at the top by loose hinges, so that when the framework falls towards the shooter, upon leaving go of it the duplicates (weighted at their foot) fall first, thereby catching and supporting the horse and preventing it falling into the mud or water, as would otherwise be the case. The skin is not securely fastened in the middle of the splines, but a space is left sufficient for the shooter to insert his hand or arm, and to facilitate his holding it. Some of these "animals" have their heads adjusted in such a manner that the operator can move them up or down, as he desires, by strings or other arrangement.

Some also are made rotund and not silhouette, the shooters, two in number, walking inside the animal and shooting from loopholes made in its side.

When approaching birds it is best to proceed leisurely, in a kind of half-end-on direction, taking plenty of time, always, if possible, working up wind, and going at a very slow pace. If these directions are carefully carried out the birds should hardly notice the fiery steed or domesticated cow, as the case may be, and the aforesaid animal can quietly approach nearer and nearer to the unsuspecting fowl, apparently grazing to its heart's content and perfectly harmless, until, with a decidedly bellicose snort, it deals forth death and destruction to the feathered tribe around.

Birds, however, who have been once or twice deceived by this innocent-looking beast, generally take good care to give it a wide berth for the future. But every enjoyment has its drawbacks, and at times, when the stalker is intent on his endeavours to successfully approach a flock of plover or duck in the fens or a marshy district, he suddenly becomes aware of a trampling of many feet in his immediate vicinity, the general stampede alarming not only the birds, but, in nine cases out of ten, himself also. Upon turning to ascertain the cause of the unexpected tumult, he is confronted with a sight not easily to be eradicated from his memory. Within twenty yards a score or so of semi-wild animals, which have, maybe, spent the whole summer alone and unattended on the marsh or fen, with steaming nostrils and dilated eyes, meet his gaze. This interview, as a rule, does not occupy more than a few seconds, for, with uplifted tails and lowered heads, they make tracks for the apparent usurper of their domains. When last the author was thus situated, a pressing appointment suddenly dawned upon him and he left hastily, without in any way apologising for the abruptness of his departure.

Thirdly, another plan is the ancient one of the stretched horse or bullock skin (see Fig. IX.). The *modus faciendi* is as follows : — Having obtained the dressed skin, or painted canvas, seam it up where it was originally opened. Cut a slit at the shoulder (or elsewhere, according to fancy) for the protrusion of the gun barrels, distend the figure with the assistance of hoops, sticks or splines, and there it is complete. This latter device is the more convenient, as it can be rolled up, and porterage is thereby greatly facilitated, whilst it is distended at a moment's notice by means of the hoops and sticks. The forelegs are rather substantial ones, and attached to the real hoofs, whilst the legs and body of the shooter form the hinder quarters. The greatest drawback to the device is that one is almost always obliged to walk in a stooping position, which causes great fatigue, to say nothing of the stiffness one feels in the back for several days afterwards, more particularly if unaccustomed to this mode of sport.

FIG. IX.—A HO(A)RSE VOICE.

# CHAPTER XI

## SHORE SHOOTING

HORE shooting is a branch of sport by far the most popular with the majority of estuary frequenters, though it is rarely recognised by scientific puntsmen, except under occasional and peculiar circumstances. It is followed by many who have neither the time on their hands nor the appliances wherewith to work otherwise, and, on finding themselves in a favourable district, take advantage of it with more or less success, the varied contents of the bag lending an additional charm and making up, in a great measure, for its usual lightness.

A PRICKED TEAL.

In most places on our coast little else but shore shooting and shooting from boats with shoulder guns can be carried on whilst the professional gunner continues (as he always has done) to turn up his nose at the humble wash-follower, whom he contemptuously dubs a "shore snobber." In one respect, however, he is distinct from his traducers, in that he requires few requisites for his craft or art, the principal being a reliable full-choke double 8-bore or 10-bore, a serviceable rain-coat and a hardy, well-trained water-spaniel or retriever, which are indispensable; thus equipped he can at once proceed to his happy hunting-grounds, where success depends upon the skill and the patience he exhibits, and the number of birds there are to be found.

116

Some people content themselves by merely walking along the shore, picking up *en route* whatsoever birds cross their path, from the gyrating tern to the croaking hanser (heron), without taking any trouble to lie in wait, stalk, or go a yard from their path to obtain better chances.

Others, visiting a shore freely indented with rocks, boulders or broken promontories, obtain at times splendid sport by concealing themselves behind various obstacles, and whenever these project far enough out into favourite bays or other places frequented by birds, the shooter can follow up the receding tide, taking fresh vantage posts further out on the uncovered flats. In this method widgeon, which do not like to miss a moment's feed that there is a chance of availing themselves of, and which on tidal estuaries flight at tide time instead of dusk, often offer good opportunities to the shooter by leading along the wash close inshore preparatory to pitching upon the first portion of grass that becomes uncovered. Whilst curlew, oxbirds and other waders keep one well employed.

Another plan, perhaps less known, is "tubbing," and many there are who in England, Ireland and Scotland earn a livelihood during the winter months by this means. It is simple and effective. It consists of a continuous row of old casks sunk into the sand equi-distant from each other (about 100 to 150 yards, in accordance with the rise and fall of the tide), each being ballasted and surrounded with loose stones, and a seat arranged inside. As the tide recedes and the long stretches of flats become available to the birds, the tubbist wades out to cask No. 1 as soon as it is visible, with bailer, and a dry cap to cover the otherwise damp seat. Bailing the water out and putting all to rights, he ensconces himself inside, blazing away at anything that passes within range, either gathering the dead birds at once or (when the wind is in the right quarter) allowing them to drift ashore. He remains in tub No. 1 until the continuing ebbing tide renders tub No. 2 available for use, when the same tactics are repeated, thus following the line of casks till tide turn, when

TUBBING ON AN ESTUARY.

he retires in precisely the same manner that he had advanced, with the exception that the tubs are ready for immediate occupation, and they do not require re-bailing.

During stormy and unsettled weather considerable sport can be obtained by this dodge, but on a public estuary certain risks must be run of being shot by a punter. For it must be remembered that from the angle at which a staunchion gun is fired shot travels considerable distances, and the fact that the head of the tubbist is on the exact level at which the big guns are discharged does not add materially to his comfort.

Fourthly, there is the man who erects huts of rough boughs covered with sods or sand, allowing them to become overgrown with grass like the winter dwelling of the Laplander. Their usual situation is a promontory jutting into the estuary, or some similar commanding position, and their use is to afford the gunner a retreat at high-water time ; the few birds that may then be leading about being thus intercepted. But this plan is not half so successful as " tubbing," although the two are often combined.

On larger estuaries, during the last few hours of flood, the birds—curlews in particular—collecting in their hundreds and thousands, select some open spot for rest and repose, where, posting their sentinels, they are in absolute security, defying every effort at approach. Every dodge and ingenious device imaginable may be resorted to in order to take them unawares and to endeavour to place a " home thrust " into their midst whilst they are so engaged, but all to no purpose ; for although, in contradiction to the infallible weasel, they can be caught napping, their sentinels and outposts are ever on the alert, and, whether it be night or day, however light or dark, they invariably raise the alarm, and the mighty cloud of birds departs, so to speak, under the very nose of the chagrined shooter.

On the smaller estuaries it is the same, with this difference, that instead of collecting in open spaces, which are naturally few and far between, the fowl make for the open sea, there to sleep and plume themselves, whilst the waders adjourn to moors, morasses, marshes or swamps that may be contiguous, never forgetting to return to the flats as soon as the first ebb of the tide commences.

Fifthly, there is the system introduced by that well-known wildfowler, Colonel Hawker, of utilising a dressed-up carriage for a swivel, which, without doubt, can be denominated under the heading of shore shooting. But it can never be used unless the ground consists of hard ooze, such as that found on portions of the Dutch coast (on the Scheldt, for instance), or on the hard sandy bottoms of our Scotch estuaries, and in East Anglia round Blakeney, Wells and Hunstanton. In the famous Colonel's book, *Hints to Young Sportsmen*, will be found drawings with a full description of this ingenious contrivance, and it is only necessary to add that if these directions are carried out, and the exterior appearance of the arrangement made to suit the surroundings of the neighbourhood intended to be visited, success should follow. But on account of the numerous unforeseen difficulties always springing up, this happy outcome is extremely doubtful, whilst the manual labour will be found something awful.

Sixthly, there is the shore shooting proper, the following of the high-water mark. It is no constitutional stroll of an inactive, unenthusiastic powder-burner, but, with ears and eyes constantly on the alert, the shore shooter proceeds, treading as noiselessly as possible, stopping every now and then to sweep the flats with powerful binoculars (not a necessity, but nevertheless a good help), whilst he carefully scans and searches every nook and corner, every marsh, pond, or swamp, and on his way he takes full advantage of every rise, bank or elevation in the ground within his beat.

Sneaking stealthily up to, or round the likely places, he peers cautiously over before showing himself in bold relief against the skyline ; and woe betide the unfortunate bird that may be there taking a quiet siesta, or afternoon feed, chuckling to itself on its apparent security.

In these shore peregrinations the bag always contains a variety ; oxbirds, curlew, wimbrel, a duck or two, snipe, half a dozen plover, perhaps a couple of " seapies " (oyster catchers), and maybe a pricked goose; with any luck at all it should always contain a dozen different specimens of the feathered denizens of the shore. It is not altogether unknown to find a goodly-sized pike in the shore-shooter's bag, as they may often be shot in the sluice dykes adjoining the marsh walls. It is even on record that a wall-shooter actually shot and bagged a fair-sized skate which was floundering on the flats; another, that he had killed a seal with one barrel and a Jenny wren with the other. A favourite plan is to carry along a spade and dig a hole in the sand, in which to await the arrival of the birds, or utilise a stalking-horse.

Decoys are also often resorted to in various ways, according to the fancy of their worker or the nature of the ground.

A simple invention of the author's consists in so dressing a rain-coat that it answers two purposes; one as a shelter against wet weather, the other as a shelter against the birds. This is brought about with the greatest ease imaginable. The waterproof, a light one, is painted yellow on one side (the same tint as sand usually is) and a dullish brown on the other, with brighter spots daubed about it haphazard, representing, as near as the artist can, an estuary beach. This will be found to answer amazingly, for when extended full length on the shore under a covering of this kind, not moving a muscle until the birds are well within range, the deception is complete, and many are the surprises, with accompanying telling shots, that it assists in bringing about.

The seventh method is perhaps the most enjoyable of any, as provisions and minor luxuries desired can be carried without being in the slightest way impeded thereby. It is managed with the aid of an assistant in a small punt, or other craft suitable for the purpose, which is also often employed to drive the birds over the ambushed shooter; but its real intent is to meet him at certain preconcerted rendezvous, poling him up creeks and bays otherwise inaccessible, where the banks or sides may be sufficiently high to afford a partial shelter. Thus the birds which rise therefrom may be bagged and many chances at others leading over taken advantage of.

If a rowing boat is used instead of a punt, row-lock holes
on each quarter will be found a great advantage in many
more respects than one, not only to scull by, but also to steer
with in case a sail is used.

This constitutes a fair summary of the various phases of
shore shooting, but as the circumstances met with in this class
of wildfowling are so various and multitudinous, it is impossible to lay down any fixed rules to regulate the actions of
their would-be follower; the results depend greatly upon the
judgment which each man introduces into the working out
of his aims, which, together with skill, comes alone from
constant and continual practice and observance; although
large bags are the exception and not the rule, capital sport
may sometimes be obtained.

But to uphold true sport let the shooter abstain from
shore pottering, armipotent sailing boats and launches, if he
is visiting a district where a far higher art can be indulged
in, and let him either start punting himself or join another
who has already acquired the necessary experience and
equipment.

By thus reversing positions he can readily imagine what
feelings are paramount in the mind if, after hours' and hours',
perhaps weeks', persistent toil and perseverance, the cup of
success, on being raised to the lips, is ruthlessly dashed away
by some 'Arry out for 'is sportin' 'oliday snapping at a harmless, unoffending and unpalatable gull.

SHORE NETS AT WELLS.

BEFORE THE RECKONING.

# CHAPTER XII

## FLIGHTING

### The Morning Flight.

THERE are many inland waters and private lakes where wild-ducks are only occasionally disturbed, and then in such clumsy fashion that but a minimum of sport is obtained in comparison to the results which a little skilful management would insure.

The water is usually visited about two hours before noon, when all the fowl are peacefully resting after their night's exertion in search of food, and placing guns on promontories, in boats, or wherever the keepers advise, they blaze away for a few minutes to their heart's content, after which the fowl are either conspicuous by their absence or wheeling high in the air premeditating departure; for every duck is thoroughly frightened, which is the worst result of this proceeding.

Whereas, by a morning or evening flight (both completely different methods of wildfowling) skilfully arranged and carried out, only a portion of the birds are alarmed. Thus the "lead in" does not become broken, and in a few days may be as strong as ever; for any person conversant with wildfowl, their habits and instincts, is well aware that if the "lead in" becomes broken, sport for the remainder of the season is over, the reason for which is not very difficult to discover.

Wild-ducks predominating in Broadland are mallard and teal, which habitually retire into the sedges and thick aquatic undergrowth during the daytime for rest and repose. Towards evening they draw out, becoming loquacious and uneasy previous to flighting for various marsh dykes, flight ponds, or other feeding grounds, from which they do not return until the first streak of dawn shows itself: arriving at intervals, according to the distance they have to travel, some of the wider rangers not turning up till long after daylight.

The screens, shelters or stands used in morning flighting and other wildfowl shooting are made by river watchers during summer, and consist of small platforms erected just above the water, carefully walled in with reed hurdles, and furnished with seats.

They should be so placed in a small patch of reeds, rushes and similar vegetation, that an experienced eye has difficulty in detecting their whereabouts, even when the gun is firing.

Having cantered over these preliminary details, let us take another imaginary trip. We arrive at the residence of our host the day beforehand, or, perchance, are visitors staying in the house. No billiards or whist after dinner, but a cigar and a quiet chat, followed by ignominious expulsion to bed like so many schoolboys home for their holidays, only, however, to arise again, apparently before our eyes are closed, at an abnormally early hour on a chill November morning, meeting in the gun-room our last night's companions, sipping steaming coffee and tugging away at obstinate shooting-boots by the candle's sickly and flickering light.

The keepers, who have already planted decoys, are in waiting at the boat-house or other prearranged spot, and soon place a gun in each of the shelters most favourable according to the state of the wind and weather, where it only remains for us to light the soothing briar and await the incoming birds.

With the first glimmer of rosy light that shoots athwart the eastern horizon a few odd pairs and one or two solitary fowl put in an appearance, and the echoing report of our heavily-loaded gun seems to arouse the entire bird life around us. Herons rise with their hoarse "Frank! Frank!" moorhens utter the most weird shrieks, whilst a large number of coots make a frightful spluttering in their endeavours to take wing and collect *en masse* in the centre of the water, where they remain quite awake and suspiciously on the watch. As the light increases so does the confidence of the incoming fowl seem to decrease, and they wheel round and round several times preparatory to alighting, which is exactly what is required of them, for, in so doing, a good opportunity often offers itself to one or another of the guns, the fowl invariably lowering to the decoys, which are conspicuously anchored between the stands.

Also, as the daylight progresses the trips increase in size and number, causing our firing to become hotter and hotter—in fact, we find that it is the only warm thing about us. In the middle of all this serenading and slaughter it is sometimes surprising to see little "trips" of fowl (more especially of teal) whisking in and dropping under one's very nose before one has even had time to get the gun to shoulder or realise their presence; more particularly is this the case if the place has been undisturbed for any prolonged period. Moreover, it is remarkable how persistently some of the birds will lead round again and again, dipping to the water and rising again as if it were too warm for their feet, whilst large bags and capital sport reward patience.

The daylight having advanced, the keepers revisit the shooters, accompanied by their retrievers and water-spaniels, the dead are collected, the reed beds hunted for cripples, and the rands round the edges of the broad walked through and searched for those slightly-tipped fowl, which invariably make for dry land.

Such a morning's work as this, for real sport and enjoyment, far excels a big day's covert shooting with its large bag of more easily-manipulated game, which can be so far controlled to the will that results are reduced to a certainty, or even to partridge driving, taxing as it does the skill of the shooter to a much greater extent.

A sportsman of the old school, when he has thus thoroughly disturbed his ground, after breakfast, instead of gorse, hurdles and hot corners, marshals his guns back to the rough ground contiguous to the site of the morning shoot, intersected as it generally is with bogs, reed beds, swamps and alder carrs, where, with a sufficient number of beaters, spaniels and retrievers, every yard is thoroughly walked, and all wounded or pricked fowl, which would otherwise waste away and die, are picked, besides taking toll from pheasants, wood-pigeons, snipe, and the other inhabitants of such aqueous regions, which (when laid out for inspection at the close of the day) are at least rich in the variety of their species.

## Evening Flight.

This, it will be seen, is a complete antithesis to its predecessor, " Morning flight." In the morning the birds are mostly intercepted upon arrival at their diurnal resting-places, whilst in the evening they are waylaid on their journey from the aforesaid strongholds, or else upon the actual feeding grounds themselves. But the great and most noticeable advantage that the evening has over the morning flight is that the feeding grounds, extending over such vast expanses of country, enable it to be practised evening after evening for an indefinite period, so long as open weather continues, provided the shooter is within reach of a good habitat; but, on the other hand, the morning flight, as described, can only be occasionally indulged in, and then one must have absolute control over the favoured spots, for unless this is carefully attended to the haunt is broken and sport for the season is at an end.

In frosty weather the habits of wildfowl are completely revolutionised. When pressed by hunger they will seek food regardless of the hour, whether by day or night, and under any fairly favourable conditions or circumstances. On finding themselves gradually forced from their inland resorts they circle nearer and nearer to the saltings and estuaries, until these alone remain unfrozen, when, if they are very much harassed, further migrations occur.

As soon as the frost breaks, old habits are quickly resumed and condition regained in a manner which is perfectly marvellous. Besides, they feed so gluttonously that it renders them more drowsy and less vigilant, hence easier to handle than during the normal wild weather. Then is the time for our friend the flighter and other wildfowlers to gather a harvest, for this change, besides possessing the above-mentioned advantages, causes larger "companies" to scatter into smaller "trips," spreading widely in their eagerness to discover which place will first provide them with the most luscious food, the search for which they continue for a time preparatory to settling down to former regular habits and customs.

Flight shooting is a sport which is conducted under a variety of circumstances and places, and if tidal flighting, or that on estuaries, is taken into consideration, times may also be added; but inland the long-winged fowl invariably flight at dusk, and not at any definite hour, as is sometimes erroneously stated to be the case. This fact can easily be ascertained by observing the habits of tame wildfowl, whose demonstrative signs of liveliness and uneasiness, which gradually increases as eventide approaches, will be only too apparent. It is instinctive in the species to visit "fresh fields and pastures new" at nightfall, however abundant food may be in the locality wherein they have passed their hours of idleness, and instances come under notice where fowl flight from one place to another, and *vice versa*.

To touch upon the most essential requirements of evening flighting.

First, and most important, a would-be flighter must have a well-trained, hardy, courageous retriever, not necessarily too steady, but rather inclined to the contrary—*i.e.*, not to leave the heel until told, but, when permitted, to range wide. The dog requires a different training to that of the ordinary fielder, and it should be regulated more or less according to the requirements of the locality. It must be taught to instantly drop at a sign here, there or anywhere, and to remain steadfast until released by its trainer.

The clothes worn for flighting should be assimilated as much as possible to the surroundings of the neighbourhood intended to be worked, and in texture according to season; with boots strong, high and impervious, even to the far-reaching snow slush. A gun sling will be found a valuable addition, although it is not generally used, to which (besides a mackintosh) the more luxuriously inclined can string a light, revolving cane seat.

Moonlight nights are not auspicious, because fowl are then most irregular and erratic in their movements, whilst fine, still nights (not moonlight) have also their disadvantages, as at that time birds fly high and out of range. Most auspicious are strong winds, dark nights, and lowering weather, when the birds fly low and come early. But the weather does not apply so much to tidal flighting, and perhaps it would be more comprehensible were the subject divided into two headings, "Flighting Inland," and "Flighting on Tidal or Salt Waters."

## *Flighting Inland.*

This class of flight shooting commences in August, when young ducks resort to the cornfields and ponds, later to the stubbles and stacks or mosses, according to the locality. They may be intercepted either at morning or evening flighting towards or, perhaps better still, on the actual feeding grounds, with which one must necessarily be well conversant before success can be assured.

The glorious summer evenings and mild, temperate weather of August renders flight shooting a sport accessible to many who through age or ill-health would be unable to withstand the roughness and rigour of the climate of the later months. Moreover, the pleasure can be sometimes enhanced by arranging a party, which is easily done when conversant with a favoured haunt and pools used by fowl. Blinds or shelters are erected in the most favourable positions, and on the eventful occasion when the birds arrive comparatively early they meet with a warm reception.

In the early part of the season fowl come in families and larger parties than is the case a month or so later, whilst their approach is generally heralded by " the sound of the distant and random gun " of other flighters occasionally firing.

Like snipe, wildfowl seldom remain during winter in the district where they have been bred, but they pass southwards, others taking their place. Gargany, shovellers and other fowl give ample proof of this to anyone who is at all observant.

As the season advances positions are shifted to the stacks, stubbles and mosses, where the birds have become far more wary, which, though considerably increasing the enjoyment of the sport, has a tendency to decrease the bag. This system is also worked by constructing hides at a wet spot, by means of sunken tubs in place of the stuffed hurdle or other arrangement.

The sere and yellow leaf indicating the nearer approach of migratory birds, more attention should be given to the lower and moister grounds, where the shortened days and rapidly-darkening nights render a hide not at all imperative, as a gate-post, low bush or tuft of rushes suffices, provided the shooter, as before mentioned, assimilates his clothes to the surroundings, and at the near approach of fowl keeps his body as motionless as possible. Indeed, in broad daylight, if the wildfowler stands perfectly still in the open, birds will

I

lead past within easy range, not swerving until the gun is raised or some other movement made.

Bear in mind, however, that the shooter must take his stand according to the class of fowl he more particularly wishes to secure, as different varieties prefer different localities, according to their species, *e.g.*, mallard, teal, etc., prefer comparatively dry ground to widgeon and others, which revel in more open, aqueous wastes.

For a variety, the best position is some rushy promontory jutting out into the bright water, or a lee shore; for wildfowl, previous to alighting, are always wont to swing round more or less to leeward. Having taken a stand, one is generally first put on the *qui vive* by the "scape" of snipe, high in the air, which, as the gloaming deepens, swoop lower, and a few are often secured before the regular flight of fowl commences. A peculiarity of snipe may often be noticed, they now and again suddenly pitch down from the air like a stone thrown to one's very feet. This is really astonishing, the more so to those who see it for the first time.

When snipe are occupying the attention large stands of plover will most probably be also observed passing high overhead, but one knows they will come lower and singly later on. Teal also are early arrivals, usually dashing past with a rush, reminding one of an express train; and so rapid are they in their flight that when going thus late in the evening it is next to impossible to hit them.

Mallard, after the snipe, come throughout at intervals, whilst widgeon and single peewit latest of all. But, of course, times and orders of arrival vary considerably according to the season, state of weather and locality.

One peculiarity is pretty sure to attract attention during autumn. A drake mostly leads the trip, but in the spring he politely yields his position of precedence to a (lady) duck.

The setting in of a genuine frost is intimated by the green plover or lapwings, which depart to a bird towards the

more genial atmosphere of the Gulf Stream, they being seen
no more until early spring. Inland the big lots of fowl
leave first, but a few homely ones invariably keep back,
frequenting springs, rivulets and open places, where they will
hang about, contentedly shifting from one to the other, accompanied by a few odd snipe, woodcock or other soft-billed
birds, until absolutely evicted.

Regular haunts being deserted, the flighter pursues the
birds in such a manner as is most applicable to the locality in
which he finds himself.

Flight shooting is never, or perhaps it would be wiser to
say hardly ever, practised during the day time, and the only
other instance within the author's knowledge, besides that
mentioned in the *Moor and Marsh* of the Badminton Library,
page 227 (which, by its description, sounds like West Norfolk),
is one mentioned by a friend, who in describing an estate where
there was a large lake near the house on which the fowl were
never shot, and at some distance away a chain of ponds more
or less frequented by the fowl, goes on to describe how they
drove the birds from one to the other, intercepting them on
the way.

## *Flighting on Tidal or Salt Waters.*

This has already been partially referred to in the former
chapter on shore shooting, which it is impossible to avoid
mixing up to a certain extent with this system of flighting,
for, although the latter occurs solely between sunset and sunrise, flight shooting inland is strictly confined to the gloaming,
except on light and moonlight nights, when it extends some
hours later, and, under those circumstances, is usually not only
unsatisfactory, but also uncertain.

In the neighbourhood of estuaries the state of the tide is
the greatest factor in the movements of the birds. For instance, if it happens to be three-quarter flood near sunset, the
birds will seek favourite feeding grounds close by until the
tide has well ebbed, when, if they have not sufficiently fed,

they will flight, although it be night time, to the goose-grass flats.   On the other hand, if it be one-quarter ebb, they will mostly leave their fresh-water haunts for that of the salt, which they seem to prefer.   Mallard, as can be observed anywhere, show a greater preference to fresh-water food than widgeon, which is indicated by the fact that in some parts of Scotland the former are called " moss ducks."   Again, mallard, when they do frequent saltings, are wont to feed much closer inshore, amongst the more luxurious grasses, than widgeon, whose habits have been previously referred to in the chapter on shore shooting, which also applies here.   Therefore, much greater knowledge of the ground and judgment in selection of a position is necessary for flighting by tidal and salt waters than for inland flighting, where there are not dual feeding grounds to deal with.   Taking it all round, the difficulties of the former are so great as to astound those who have not thoroughly attempted to master them.

Flighting in the neighbourhood of estuaries is much more precarious than flighting inland (except when frosty weather prevails), that is to say speaking strictly and discriminating between the many who take rough shooting in a rough manner to those of the few who practise it with deep thought and judgment, coupled with skill and perseverance.

Yet the latter division of flighting does not show so much sport as the former, but *chacun à son goût*.   However, where punt gunning is pursued shore flighting cannot be conducted without enormous injury to the gunner; even on estuaries where there is no punting it is a difficult sport, unless there are certain spots in favourable positions where hides can be arranged, or one can mark the line of flight taken by the birds in their passage to and from their salt and fresh water feeding grounds, when they can be successfully intercepted according to the particular state of tide, wind and weather.

In some districts the birds are wont to lead along the seashore, or over certain promontories, but in others their range is so wide that it is almost impossible to do much from a satisfactory point of view to a good fowler's notions, as such an one objects, above all, to constant snapping at impossible ranges on the offchance of pinioning one or two birds, with the probability of pricking, maiming, or needlessly causing suffering to many others; a system of pot-hunting which fosters unpleasantness, and brings wildfowlers into disrepute amongst those who are not aware that no one deprecates it so much as does the truest of true sportsmen, a good wild-fowler.

### *Decoy-Flighting Pools.*

These pools, when properly made and used by fowl, are as carefully watched and jealously guarded by their owners or lessees as are the regular decoys—now, alas! so few and far between.

To the sportsman they have distinct advantages over other decoys, as the fowl are killed in a sporting fashion instead of having their necks wrung wholesale by one man, with no gun-powder expended over their downfall. The water need not be made anything like so large as an ordinary decoy pond or lake; if it was it could not be properly worked. And instead of being star-shaped it should be made triangular, with the base facing westwards, for reasons which will be shortly given.

There are several of these pools in Broadland where the owners of some of the large tracks of bog and swamp have dug them out with a double purpose—to secure the excellent sport they afford all through the winter, and to fill up the holes, dips and low-lying levels on their marshes with the soil excavated. Thus these decoy-flighting pools cannot be called extravagant luxuries for the landowner, because, although he gives up an acre, perhaps a little more, yet he gains a con-siderable improving value to his marshes, quite equalising the outlay expended, whilst at present-day rentals the existence of the pool would be greatly to his advantage. Again, the ground selected for the site is generally a coarse, rough swamp or marsh, the product of which is valueless as fodder, and only used for litter in the bullock-yards. The quieter and more secluded the position, the better and the more it is wooded round, so the more freely will wildfowl take to it and use it.

As before mentioned, the best shape to lay out or form the pool is triangular, with the base westwards and the two sides north-east and south-east respectively. The base or westward side should have a shelving shore, and the other sides should be cut straight down, allowing for deep water.

The reason of this is that the fowl which use the pool, when lighting, will favour the shelving shore, where they are accustomed to be fed; and as the sun sets in the west, the flight shooters, who are posted along the north-east and south-east sides in their screens, get the full benefit of the lingering light from the late-set sun—a very great advantage. So long as no trees are planted within about thirty yards of the shelving shore the light from the sky is not impeded, whilst osiers and alder-scrub can be planted nearer if desired.

There are pools dug and made which are square, oblong, formed like a capital S, round, and all shapes and sizes, but the triangular form is best.

Should the pool be dug from a bare swamp it will be as well to plant round it freely, leaving an open space near to the western side, on account of the light. Between the outskirts and the water's edge, rhododendrons, laurels, young firs, etc., may be set fairly thickly, as they not only help to hide the shooter or onlooker, but they at the same time shelter the water and afford good facilities for nesting to the birds, besides lending themselves considerably to ornamentation.

A thin belt of reeds may be encouraged on the north and south-east sides, but should they appear on the western side they must be immediately cut down. June is the best month for doing this, as then it kills the reeds, and they rarely grow up again.

All round the pool a wall about three feet or four feet high is made with a corresponding trench, provided the land is not swampy or moist, in which case no trench can well be made, as it becomes a ditch; but should the land be fairly dry the

soil taken out to make the trench forms the wall between it
and the water. If this wall or bank is sufficiently high for a
shooter or observer to walk behind and watch the birds without being seen, it answers the purpose required; if not, or if
the soil is such that the wall does not answer the purpose
named, then reed screens are made and fixed up in the weak
places. The screen may also be continued for part of the way
(just to cover the corners where fowl would hardly ever light

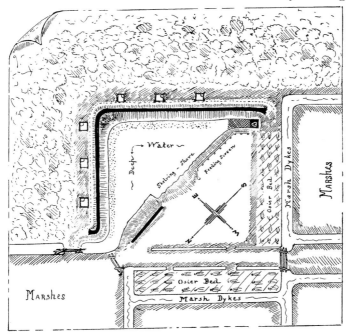

when coming in at flight time) along the western shore and
quite close to the water's edge, so that a keeper can steal
softly down and throw in the maize or Indian corn and
acorns without disturbing any of the wildfowl which may be
in the pool.

The rough sketch Ground Plan shows one of these decoy
pools, which was artificially made from a bare marsh and has
now been most successfully worked for a number of years.

Having completed the decoy pool, attention is turned to the more interesting process of working it to advantage from a sporting point of view.

A fair-sized duck pen is made in one corner of the pool on the shelving shore, so the birds confined therein can use the land or the water at their pleasure, and rush tufts are allowed to grow in this enclosure in moderation. Half a dozen or more wild ducks are procured and properly pinioned, and are placed in the enclosure with one or a couple of tame drakes. They must be well looked after, carefully fed and tended, so that when, a fortnight or three weeks later, one side of the pen is taken down and they are left to their own devices they will prefer to stay in the sheltered waters of the pool rather than stray further afield, where they would certainly fare worse. During this time—in fact, all the year round—an abundance of food must be supplied to the fowl, which should be thrown into the water over the top of the feeding screen [marked on the Ground Plan], so that rats, crows and other vermin cannot get at it and eat it up so easily.

Should there be any wildfowl in the neighbourhood the ducks will not be there many days before they attract the attention of drakes, which will immediately pair off with them; and on ascertaining the fact that their ladyloves are unable to fly they will be quite contented to remain and enjoy connubial bliss within and around the limited precincts of the decoy pool.

In the early spring ducks are in great request by mallard, and the offers placed at the delicately-webbed feet of the lonely widow ducks in the pen will be not only numerous but demonstrative and noisy. In peeping through the screen it is no uncommon sight to see close on half-a-score of handsome young Masher Mallard "doing the polite" to one bashful duck, whilst the tame drake has been edged quite out into the cold.

The birds, as is customary with wild duck, pair off and nest very early, and when the months of August and September arrive the heart will be gladdened by the sight of twenty-five to fifty wildfowl constantly wheeling round and round the pool. The temptation to shoot them will be great, but it must be resisted, and they must be left entirely alone and undisturbed, feeding being increased in accordance with the numbers that require it. Should the birds flight out to neighbouring waters, or to cornfields and stubbles where you have the shooting rights, and you wish to take toll from them, there is no reason why it should not be done by concealing yourself in their line of flight or on their feeding grounds; but it is not advisable for a shot to be fired, either by night or day, within a quarter of a mile of the sanctuary.

In October the migratory birds begin to arrive, and by the first week of November a strong *lead in* to the decoy pool should have been procured. Or, in other words, the semi-tame home birds should have made their presence known to the migratory fowl, and to the birds inhabiting other waters, which travel afield at flighting times in search of food. They do this either by visiting neighbouring waters where their feathered relatives congregate, returning in company with them, or by their incessant quacking and circling round their own secure retreat at flighting time, as is their wont, induce other fowl to lower their line of flight and visit the water. The strangers are generally so pleased with their first visit and the bounteous hospitality of the feeder that they are certain to come again on the following evening, more often than not bringing other fowl with them. Thus does the fame of the diminutive piece of water spread through local duckdom.

*It is this lead in which is the secret of the success of a decoy-flighting pond.* It is the one and only pivot upon which the whole sport depends. Therefore, the reason why the water is left so long quiet and undisturbed should be apparent.

On one pool the fowl were shot during the month of September, but the experiment was never repeated. About five-and-twenty birds were bagged, but the remainder took fright and left the water, few if any returning; no home birds were left to establish a *lead in*, and despite constant and plentiful supplies of food all through the winter months hardly a duck put in an appearance, whilst all idea of sport for that season was rendered a dead letter.

If the instructions laid down are conscientiously followed, and the decoy pool is located in a neighbourhood where there are fowl, a strong *lead in* will become a certainty, although it must not be taken as an accepted fact before the first week of November arrives, however forcibly a keeper may argue to the contrary.

The screens which are used to hide the shooter are generally erected during the close time, and consist (as before mentioned) of reed hurdles or rush litter interwoven between growing twigs; anything will do so long as it acts as a successful hide and partakes of the nature of the surrounding foliage.

Now, as the time for using them draws near, each screen should be supplied with a seat, having a rough lid attached in order that it may always be found dry.

Having decided upon the date for commencing to shoot, the keeper should be instructed to visit the pool during the afternoons three or four days beforehand, and to show himself upon the bank. This frightens the fowl, which rise and soon make themselves scarce, but they will return at flight time, which is what is required. Furthermore, when frightened in this manner they rise in a large bunch and fly away; but again, they return in twos and threes, and it is seldom that more than seven come together.

A little after sunset the flight shooters put in an appearance and take up their respective stands in the screens before mentioned, which are comfortable quarters indeed after a damp, cold walk over the bleak marshland, whilst the evergreen shrubs growing around should be a complete shelter from the marrow-reaching North-easter (the most favourable wind for this class of sport).

By imperceptible degrees the light gradually fades away and the watchers are awakened from their reveries by the weird cry of a lapwing or the scaping of a snipe warning them to be on the *qui vive*.  Presently there is the unmistakable whistle of pinions, followed, a moment later, by a rushing sound in the air, and two or three wild duck alight with a mighty splash in the centre of the water.  The gun stationed in the south-east screen, or perhaps the keeper, immediately puts into motion a bell, which is sometimes placed on the western shore with a communicating cord or wire.  This frightens the fowl so that they fly up over the guns and away from the bell or rattle (whichever may be used), offering good sporting shots, which in the uncertain light are much more difficult than one anticipates.

After the first two or three arrivals there is generally a short interval, then the body of the fowl arrive in quick succession, and if the circumstances and elements be favourable sport should be fast and furious for upwards of an hour.

If the wind blows from the west it may be as well to place one gun, at least, in a screen behind the shelving shore. Early in the evening he can put the fowl over the other guns, and later, as the night lowers and the darkness deepens, he can draw out from his screen, continuing to put up the fowl as occasion requires.

Working in this manner, the fowl, if allowed to alight first (the most killing method), will, on being alarmed, jump from the water and spread out in all directions; the shooting is thus equally divided and the sport increased.  It is always more or less dangerous to shoot at fowl on the water, and at best it is a pot-hunting process.

Instead of having first ordered the fowl to be frightened out by the keeper earlier in the afternoon, had the wildfowlers crept stealthily down to the pool, taken up positions, and, acting on a preconcerted signal, fired simultaneously at the birds on the water, and as they rose therefrom the result would have been that seven or eight would have been bagged and *all* the fowl frightened away for some time to come. Whereas, by acting on the lines suggested, the shooters, to the number of quite half a dozen, can visit the water once or twice a week all through the season and have the opportunity of firing some twenty shots or more at each visit; whilst the bag will naturally be heavy or light in accordance with the straightness of the powder.

One peculiar fact is noteworthy. A decoy pond may be worked and shot for many years before an opportunity presents itself of shooting any of the half-bred wildfowl flighting into it at night. They seem to tumble to the arrangements, and although they are always to be found in the immediate neighbourhood of the pool they never lift into it during the evening whilst the guns are concealed there with the dogs.

IN MEDIAS RE(ED)S.

# CHAPTER XIII

ALMOST all the rivers which carry their freshets to the sea find an outlet into the Yarmouth Roadsteads. Roughly speaking, there are between forty and fifty Broads, having a total area of about 4000 acres, any one of which may be reached from the rivers which converge at Great Yarmouth. No wonder the tide runs strong, and the local wherrymen are wise in their generation when they demur at orders which direct them to proceed without regard to ebb or flow.

From the experience gained in coming from Oulton, the advantages are foreseen of laying plans for navigation with a due respect for the tide time-tables. Leaving gay old Yarmouth behind with its ancient walls and turrets, its quaint rows, streets, curious houses, its hospitable inhabitants and pretty fisher-girls, we somewhat reluctantly proceed upon our way up the North River towards the heart of the Broad District. For ten miles the going is anything but comfortable, the river is narrow, mud banks jut out into the stream at many points, often being found quite in the middle; plenty of other craft are met with, passed and repassed, to the hindrance of themselves as well as others, and the scenery is neither attractive nor interesting.

Along the whole stretch of river to Acle, a distance of twelve miles, little worthy of note on either hand is passed. To the south, a flat expanse of marsh land extends for miles, with nothing to break the sky-line except an occasional water-mill; on the north the upland is visible, and after passing the Two-Mile House the ruined tower of Caistor Castle may just be seen rising therefrom. Leaving the three-mile, four-mile,

five-mile, six-mile, and seven-mile houses behind, we come to
Stokesby Ferry, a group of tumbled-down cottages erected
upon the banks of the river in picturesque confusion, attractive
to the artist but to no one else.    Next comes " Muckfleet," a
grown-up dyke only kept open by the water running from
Ormesby and Filby Broads, which stretches of water have
much to attract the angler, but the shooting on both is
strictly preserved.    This dyke is four miles in length and
navigable to a dinghy.    He who is venturous enough to row
up it will require much refreshment and many rests, the way
being laboursome and difficult.

Turning, a point of the winding stream Acle is before us,
and we lay-to within a hundred yards of the ancient stone
bridge.

This stretch of the river from Acle to Yarmouth has little
to attract the sportsman.    Occasionally an odd fowl may
be met with in the river, but on account of the traffic this is
a rare occurrence.    The rands are not sufficiently attractive
to snipe, although they are to be met with.    Ruffs, reeves,
sandpipers and stints now and again visit the waterway,
but lapwings are at all times passing and re-passing there-
over.

Many a weary hour has the author spent navigating this
stream in the hope of obtaining sport with the gun, but never
yet has he been successful in marking in his register a red
letter day.    Should there be a marsh close to the river with a
bright spot on it (in other words, an overflow of water) without there being others similarly covered within a considerable
distance, the flight shooter may anticipate an hour's good
shooting when the evening draws to a close, as peewits love
these places which are most attractive to them at sundown.
As a stand for this sport it is best to select a gateway, where,
by crouching down as near to the gate-post as possible, the
birds are unable to distinguish the outline of the flighter; but
he will have his work cut out in making a bag, more
especially if there happens to be a bit of a breeze blowing at
the time.

It is extraordinary how difficult peewits are to shoot at night when the elements are rough ; like leaves blown by the wind, they hover, whirl, and twist about in all directions. To attempt to follow-on is useless ; it is only the smart snap-shot which brings them lifeless to the ground. When on an expedition of this kind it is advisable to carry a long pole having a small board about four inches square or round firmly attached at one end. This pole is used for jumping the ditches, and the object of the board is to prevent the pole sinking too far down in the ooze, which everywhere abounds. With a pole such as described, light, and only ten or twelve feet long, with a sling in which to carry one's gun, a fairly active man should be able to take a bee line in all directions over the marshes and their incomprehensible network of dykes and drains. Of course, the shooting on these marshes is private, but little, if any, game is ever found there. Wildfowl and seabirds claim them as their own, and at night are feeding to their hearts' content upon them in all directions. Should the trespassing visitor be approached by a marshman or others, he will find that a civil explanation, a pipe of tobacco and the price of a drink goes a long way to open up the marshes to him, as well as to find him sport. The owners of the marshes do not, as a rule, object to the visitation of the flight shooter, unless there be game in the neighbourhood which they are preserving for themselves or friends.

The angling between Acle and Yarmouth is practically a dead letter, although in the reaches near Acle Bridge good bags are made. The visitor will do well to visit the Angel Inn, which stands on the banks of the river immediately adjoining the bridge, where good accommodation is obtainable as well as boats, baits, luncheon, tackle, guns, traps and every other requisite. The village of Acle is worthy of a visit. It lies about one mile from the river, and contains two good village hostelries, where accommodation for man and beast can be obtained, namely, "The Queen's Head" and "The King's Head."

The shooting in the neighbourhood of Acle is mostly divided into small holdings, many of which can be hired at about one shilling an acre all round. Partridges are most in evidence, and the average bag for four guns would be about twenty brace a day, together with half a score of hares, for which the neighbourhood is celebrated.

Acle Bridge is a solid stone structure supposed to have dated from the time of the Romans. If one has never seen these Norfolk bridges, an inspection should be made from above as well as from below. A little way from the bridge is the entrance to Upton Dyke leading to Upton Broad, where, in times gone by, many rare birds have been collected. The broad is enclosed by trees and is difficult to explore, unless a permit is obtained from the owner and the use of his boat granted. This is one of the broads which is rapidly growing up, and in a few years' time it will become converted from open water into a wet bottom carr.*

The dykes, rands and swamps which surround these broads and fleets are interesting to the lover of nature as having once afforded undisturbed homes to plants, insects and birds which are now almost entirely numbered with the past. It was here that ruffs used to choose their hillocks on which to fight for the reeves which collected round the base of the hillock, watching the combat with interest and admiration, in the end falling easy victims to the horse-hair snoozes so artfully set by the cunning marshman. The bittern and the black-tailed godwit also frequented these haunts during the incubation season, but now, if one of these comparatively rare species is seen a dozen men with guns follow everywhere hunting it to death.

The Acle Reach is a capital fishing station and easy of access from Yarmouth or Norwich by rail, whilst traps can be procured at the village or at the bridge to drive to or from the river. The reaches just above the bridge also afford

---

* In Broadland—a marshland covert.

excellent sailing, and the regattas are visited by over two hundred yachts and other craft at every fixture of the local yacht clubs. For the fishing it is advisable to inquire from the local watermen, or, better still, take one of them in the boat before setting out, as the swims vary so in accordance with wind, tide, moon and other circumstances, that however correctly described the visitor would most probably go away dissatisfied if he had not taken further assistance upon the spot to guide him.

Beyond Upton Dyke there is almost a straight run past Fishley Mill to Thurnmouth, three miles from the bridge, and fifteen from Yarmouth. The river now bears away due west for two miles, to St Bennet's Abbey.

From Thurnmouth to St Bennet's Abbey the fishing is good, and plenty of peewits may be killed crossing the river if a constant lookout is kept and the boat is fairly well concealed. The rands provide snipe in November, but beyond this there is little other sport.

St Bennet's Abbey is situated on the River Bure, on a rising knoll of land near to the point where the River Ant joins the Bure, and facing the three entrances to South Walsham Broad. On all sides it is surrounded by marshes, and at one time, no doubt, this knoll of land must have been an island rising from the swamps. In many places on the land (which is several acres in extent) may be seen traces of the old walls and of the ruined Abbey, which, about a hundred years ago, was converted into a windmill, now also in ruins. The lofty archway (built in the days of Canute) is still standing, and in the cool recesses of the interior of the mill may be seen portions of ancient carving and other objects of interest to those who study the history of former times. To the west of the windmill the remains of fish tanks used by the monks can easily be traced.

The river reach, on which the abbey stands, is noted for perch, probably accounted for by the hard, gravelly bottom which exists in many parts of it.

This is a region of good fishing of all description, no

K

matter what direction fancy takes ; the Ant and its tributaries may be especially mentioned.

The shooting round St ·Bennet's Abbey is very good, and
fortunate is ˙the man who can hire sufficient of the rough
swamps favoured by snipe to occupy a whole day's beat.
Within a̤ gun-shot of the ruined walls excellent sport may
also be obtained upon the marshes, which in this neighbourhood are cultivated by the farmer to his advantage during
a dry season.  In standing beans hares are mostly found, but
the cover is so dense and high that they are very difficult to
shoot or to drive into the open.  On some of the stubbles of
these marshes are many coveys of birds, and until quite late
into the autumn they are easy to obtain, on account of the
quantity of cover which everywhere abounds ; but it must be
remembered by the visitor that this class of shooting is of
marketable value, consequently it is preserved.  Inquiries in
the neighbourhood will soon make known what tracts there
may be undisposed of, their rentals, and all concerning
them.

This shooting has a special charm ; a half day on the
uplands, together with a half day on the marshes, producing
a bag of great variety.  The unusual nature of the surroundings, the difficulty of the shooting by reason of the variety
of the quarry, the passage of the broad dykes, the negotiation
of the smaller ones by means of a jumping pole, all add to
the experience which an ordinary common or garden shoot
lacks.  Not only this, but when any ordinary mortal would
consider sport at an end, the evening flight can be relied upon
for a few shots.

The shooting above referred to lies more to the north of
St Bennet's Abbey than to the south.  On the south side of the
River Bure the marshes are all laid down to grass, and one
must tramp many miles to obtain sport, unless exceptional
fortune favour the shooter.  This does not apply to the
swamps which lie contiguous to the broads, which are strictly
preserved, and generally let with the upland.  At all times
of the year they furnish a most interesting observation

ground to the botanist and ornithologist, as well as sport to
lovers of the gun.

South Walsham Broad, which is situated about a mile
from the river, under the uplands, is divided into two parts,
the Little and the Great Broad. The public claim the right
to shoot upon the Little Broad, which is, of course, disputed
by the surrounding owners. The Great Broad, which is connected with the Little Broad by means of a narrow dyke,
is strictly preserved, and is at times well stocked with fowl.
At the westernmost end, separated by another dyke, lies
Sotshole Broad, a mere pulkhole grown up in summer with
water lilies and weeds. These broads are surrounded by woods
very picturesquely situated. For some years it has been the
custom of the lessee of the shooting to breed a number of
half-bred wild ducks, which afford excellent sport when the
season opens. During the autumn, pochards, widgeon, teal,
duck and mallard, tufted duck, shovellers, and many species of
long-winged fowl are nearly always to be found here. After
the first shot is fired the foreign fowl circle high in the air,
and they understand all too well how to take care of themselves. Many a day's excellent sport has the author had
upon these waters, the memory of which is not likely to be
effaced by time, and as the years roll on they are looked back
to as sweet pages of a happy past.

One of the most enjoyable sports Broadland affords is
evening flighting. It is good between two of these broads.
Warmly clad and provided with long marsh boots one sits
upon a hummock of hassock grass concealed from view by
a rudely-made screen of reeds, or a net-work of improvised
boughs and bushes, bent and twisted into a leafy curtain,
before and around. A well-trained Norfolk retriever crouches
as near as circumstances will permit, its ears pricked, its head
on one side, and its whole attitude showing that the dog has
as much interest in the proceedings as its master.

As the shades of evening draw to a close, and the mist
rises from the water and swamps, rail may be seen stealing
noiselessly from their haunts amongst the labyrinth of rush

and sedge, stepping gently over the broad water-lily leaves, and picking insects from the herbage as they seek their evening meal; the water-hen chirrups to his mate, they also seek supper before retiring to rest in the low alder bushes; white-faced coots, which during the day have been splashing in the broad, betake themselves to some favourite island in the sedges, where they prune their dusky feathers and make their toilet with the perfect security that evening-tide brings; wood-pigeons or ring-doves pass and repass, taking their flight either to the fir trees, where it is their intention to pass the night, or else to some well-known bush, which they make use of to descend to the water's edge to take a nightcap to assist the digestion of the contents of their well-nigh bursting crop; the heron returning from the marsh utters his harsh "f-f-f-rank," and should he alight upon a fir tree near to the ambush, he will disgust one with the un-gentlemanly utterances which he gives forth before he takes himself to rest; the water vole contentedly munches the sedge roots, and perchance the splashing of an otter is heard as it enters the water.

At the beginning of the night these and many other sights and sounds of interest may be noted by the flight shooter from his ambush. Thus far, he will content himself with observing only; he will not disturb the scene by drawing trigger, he will await the coming of the fowl or other quarry more worthy of his cartridge. Perhaps his first shot will be at a woodcock, which flits silently from some low-lying alder carr to a favourite clump of holly trees upon an upland bank adjoining the marsh land. Perhaps it will be a snipe, both of them difficult shots in the uncertain light of evening-tide.

The retriever which has had a careful training will not permit these incidents and signs of life to pass by un-observed; very little will escape its attention, and if he be watched, many a sign will be brought to notice which would otherwise have escaped. Suddenly he cocks his head on one side, looks up and surveys the horizon around him; his ears are delicate, he has first detected the faint whistle of the wings of wildfowl, and shortly we also shall catch the unmistakable whistle of mallard on the wing. Minutes seem to pass, which in reality are but a few seconds, and before we have been able to distinguish the fowl they are on us with a rush of wings that would startle the unexperienced shooter, and they alight on the water with a mighty splash which causes the pulses to throb and the veins to be on fire with suppressed excitement. Should the fowl fly between us and the western sky, there will be little difficulty in spotting them, but it takes a good man to kill dead a right and left when the evening is far advanced.

Sometimes when fowl have been much shot at, or the wind is light and the weather fine, they will circle several times round the water before alighting, and it is a good rule to follow, "never to pull trigger unless the gun is prepared to lay even money with himself; like a well-known sporting duke, either his left-hand pocket against his right, or to lay it "on the nod" with his four-footed companion.

Each shot creates a hubbub all around, which at first is quite unexpected. The water birds which make their home in this particular neighbourhood commence shrieking, and uttering loud cries of alarm, spluttering into the reeds with a great rumpus. The retriever should require no direction; he has noted the result of the shot and silently leaves, soon bringing to our feet the slain, which he retrieves with great pride in his work. No sooner is he back than he is off again in another direction to fetch the second bird. Other shots follow, sometimes successfully, but more often otherwise, and thus we sit, without moving from one position, until the last light of day has faded from the sky and only the stars twinkle overhead, or the night wind howls and the darkening scud comes on, and we are unable to see by the watch how quickly the time has passed.

According to circumstances, the bag is heavy or light, and the expenditure of cartridges large or small; but whether sport is obtained or not, the satisfaction is great at having had the opportunity of passing one more evening upon the marshland, in the midst of the life which we love, and having added to our experience by noting the hundred and one minor incidents which are always fresh and interesting, however often they may have been seen before.

The foregoing picture is but a reminiscence of Broadland life at the close of day, or an evening on the flighting ground, but should the visitor not be fortunate enough to obtain permission from some owner or other to participate in that sport, he can, if he be so minded, by leaving his gun and dog behind him, betake himself in a "dinghy" or punt to some well-known stand upon a water to which he has access, and by concealing himself in the rushes, watch the scene, and in his imagination picture what he would do could he only carry his wishes into effect.

Whilst moored at St Bennet's Abbey it is well to sail in the dinghy to explore the ramifications of such broads as lie in the district, and in doing so to spin a spoon bait out aft. This process should be rewarded during the day with several runs both from pike and perch, which are taken home for consumption on board.

The fishing on South Walsham Great Broad is preserved, but it is not difficult to obtain the necessary permission, and very large takes often reward the patient piscator.

Leaving St Bennet's Abbey, we turn a bend of the river reaching southwards, and arrive at the dyke leading to Ranworth Broads. Like South Walsham, these broads lie about a mile from the river, and the fishing and shooting is preserved on each, although the public claim a right to fish on Ranworth Little Broad. During the autumn and winter these broads are noted for the pike they contain, which run from thirty pounds in weight downwards.

Ranworth Great Broad, which at one time contained several decoy pipes, is noted in Broadland for the wildfowl that collect there during the winter.

From Ranworth Broad several other minor waters are navigable. The whole neighbourhood is strictly preserved

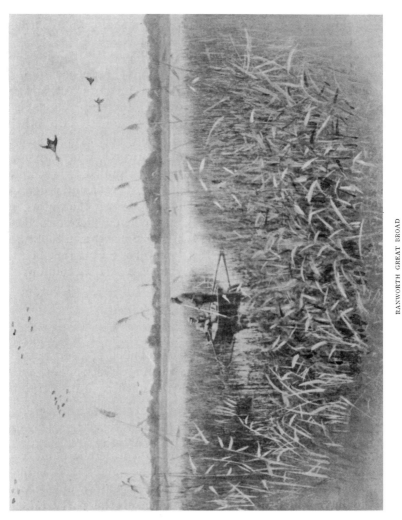

RANWORTH GREAT BROAD

and an enormous head of game kept up, a fact soon brought
home to the visitor by the quantity of birds of all descriptions met with everywhere.

Returning once more to the river, its winding course leads
to Horning Ferry. This part of the river runs through a
district of bogs and swamps, which have been reclaimed from
the main stream by drainage at a great expense to the
owners. The swamps extend over thousands of acres, and in
many places snipe and other wildfowl are found in abundance.
Well do we remember, when in company with two other
friends, we had a day's rough shooting on these very swamps.
Starting from the Old Maltings at Ranworth Quay, we em-
barked in a flat-bottom lighter which was pulled by a couple
of marshmen through the many clumps of reeds and sedge to
the entrance to a broad dyke. On the way over the water we
had several shots at snipe, coot, moor-hen and other birds
Then we were landed on a bog whilst the marshmen took the
boat round a labyrinth of dykes to meet us at another point.
We floundered along as noiselessly and as best we could over
the flooded bogs, the litter from which had been cut and
gathered, picking up on our way snipe and other water birds,
but missing many more than we shot at.

Occasionally we would conceal ourselves in a clump of
reeds or in a friendly bush as a large bunch of peewits or a
few fowl took their line of flight in our direction, but more
often than otherwise were these tactics unsuccessful. Joining
our friends in the boat we were next deposited on some finer
marshes used for grazing, where we were able to add seven
and a half brace of pheasants and a leash of partridges to the
bag. Taking to the swamps again at a different point, we
beat some 500 acres, flushing a large number of snipe,
but not securing more than five and a half couple. We
should have killed more had not some of the party taken
occasional headers into places where they should have set
their feet. This necessitated a large consumption of whisky
which, it is perhaps needless to add, did not tend to promote
straight shooting; but the sport these swamps afforded

was of the most enjoyable description. It was not an uncommon occurrence to have a right and left at a snipe and
a pheasant, or at a pheasant and a duck, and the flora
through which we pushed our way was delightful even to
one who has no knowledge of the subject. A day such as this,
coming as it did in the middle of the shooting season, and in
itself so different in comparison with the ordinary day's sport
to which we were accustomed, was the more appreciated and
in consequence the more enjoyed.

MAISON D'EAU.

# CHAPTER XIV

## A RIVER YACHTING RESORT

A SKELETON WATERMILL.

THE low-lying landscape of uninterrupted marshland stretching away from Yarmouth to Acle is monotonous even to the sportsman, steam drainage having rendered the marsh unattractive to most species of wildfowl. Occasionally in the autumn, after a wet season, snipe are fairly abundant, and may be shot from a boat on the river as they rise from the rands, but as a rule, in summer, nothing catches the eye of the gunner save perhaps the lazy flight of a solitary heron in the remote distance, or a few lapwings as they cross the river from time to time.

Shooting on the rivers and broads, owing to the crowds of armed Cockneys which appeared when these waterways were first brought under the notice of the public, fell into evil repute. This was perhaps hardly surprising when irate landowners found their cattle wounded by bullets, blinded by charges of shot, the sails of their yachts perforated, and the roofs of their watermills damaged by projectiles discharged from the weapons of these would-be sportsmen. No language is too strong to denounce such offenders, and no treatment

154

would be too harsh to serve out to those guilty of such
wanton cruelty and mischief. However, as these lines are
more likely to be perused by sportsmen than by others, it
is not necessary to dwell upon the abuses that firearms of
every description have been put to in this locality.

As Horning is approached the scenery undergoes a welcome change. The landscape becomes more undulating, and
in some places is densely wooded. The river is bordered by
a broad margin of reed-covered swampy marshes, studded
here and there with innumerable clumps of alder and secluded
pools and dykes—a veritable paradise for wildfowl.

Visitors, however, must not imagine that they are at
liberty to roam and rove to their hearts' content through
the tempting tangle of undergrowth and aquatic vegetation
which stretches away on either hand from the riverside to
the middle distance. But should they select a favourable
retreat by the river bank at sundown, they will, with
moderate luck, be rewarded for their patience when the
wildfowl leave their swampy haunts for evening flight.

Early in August, after the duck have been disturbed on
the private broads abounding in this district, they may
frequently be seen on the wing in considerable quantities,
wheeling with uncertain flight within easy range, but sportsmen must remember that when retrieving birds dropped
beyond the boundary of the river wall their guns must be
left behind, and it is not legal to avail one's self of the
assistance of a dog.

With respect to " flighting," most careful observation is
necessary to determine the exact point of ambush, and
one more often than not finds the spot selected is just
out of range. However, in this as in everything else,
success is bought by experience, and one or two failures
may result in the discovery of the precise position which
will be favourable to making a bag. So long as the feeding
ground continues satisfactory and the fowl are not harassed
too much they will take the same line night after night.
From this it is patent that it is of the greatest importance

to take note of the particular locality which affords the attraction, also to glean all information possible from local flight shooters, who will be found agreeable companions, and, if treated with due respect, fairly communicative.

Personally, when shooting in a new district, or late in the season in a known district, we always prefer their company for a few nights in order to make ourselves well up-to-date in the lines of flight. On these occasions we lean together over a marsh gate or barrier, listening with interest to the many anecdotes they always have at the tip of their tongue, learning much of the habits of the denizens of marsh-land, until the time arrives when we must separate to take up our respective stands for the evening.

About two hundred yards down stream from Horning Ferry is a bend of the river which lies nearest to Ranworth Broad and the innumerable pulkholes in the bogs and swamps, where an excellent stand for flight shooting will be found, and many is the fowl the author has dropped of an evening, with a mighty splash, shooting from this point; but the rands around are so boggy and dangerous that few birds can be recovered without the aid of a good dog. During the daytime little or nothing is seen; almost all the shooting is done when the sun has set and the air is alive with birds, which one not accustomed to flighting may fail to notice.

Horning Ferry, situated about a quarter of a mile from the village, and about a hundred yards or so from the up-lands, is one of the most interesting spots in Broadland, not only on account of its position, but also by reason of the everyday country life to be seen when staying there. Many a time during the day the old ferry boat is cranked over the river with its living freight of horses, traps, beasts or stock, which are being conveyed from one part of the marshes to the other. The eccentric costumes of the Cockney and other yachtsmen, who make this a favourite camping ground, cannot fail to attract attention. The sporting annals of the inn, dating back so many years, may well be dived into, and the rustic dances of the labouring classes on a Saturday evening in the low-roofed and brick-floored tap-room are worthy of encouragement. It is generally agreed that the time devoted to Horning Ferry is well spent, and as enjoyable as any part of a cruise in Broadland.

The Ferry Inn is a charmingly picturesque hostelry of considerable antiquity, which contains in its visitors' list the autograph signatures of many notable men, amongst whom may be mentioned the Duke of Argyle and the Marquis of Lorne. For many years the Ferry Inn was in the hands of Mr Thompson, a sportsman of the old school, whose splendid physique, genial countenance, and unlimited stock of sporting yarns were known to every " Broadsider " in the county. We can remember how " Old Thompson " used to make our piscatorial bumps throb with excitement as year after year he would relate that the giant pike, supposed to be at least 50 lbs. in weight, was still pursuing its unchecked career of piracy and plunder. This marauder of the deeps round Horning defied the strongest gimp, and if only half the tales heard were to be believed, it had appropriated enough fishing tackle to start a small shop with. It was not, however, by legitimately acquiring the various gee-gaws provided by confiding anglers that it gained its reputation for potential greed; many a pheasant and. duck was supposed to have disappeared in its capacious maw, much to the astonishment and chagrin of those who had shot the birds; but at length this advanced type of *Esox lucius* met with an untimely end in the trammels of a bow net. It is always so with noble fish. Its gross weight proved to be 34 lbs., and the scene of his depredations knows him no more.

Poor Thompson, having in due course become a martyr to rheumatic gout, retired, fearing that the winters of this marshy land " might double him up for ever." The Ferry Inn since his retirement has changed hands once or twice, but is still an excellent retreat for those who desire to indulge in fishing and shooting which the locality offers, although, of course, the place, to those who knew it in the palmy days of the old sportsman referred to above, is hardly the same.

When our wherry, the commodious *Warrior*, arrived within sight of Horning Ferry, the sun was sinking into a glorious bed of rose-tinted clouds, before which a thin white curtain of marsh mist was rising, whilst the masts of the numerous craft of all sizes which loomed above it looked gaunt and uncanny because the hulls of the vessels to which they belonged were invisible. The wind, as is customary in Broadland at that season of the year, had died away to a whisper, and the bats and water voles emerged from their gloomy haunts to enjoy an evening meal.

The quant had to be used freely, and with its aid we gradually crept nearer and nearer to this apparent oasis in the desert of marsh mist which now enveloped us.

At last we were alongside the other craft, whose respective crews were soon busy preparing dinner and putting up awnings for the night.

Selecting a berth as near to the green fronting the inn as possible, the rand anchors were secured fore and aft, and we made tracks for the hostelry for a preliminary reconnoitre with sherry and bitters by way of an *appetissant*.

The bar parlour is generally crowded with thirsty yachtsmen. On this particular occasion two of them were nailing a notice to the wooden partition, headed *Le Palais Gaieté de Cœur*, and, in effect announcing that a grand concert would be held that evening in the club-room, to which everyone was invited, the terms of admission being a contribution of some kind or other towards the general entertainment.

When first reading this we wondered what hour would be suggested for ordering the " gigs," but on looking a little lower down a footnote was observable.

*N.B.*—Should the Landlord of this Hotel produce chuckers-out at the hour of ten, or before, the Concert will be continued on board the Good Ship *Nautilus*. By order of the Worshipful President, Bacchus Neptune Appolloman, Esq.

Of course we consented to go to the concert, as did almost

everyone else from the yachts moored in the neighbourhood, and the event promised to be one not lacking in amusement.

A detailed description of that evening, although it might certainly come within the category of Broadland sport, is hardly such subject-matter as should be included within the pages of the present volume, and it is therefore skipped.

Visiting first the low-roofed kitchen, we watched for upwards of half an hour the many and varied step dances of the Horning rustics. An American hand organ provided the music and a liberal supply of nutty brown old ale, with a dash of gin in it, promoted the energy of the dancers to an extent amazing to onlookers. At first glance the dancing appeared to consist of nothing but a great rattling of feet upon the well-sanded brick floor, with much stamping and occasional exclamations and gesticulations to vary the monotony, but the more careful observer would note that regular steps were made and that the dance in progress was one which required both practice and skill to perform.

On the whole it was quaint, peculiar and unapproached, except perhaps by the dances in the wilds of Andalusia as rendered by the *Jitanos* and Spanish peasants. On entering the so-called *Palais Gaieté de Cœur* we were hailed with an enthusiastic welcome, although the room was so crowded and filled with tobacco smoke it was difficult to distinguish anything or anybody. At the moment a member of the company was engaged in singing "The Tarpaulin Jacket," in the chorus of which everyone most lustily joined, whilst several members of the audience were sitting upon a luckless individual who still insisted in attempting to recite "The Lifeboat" as his contribution. When howled down he would not accept the verdict of his listeners, but made repeated attempts to renew his offer by starting upon the first verse, regardless of what was going on or the objections of those around him.

Doubtless we should have stayed longer than we did, but the heat and smoke were so oppressive we were glad to seek the fresh air outside, and, muffled up in our mackintoshes, we sipped our grog on a garden chair, listening to the rowdy voices within the house and the weird cries of the waterfowl which filled the air without.

As had been feared, the landlord's chuckers-out *did* appear on the scene and bundled the whole company off the premises at ten o'clock p.m. to the minute, but not before several of them had secured stone jars of beer and other refreshments, with which they intended to continue their merriment and debauchery far into the night. Prominent amongst them we could hear the would-be reciter of "The Lifeboat." He had apparently annexed a stone jar of old beer, which was claimed by a man from another boat, and an altercation ensued amusing in the extreme to listeners.

One hiccupped out snatches of the recitation in a confused jumble, the other used bad language and abusive epithets, whilst both tugged hard at the two-handled jar, disputing its ownership. Suddenly a splash announced the fact that there was a man overboard, whom we were perfectly correct in assuming was the gentleman interested in the lifeboat. He was fished out, however, with boat-hooks, amidst much laughter and expressions of mock condolence, after which the party, excepting those who were visiting the *Nautilus*, broke up into little groups and made their way to the cabins of their respective craft for a final nightcap before turning in. Having one of the largest cabins, we invited several of the quieter members to accompany us on board, and when we were seated comfortably in cosy corners of the cushioned lounge, the conversation immediately turned to the subject that was ever uppermost in our minds —namely, sport.

Amongst our guests was the son of a Broadland squire, one of the few that had managed to live upon his own acres and farm them in spite of the depressing times. He was a keen sportsman in every branch of the art and had known all the broads and waterways from childhood. With the natural grace and easy confidence of a Norfolk gentleman he soon grasped the topics of conversation which interested us most, and after a few preliminary anecdotes he leant back in his seat, blew a ring or two of smoke from his pipe, and narrated the following peculiar and unaccountable experience :—

### A Shooter's Confession, or the Gun with the Bent Stock.

During the month of November, in the year 189—, I had been to stay the week-end with a friend in the heart of the Broad district, and at breakfast on the Monday morning, prior to my departure, he urged me to prolong my visit a few hours.

He spoke of wildfowl. He said he could lend me boots, clothes, gun and cartridges, and he guaranteed good sport.

I was sorely tempted. Surely a few hours could not matter so materially to the mission I had undertaken for that day ; besides, could I not make up the leeway by burning the midnight oil ? Such a chance as he offered—even pressed upon me—might not present itself again for some time to come. I was weak, and yielded to his persuasive eloquence and his generous hospitality ; thus was it arranged for me to catch the afternoon train instead of the earlier one that in duty bound I should have taken.

After breakfast we repaired to the gun-room, where I was rigged out in long indiarubber boots, a loose-fitting yellow-coloured Norfolk jacket, a tweed hat to match ; and I was offered a selection from several guns of various pattern. " This," said my host, " is an excellent wildfowling gun; in fact, there never was a better one made, but unluckily the stock has too much bend, and I have postponed its alteration so long that it has not yet been attended to. However, if you think you can shoot with it, you will find it a beauty." " If I thought I could shoot with it !"—what a suggestion ! I— who had started shooting when scarce eight winters had passed over my head; I—who had handled guns of almost all descriptions, and under the most varying circum-

L

stances. The doubtful tone of his voice at once decided me. I would take this gun in preference to any other if I never touched a feather. (I did not say so openly; I only thought it.) I would show him that, bend or no bend, it mattered not to me, for that day at least the gun with the corkscrew stock which he meant to have altered should so excel its former self in its death-dealing propensities that its owner should seriously reconsider the advisability of altering it at all.

Gentle listener, bear with me to the end of this narrative, and you will see how my egotism was so ruefully taken down, and how all such vain thoughts should be suppressed the moment they enter the brain, in case the tongue should be weak and foolish enough to betray utterance.

Our sporting toilet was scarce complete when the dogcart drove up to the door, and we were bowling smoothly along a good turnpike road towards the reed-grown waste of bog and open water, surrounded by fair woodlands, which marked Ranworth Great Broad.

Our appearance was not expected, but the preparations for our sport were none the slower carried out, and I at least had the double satisfaction of seeing more in detail than I otherwise should have done.

Fortified with a nip of home-made cherry brandy, our steps through the glade, which wound its way among the nut bushes of the old rookery, were elastic and hurried. We were eager for the fray, and the noise made by the wildfowl on the open water, of which we caught an occasional glimpse through the undergrowth, only inspired us the more. The retrievers were in ecstasies. All of us were sanguine, and felt the hot blood of excitement and expectancy coursing through our veins, except perhaps the keeper and the boatman.

At the home farm my host had stopped and invited the bailiff to accompany us, which invitation had been cordially accepted. A more jovial companion, a keener sportsman, or a better shot than he was I have rarely met.

Arriving at a tumble-down old boathouse we were greeted

by the decoys. The quacking they gave tongue to when they saw us, which they kept up incessantly all the time we were there, was really worthy of a better cause, so far as the well-being of their wilder congeners was concerned. A few of their number were white, but the majority of them were the small cross-bred wild ducks. Tame! They were all so tame you could catch them in your hand. They took no notice of our dogs. ´ You had to take care not to tread on them; but if hustled, they would fly away as strongly apparently as wild ones would have done. About a dozen of these the keeper caught without ceremony, putting them into a couple of bags, which he placed in the boat.

My host was then rowed to an island on the north side of the water, and half-a-dozen of the over-confiding call ducks were anchored down outside the fringe of reeds which surrounded his small domain. They were tied to bricks, with about six or ten yards of twine apiece as tether ropes. On the island a shelter or screen had been constructed with reed hurdles, and so skilfully was it arranged that at a distance of a few paces it was well-nigh impossible to distinguish it from its surroundings.

My agricultural friend and myself were then conducted by a narrow, tortuous path, picked out through the low-lying alder carrs and sedge-covered swamps, to our stands, which were situated at the further end of the broad, and, by the way we traversed, distant perhaps a mile from the boathouse.

Half-an-hour we were allowed to get to our positions. That short space of time seemed an age to me.

The path itself was interesting Treacherous bogs were spanned by faggots sunk deep into the slime, and fixed together by wire or willow bands. Rank vegetation, having entwined and twisted its tortuous roots well into these faggots, had caused soil of a kind to be formed, and cut litter having been freely scattered on the path, walking was rendered easy, dry and noiseless.

About every fifty yards little becks or drains had to be crossed by means of moss-grown bridges, which were merely tree trunks halved and thus made use of. When near the haunts of the fowl, high reed screens had been placed at all angles to shield the shooter, and litter had been scattered with a free hand.

Occasionally we passed secluded pools, overhung with trees and alder bushes, too secluded for wildfowl, but beloved by the rail and moorhen, many of which we disturbed as we wended our way stealthily along. Wood-pigeons were there in plenty. Pheasants ran on the path before us and behind, like chickens in an orchard, and all the while we could hear a perfect babel of quacking, splashing, whistling and flapping from the wildfowl, whose nearer acquaintance we eagerly looked forward to.

At a bend in the pathway my agricultural friend left me, with strict injunctions to go the last hundred yards as though my life depended on it. Following his instructions to the letter, I proceeded, with body bent (for which there was no occasion, but in my excitement I thought it best), placing my feet with a fastidious nicety, trembling all over, and working myself into a cold perspiration from sheer excitement. This did not augur well for good results, but I had yet ten minutes to wait and but twenty yards to go. Every step I took stirred some new phase of animal life. From the reeds at my feet water-rails glided, whilst now and again I saw a duck so near to me that I could almost have touched it with my gun barrels.

I soon discovered that my path traversed a narrow peninsula of land, upon the extreme end of which my screen or shelter was situated. This made me so nervous of disturbing the main body of fowl before the appointed time that I crawled the remainder of the way as best I could, and I did not breathe freely until I was comfortably seated inside my little three-cornered hut. Finding I had five minutes yet to wait, I lit a pipe to quiet my nerves a bit, laid out a row of cartridges, placed my gun in readiness, and then placing a flat stick in the reed screen, twisted it round in order to make a peephole through which I could reconnoitre.

What a sight!

I could see hundreds of mallard, widgeon, teal and water-birds of all descriptions swimming, bibbling and splashing about in the water all around me. On my left was a family party, which I thought I could decimate entirely if they would only wait until the appointed time came round.

I looked and looked until I dare not look any more or I should be tempted to outrage the laws of hospitality, throw discipline to the winds, disobey orders and fire. Taking my eye from the peephole I loaded my gun. (I had not dared to load it before; the temptation would have been too great.) Then I fixed my eyes upon my watch and counted the seconds.

Hardly had I done so when the roar and mighty splashing of five hundred mallard rising from the water together and winging their way heavenward alarmed me.

This I afterwards ascertained was caused by my agri-cultural friend, who had fallen into a slough of despond and had cracked some faggot sticks in his endeavours to get out and reach his shelter without further mischief. It was a pity, but accidents will happen, as it is said, in the best-regu-lated families. My family party was scattered and all hopes of a wholesale sitting-shot were gone.

Unfortunately the elements were not in our favour; it was one of those still muggy days than which nothing can be more disadvantageous for wildfowl shooting on inland waters. Every sound could be heard, and was magnified the more by the telephonic qualities of the unruffled water, and there being no wind the fowl flew high and circled longer before they descended.

Three minutes more! Overhead the air was dark with fowl of all kinds, flying low, high, in bunches and singly. Enviously I looked at them, eagerly I handled the "excellent gun, with the bent stock," and in my own mind I cogitated upon the probabilities of the life value of the various fowl who ventured so near my resting-place.

At last the long-waited-for signal was given. The loud

roar of my host's 8-bore echoed and re-echoed over the water. I heard the rush of another large mass of fowl rising, and, peering over the screen, I noted with exultant joy that they were heading straight for my hiding-place.

How many, I asked myself, should I get with my first two shots. I noticed a thick bunch of at least two hundred duck and mallard. Surely it would not be less than five with the right barrel and three with the left.

Vain thought! greedy shooter! (I cannot designate myself "sportsman" when I counted on this wholesale browning.) Nearer they came, and still nearer. The big bunch was lower than the others were. In my eagerness I pushed the barrels of my gun over the top of the reed screen, and the next moment I cursed my rashness. The fowl saw the movement, slight as it was, and they shaled * upwards.

So eager was I to make that family shot that I misjudged distance, and without aiming at any one of them in particular I fired.

Where was the rain of dead and dying?

What, not a feather!

Annoyed beyond measure, I fired again, with a like result.

" Ten thousand devils tear me," I thought, what a beginning, what absurd and juvenile eagerness, could I really have been guilty of such? could I really have fired at that " wall of ducks " without drawing a single feather? I could hardly believe it.

But my senses were soon brought back to the reality of the situation by seeing a beautiful right and left made by my agricultural friend, whose stand was a little northward to my own. It was a really pretty shot; it inspired me to follow his example. I had not long to wait for an opportunity. A bunch of five teal whisked round a clump of trees and rushed towards the surface of the water like witches in a hurricane. Again I sent two barrels aimlessly after them, and again I cursed my too eager disposition.

* *Patois*, signifying a gliding movement, somewhat similar to the gyrating course taken by a propelled piece of slate or flat stone.

Before I had properly loaded a single mallard passed me ; he presented a lovely shot, a full broadside, and he was not more than thirty yards away from me. This time I was really in earnest. I took a long-sighted aim and carefully swung my gun in front of him, steadily drawing on the trigger the while.

Bang !—the echo travelled far and wide, the smoke cleared away, but no duck fell ; on the contrary, I saw him mounting higher and higher above the reeds' and topping the alder carr behind me.

Once more I shot with as much care as before, but, alas! with the same result.

To say that I was disgusted is stating my feelings moderately. What was wrong ? Was it the cartridges, was it the gun, or was it the atmosphere ? These and dozens of other equally absurd questions I put to myself, covering everything except the real reason—the want of skill in the shooter, which was myself.

I am not by any means the only one who has thus erred under similar circumstances, instances in proof of which every sportsman can call to mind who has had any experience. But that fact is a poor consolation, and to lose one's temper and blame one's appliances only drives one from bad to worse. So it was with me. The more pains I bestowed upon my aim the cleaner I missed the object. Had I mauled one or two birds it might have given me a clue to better results, but even that (fortunately for the unfortunate wildfowl) was denied me ; and although I stood in my allotted stand and blazed away at wildfowl in every conceivable position for upwards of an hour to the benefit of the cartridge-maker, I never drew blood—at least, not to my knowledge.

My agricultural friend in the next stand exasperated me, although I could not but admire his skill. He dropped his birds seemingly from the clouds, and every one appeared to fall stone dead. Some even crashed through the yellow brittle reeds within a few yards of my stand, and, to add to my annoyance, splashed me with spray when they fell into the water.

In the distance I could see the little island on which my other friend was stationed, at intervals I heard either the roar of his 8-bore or the almost noiseless puff of the nitros from his 12, and I could see the victims which hovered round his decoys like moths round a candle crumple up in the air before the sound of the report could reach me.

When the fowl were first alarmed there must have been at least a thousand or more on the wing at one time, but after half-an-hour's serenade they made themselves scarce and disappeared almost entirely, returning in small groups from time to time, but, as the weather was so still, they circled and circled round and round the water, high overhead, before they could gain sufficient confidence to return to their former sanctuary. It was this suspicion of theirs which caused so many to drop upon the surface of the broad for the last time, and to dye the water with their blood.

As they lowered they sighted the decoys swimming about where they were accustomed to disport themselves, and gaining more confidence thereat they approached nearer and nearer, until the leaden hail stopped them altogether; at least, as I have before said, so far as my two friends were concerned. So far as I was concerned, it only caused them to fly the faster.

After a while we had a lull in our sport for about half an hour, and the keeper, who had been watching the proceedings from a distance, visited me. I noticed that he wore a worried look, but at that pastime I consider I gave him points and an easy beating.

"How many have you got in?" he asked.

What the devil should I say? He could see a score of empty cartridge shells at my feet, he had heard my incessant fusilade, my stand was certainly one of the best on the broad, and he knew from a former experience that if I shot at a barn door four-and-twenty times I should *not always* hit the roof. Even then, in my egoism, I would not confess

that perhaps the bent stock was in some measure accountable
for my execrable shooting, so I smiled a kind of sickly
smile and replied, " Well, I'm not quite sure, but I'll let you
know later on." And I thought of the motto, " *Dum spiro
spero.*"

" If it's all the same to you I would rather know now,
as I have come to take you to a different stand, where I
have anchored some decoys, and I think you will get better
sport."

For a few moments I fought within myself, and then I
said, " Well, I really don't think it's worth while wasting
time looking for any of my birds, as I don't think you will
find them. *To tell you the truth, I don't feel altogether myself
this morning*, and I don't believe I have drawn blood,
whether this (here my smile was positively awful) bent
stock has anything to do with it I don't know, but the
hideous fact remains that I have not been able to mark
down a dead bird as mine."

He was really quite distressed, and I felt for him, even
to the extent of several shillings extra tip money, which
sympathy I expressed before we parted.

At my next stand I did no better, although I had every
opportunity of retrieving my reputation. Whether the fowl
flew high or low, fast or slow, to the right or to the left, it
made no difference, and no one could possibly have been
more disgusted with the glaring exhibition I made of myself
than I was.

Then the time arrived for picking up. The decoys were
re-bagged, our friends taken on board the boat, and, with one
of us standing upon the seat in the bows, from which coign
of vantage a good survey of the reed beds could be taken,
we poled our boat through the sedges, in and out of little
bays and creeks, haunts of duck and pike, which latter we
often disturbed, and saw dart away with a rush and a swirl
of the water, in some cases sufficient to cause a slight oscilla-
tion to our frail craft.

Not the least interesting was this part of the proceedings.

Pretty little teal in full winter garb lay upon the water amongst the decaying lilies, the bright green of their wings looking as though a spring leaf had fallen upon them, whilst the drops of water scattered upon their plumage glistened like diamonds in the brilliant sunshine. Here and there lay duck and mallard, some on the sedge tussocks, others floating on the open water, all of them dead, with hardly a feather of their plumage ruffled. In half - an - hour we had collected over a score, and by a skilful cross-questioning of my friends as to the sport they

SHOOTING ROUND THE HOVERS.

had had, and by dwelling at length upon the accident to our agricultural friend in the bog, I had diverted inquiry concerning the extent of my share towards the bag. But it was not a wise artifice—the truth will always out—and had I anticipated the good-natured chaff I was certain to receive I should have blurted out the facts when I first met my friends, and not have allowed them to ferret them out for themselves.

Of course, my host very generously asserted that the blame must all be attributed to the bent stock, but this I would never openly admit, and urged in preference that it

must have been indigestion, or want of more cherry brandy
when sitting cramped up in the reed shelter. This latter
excuse was a glorious suggestion, for did it not "kill two
birds with one stone" as we say in England? Firstly, it
freed me (at least, so I fondly imagined) from all blame as
to my shooting. Secondly, my host was compelled, by the
laws of hospitality, to give me a second innings at that
inspiring beverage when we reached the keeper's cottage.
Trust this humble and modest sportsman for making super-
lative use of this his last and golden opportunity—at least
so far as that bottle was concerned. With my —th glass
I drank for the —th time—"Success to my host, and confusion
to wildfowl, and to all bent-stocked guns."

A THAMES PUNT FITTED FOR PICNIC-CRUISING IN BROADLAND.

An Upper Reach

# CHAPTER XV

### HORNING TO THE SOURCE OF THE BURE

SEVERAL days may be spent at Horning Ferry in sweet hours of idleness or fishing and flighting with varying success. The longer the stay, the more the locality seems to attract, and it is with feelings much akin to regret that at last the sail is hoisted and the old thatched roofs and rustling willows are left behind.

For half a mile above the ferry the river extends in a straight reach to Horning village. This reach is celebrated for its good fishing swims.

Horning is an old-fashioned, out-of-the-world spot, four miles from the nearest railway station, which in these days of ubiquitous trippers may be regarded as a pleasing attraction. As the quay, which runs the whole length of the village, is neared crowds of ragged urchins await the coming in keen expectancy, and commence chanting a strain, the words of which run somewhat as follows :—

Ho ! John Barley Corn,
Ho ! John Barley Corn,
All day long I raise my song to
John Barley Corn.

It is a time-honoured custom to throw pence to the children when passing.

Needless to add, they scramble wildly for them wherever they may fall, whether in the puddles of dirty water on the quay heading, or on stone heaps, or in the crevasses of piles of timber, or in the river itself ; whilst their ranks are frequently augmented by grown-ups, both male and female, with here and there an aged dame.

Thrown from the various passing craft the halfpence fly in all directions, and the eager penny hunters dig their arms into the pools and puddles as if gold and not copper was the object of their search.

The picturesque quaintness of this village is charming. Rambling amongst the old houses one can study at leisure a typical Broadland village, where the rustic maidens blush with shame when notice is drawn to their · sunburnt faces peeping out from under the large Norfolk hoods, which adds an almost irresistible attraction to their charms.

If the leafy lanes wending away from the back of the village are explored on all sides will be seen an abundance of game. Pheasants and partridges alike sit near to the road-ways, and are seen picking about on the stubbles. Hares hop across the path with perfect confidence in their security. But the shooting is most strictly preserved. A mile or so away is Beeston Old Hall, the ancient family seat of the Preston family, who distinguished themselves as Royalists during the Civil Wars. The house is a gloomy stone structure standing in an extensive park, well ornamented with magnificent old oak trees. Round it runs a lake, said to be full of large pike, some of them supposed to be as old as the house itself. The shooting is exceptionally good, and consider-ably over one thousand pheasants are shot on best days. Once when shooting a covert adjoining Barton Broad of this estate, the author shot at what he, in the shades of evening, supposed to be a rat running along the top of the bank, but which, subsequently, proved to be a woodcock.

Closer to the village lies Oliver's Broad, a small water

bounded by uplands, and affording home for both fish a
fowl. Topping the small hill of upland upon which t
village stands, a grand panorama of marsh land, wood a
water, the like of which cannot be found except in Ea
Anglia.

The river from Horning village to Wroxham runs throug
the heart of a highly-preserved game district, and keepe
are always on the alert, and concealed in the neighbourhoc
of the river to keep a jealous eye against any possible poacl
ing. Many cases have been brought in the county polic
courts for shooting pheasants as they crossed the river, an
although these cases have been argued, on behalf of the de
fendants, by some of the best sporting solicitors that mone
could procure, a conviction has nearly always been obtained
and the visitor will do well to remember that he cannot with
impunity shoot game, although, at the time he kills it, it may
be over the river and fall into it. It will be better for him to
reserve his fire for water birds and allow the game to pass un
molested. The temptation may be very great, and in some
places pheasants are very numerous, but the riparian
owners claim the soil of the river. The bench of magis
trates is mostly composed of local landed proprietors, and the
result is generally a foregone conclusion. One of the
defences raised was amusing if not interesting.

On October 3rd, in the year 1894, the North Walsham
Petty Sessional Court House was crowded to hear a case
brought against a member of the Royal Geographical Society
and of the Savage Club, who, with his friend, endeavoured to
prove himself a sportsman in every sense of the word by
bringing in evidence their shooting experience in South Africa.
There is no need to mention names, and we trust that mature
reflection, consequent from the fines and costs inflicted, has
improved their interpretation of the word "sportsmen." These
two tried to lead the Bench to believe that they shot a cock
pheasant (out of season) in mistake for a water-crow. "They
were well acquainted with the water-crow, and had shot
hundreds; it was much like our coot, but instead of having

white on the beak it had red—there are thousands of these
birds in South Africa." But was it likely to suppose that
anyone who had travelled (presumably for sport, but perhaps
with other aims in view as well) in many countries could
possibly mistake a cock pheasant for a water-crow ? or even a
water-hen for a cock pheasant as it flew " hollering " (keepers'
expression—evidently crowing) over the river between 6 and
7 p.m. during the second week in September. In this case
the magistrates rightly convicted.

In the summer of 1891 there was a great public outcry in
East Anglia, supported by the Corporation of the City of
London and elsewhere, and mass meetings were convened in
London, Norwich, Yarmouth and Lowestoft, and an Association was formed styling itself " The Norfolk Broads Protection
Association of London." Funds showered in from all sides,
but the result of the movement was, without doubt, a waste
of time, labour and money. The association selected a weak
case and one of the most difficult to fight that they could
possibly have chosen. It was known as the Hickling Broad
case, and (using the words of one of the speakers), " Those
who indulged in the harmless amusement of inhaling at their
leisure God's fresh air and the breeze of Heaven " are to-day
thankful to think that the objects which the association
claimed were not upheld. An appeal was attempted, but the
majority who gave their support to the movement were so
disgusted with the miserable fiasco that they would have no
more on't, and the whole thing practically ended in smoke.
That more protection is required is an admitted fact, and if
a movement could be made by which rules and regulations
could be enforced on the miles of waterway and broads, such
a system of government would be better for all parties alike.
What is really required is an Act of Parliament on all fours
with the present Thames Conservancy, but such a blessing
seems a forlorn hope.

It is a daily occurrence in Broadland to see large quantities
of fish rotting on the banks which should have either been
returned to their native element or given to poor people

who would appreciate them. In years gone by Broadland teemed with life, and every nook and cranny afforded shelter to some interesting species of the fur, feather or fish tribe. On these waterways one met with coot, grebe, water hen, rail and wildfowl of all description, but now so many visitors carry guns in the yachts with them, and when they can find nothing better to shoot at, choose as their mark any living thing that may come within range, not troubling to pick up the dead and wounded, and birds which are not mangled or killed during the season are driven away, to seek fresh haunts and waters new.

Not unfrequently a yachtsman hears heavy firing from a boat in front, and as he overhauls it he notices large quantities of dead and dying insect-feeding birds —such as martins or swallows—drifting past on the tide, an object of pity, and a disgrace to the unfeeling and unsportsmanlike shooters who so ruthlessly butcher them, simply for the gratification of having had a living mark to shoot at. Not unfrequently cattle are found on the marshes injured by shot as well as by bullets. It is only surprising to think that more serious accidents do not occur to human beings, as it cannot be believed that anyone would shoot at, and thus torture, dumb animals wilfully.

From the village of Horning progress is slow because the stream is wood-bound nearly all the way, but the scenery is very beautiful and thoroughly recompenses for delay. In drifting lazily, drowsily, up-stream, many pleasant recollections are brought back to the memory, and these untrammeled hours of idleness are enjoyed to the full.

It may be again well to remind the *summer* visitor to Broadland that fishing or sailing should be made the groundwork of his amusement, shooting being more or less an accessory. The coarse fishing, that is to say, fishing for bream, roach or perch, is as good as can be obtained. Jack, also, may be caught in large numbers. As a centre Horning can be highly commended. Below the village towards Acle the river is open to every breath of heaven; above, the picturesque reaches wind away as far as Wroxham Broad, which is the deepest expanse of fresh water that East Anglia can boast. In the reach below Horning remarkably fine perch are to be obtained, which often scale up to 3 lbs. or 4 lbs. One bright afternoon we had been sailing in the yacht's dinghy all the morning, but the wind having died away after lunch, it was proposed to drop gently down with the remaining breeze and spin for jack ; one hand being told off to sit clear of everyone with a 12-bore and to keep his weather eye lifted for snipe or duck. We had barely cast the lines before two patriarchal perch (one 3½ lbs. the other 2½ lbs.) were jumping and slapping about in the bottom of the boat. A third fish would have been added but for the breeze that momentarily freshened, and the boat, drawing rapidly ahead, enabled him to break away from the hook, and the annoyance was added to by seeing his great red tail and fins gradually disappearing in the depths from which he came.

When we got back to the wherry a damsel of some eighteen summers was creating a diversion by swarming up the mast of a small yacht moored to the bank, and her graceful evolutions were quickly transferred to the sketch-book, but perhaps it is advisable not to reproduce that effort in these pages.

With respect to shooting from a boat where the space is so limited, and the operator may be subject to sudden and involuntary movement, the greatest caution in handling and laying down a gun should be observed. In fact, it will not be going too far to declare that anyone in whom principles of caution are absent should not be allowed, under any circumstances, to touch a gun in a boat. Many are the distressing accidents which have occurred in Broadland. To record one will be sufficient for present purposes. A young fellow was shot in the prime of life owing to his brother having placed the gun down so carelessly that the accidental contact of a fishing line with the trigger lodged the whole charge in the unfortunate victim's stomach.

Upon looking at the map it will be seen that the river

M

from Horning steam mill is very tortuous, being connected on either side with many private broads.

On Hoveton Broad, the large sheet of water on the right hand proceeding from Horning to Wroxham, there is a colony of black-headed gulls which breed every year regularly. This broad is strictly preserved, but permission is occasionally given in the winter for pike fishing. The pike fishing on this Broad is exceptionally good, and 100 lbs. in weight is often taken in one day. Several fish of over 20 lbs. in weight each are generally secured here each season, fishing with rod and line and snap tackle.

Opposite the upper end of Hoveton Broad is Salhouse Larger Broad (also private), almost adjoining it, is Salhouse Little Broad, which contains some splendid rudd, and as this picturesque little lagoon forms a highway to the adjacent farm, the fishing, *nemine contradicente*, is regarded as public. At Salhouse Broad will be found an old and good farm. It is an excellent place for visitors, quiet, secluded, and situated in one of the most picturesque spots in Broadland. This broad has been selected by the Royal Canoe Club as a camping-ground. The rising ground overlooking the broad abounds in rabbits.

Leaving Salhouse Little Broad, after passing through a few bends of the river, Wroxham Broad is reached, the entrance to which is on the left-hand side of the stream. This splendid lake has rightly been termed the Queen of the Broads, owing to its beautiful surroundings and depth of water, the lead line showing a fathom nearly everywhere. The broad is open all the year round for sailing, but yachts, except with special permission, are not allowed to moor. The shooting is rigidly preserved, but fishing may be indulged in at the cost of half-a-crown a day per boat, which amount is collected by the lessee, a farmer living close to the broad, at whose house comfortable quarters may be procured by visitors.

Wroxham Broad by water is distant from the village about one mile, and the river winds through some charming scenery, but, owing to the traffic between the broad and the bridge, this part of the river is not, perhaps, so favourable to the sportsman as the reaches lower down. In the village, within a stone's throw of the station, and quite close to the river, are two hostelries, the King's Head and the Horse Shoes, at both of which the sportsman will find ample accommodation and all the necessary requisites he may require. At the top of the village, some twenty minutes' walk from the station, there is also another inn, called the Castle, an old-fashioned house with a bowling green. Rough boats for fishing may be hired for the sum of 1s. 6d. or 2s. per day, but for the better-class rowing boats a charge of 5s. is made, and for sailing boats 7s. 6d. to 10s. Wroxham is a very convenient spot to make headquarters so far as railway convenience is concerned, but for absolute quiet and rusticity it is advisable to go further afield to Horning, Salhouse, or, further up stream, Coltishall, a village about seven miles by water from Wroxham but only two and a half by road and rail—it ranks as one of the prettiest villages in Norfolk.

Above Wroxham Bridge the shooting is most strictly pre-served, and as the neighbouring landowners claim the soil of the river bed a shot cannot be fired without the probability of the shooter finding himself in the police court. On the other hand, the fishing is good. One can enjoy it free and unhampered in most places at very little expense.

In the bend of the river, just beyond the railway bridge, heavy baskets of roach may be taken in the summer, as the traffic below bridge forces the fish up river, where it is quieter, and the stream is not so much disturbed.

At Coltishall, a mile or so above Wroxham, roach and bream fishing can always be obtained. There are two good inns, "The White Horse" and "The Anchor," whilst comfort-able apartments may always be found in the village. Any amount of boats may be hired at a cheap rate, with or with-out men to accompany them.

Proceeding up stream we come to another good station for the angler—Buxton. Near the mills 2 lb. roach are no rarity, and in the winter the pike fishing is excellent. There are however, no boats to be hired near enough for day anglers, although permission to fish from the banks is rarely refused.

Still further up the river, beyond Aylsham, the fishing is private and preserved, and the necessary permit is more difficult to obtain than the sport merits.

Whilst exploring the upper tributaries of the Bure one of our party introduced us to a Broadland Trilby, whose charms and winning graces took the whole ship by storm.

In years gone by, when the dormant spark of sporting instinct within his breast was being fanned into a tiny flame by an early contact with birds, beasts and fishes, so oft encountered in his lonely ramblings, he had one day met this Diana of the marshes. With a fellow-feeling uppermost in both their minds, what was more natural than that such a casual acquaintance should lead to a closer friendship, which the difference in their sex, at that youthful and romantic age, soon ripened into unavowed affection.

As the years rolled on their secret meetings (so he told us) became more seldom and more wide and wide apart, and when he was sent away to school he almost lost sight of his pretty-faced little sweetheart-poacher. Not that it is wished to insinuate for a moment that she poached anything for herself, her kith or kin, but rather that she, by her superior marsh-craft, assisted him in a manner he could never have learnt for himself, whilst she at the same time gained his boyish respect, his admiration, and became the heroine of his " calf love."

For many years he had not seen her, but she apparently had not the while forgotten him, and when chance once more led him to the neighbourhood of her humble abode no time was lost by him in reseeking the cottage door to pay a call and to renew an old-time acquaintance. That call awakened sweet memories which formed many a happy reverie in his day-dreams—at least, so he confessed. She appeared as fresh, as unaffected, and as charming as of yore, although time had worked many changes to external appearances. The curiosity of our whole crew was naturally aroused and we were equally desirous to become better acquainted with the maid in question. After much persuasion he took us to her marshland home in a body. We went, we saw, and we were conquered. On the excuse of its being a good fishing neighbourhood we instantly and unanimously agreed to stay for several days in the reaches adjoining this stretch of marshland which found her and hers with an occupation and an honest livelihood. Every morning a visit was made to her small dairy, and we vied with each other in amusing rivalry by purchasing all we could, whether we had use for it or not.

She was always the same and her good-natured chaff kept us in excellent spirits, however irritably any of us might have arisen from his respective berth; but when the conversation between her and our friend turned to days gone bye there was a touch of sadness in her tone which, having regard to their removed positions in life, was dangerous, for the mutual happiness of both, to encourage. He avowed that he found her as she had ever been, happy, contented and prosperous. With such a disposition she was indeed fortunate. Let it be hoped she may thus ever be blessed.

### A BROADLAND TRILBY

Milk oh! M-i-e-l-k o-e-o-h No, it is not *the* Trilby this time: we are far away from the Latin quarter of gay Paris, and far away from the rumble and the roar of the Haymarket; we are coiled in our blankets in the snug and cosy cabin of the *Warrior*.

The sun is rising high above the horizon, chasing the dews from the grass and the marsh mist from the sedges, weeds and herbage of Broadland. We, lazy idlers that we are, have not yet had our morning dip, and the Trilby voice that calls us back from dreamland comes from "Molly," the marshman's daughter. She noticed our drawn curtains as she passed along the river wall, on her way to the cowshed; she has stolen a march upon us and brought our measure of milk to the gangway. Had she waited for us, on the morning in question, to come to the shed, as had been our custom, she would have wasted many valuable hours. We are late sleepers; we had travelled far the day previously, when the wind had been adverse to our progress; we had had much recourse both to the quant and to forcible language, and we had one and all determined ere we turned in, long after midnight, to take it out on this the following morning. But "Molly" we had not bargained for. It is true we should hardly have breakfasted without visiting her dairy for a supply of fresh butter, eggs, milk, cream and such dainties as we could purchase, but we had not reckoned on her visiting us. She, on the other hand, had not reckoned on our plans for deep slumber, and, as she explained to us in her own sweet, charming manner, "She thought as how she would spare us the journey through the wet grass, and catch us all at home together like at the same time."

Few minutes tick from the cabin clock ere our entire crew are seated on the hatches near the stern sheets, laughing and chatting with Molly. Our costumes are conspicuous for the variety of cut, cloth and colour which they exhibit; but Molly is not one of those who are easily shocked, nor is she particular to clothes so long as the heart beneath is true and honest. She ridicules the maxim, "Fine feathers make fine birds," and well she seems to know our eccentricities, as she already does our weakness for mushrooms and fruit. This morning she has anticipated our longings, and a fine well-filled basket makes our breakfast-table look appetising enough for royalty.

In our gratitude, added to a selfish feeling to retain her companionship the longer, we press her to stay and partake of *déjeûner à la fourchette*. But no, Molly always remembered her duty, and she, laughing, leaves us to prepare our own meal whilst she goes home.

No sooner has she left than one by one we silently and sorrowfully crawl back to our blankets, each to enjoy his own reverie of the bright, bonny little English maiden whom we so recently held in converse, and whom we individually and collectively so much admire and respect.

There cannot have been much variety in our dreams, but let those mind-pictures which soothed our friend (who had known her years ago) be followed in preference to others.

With half-closed eyes and senses but hovering on the borderland of unconsciousness he wandered back to boyhood with the lithe figure of Molly ever present in the pictures of his fancy—reflections of fact rather than of fiction.

He sees himself, at the early age of ten or a dozen years, crouching in an osier-bed beside the hundred-drain, bending a yielding willow wand of overgrown proportions down in a bow over the well-beaten path of a hare, he is setting the deadly noose with a practised hand, and twining grasses round the suspicious-looking portions of the poaching apparatus, when he receives a sudden fright. He is conscious that he is not alone. With the perspiration starting from his forehead he gazes round with frightened stare, and sees peering from the parted reeds of a grown-up dyke the laughing eyes, the sunburnt face, the cherry lips, and the curly locks of little Molly. "Now spring that snare, Master ——, or I'll tell——" (naming a keeper, whom he held in wholesome dread). "No, you won't get over me this time by wheedling; spring that snare and kick up the stakes." "But, Molly," he expostulates. It is no use, Molly comes from her lair and springs the snare herself. "It's all very well for you, you know," she says; "if you would only say you snared them, but you know you don't, and when the snares are found other people may be blamed, and it's not right." Whether he encircled that lithe waist and dried the teardrops on that tempting cheek, in order to console the woe of Molly on learning that there were other snares in the osier-bed, the whereabouts of which he refused to disclose, and the proposed destruction of which he would not listen to, cannot be recorded, as the picture of wandering contemplation changes suddenly.

He sees himself in the interior of an old ruined watermill, taking shelter from a storm of wind and rain, accompanied by lightning and thunder. Seated on the ground beside him is a retriever, and as he gazes upon its curly coat and hazel eyes its shape gradually changes, and again he sees that Molly is with him. The storm lifts as suddenly as it had begun, and he emerges into the bright sunshine, which makes the raindrops on the reed stems sparkle like diamonds. Hand-in-hand they stand on the river bank and gaze at the retreat-ing storm, whilst a perfect rainbow, tending to send thoughts Scripturewards by its dazzling colours, is brought the more into prominence by the heavy leaden hues of the angry-looking clouds beyond.

He suggests the fish should be well on the feed after such a storm. Molly shakes her pretty curls and inquires what kind of fish he would endeavour to lure from their natural element.

Roach, dace, bream ? " Ah ! they may be all very well to catch," says Molly, " but give me pike, perch and eels: they are better to eat and are more marketable." Yes, Molly, even in her earliest days, seems always to have had an eye to the larder. Lying down at full length on the wet board flooring over the mill sluice, she peers far down into the clear depths below : she does not require to shade her eyes, her hair does that for her ; long she gazes, and then she produces from somewhere hooks and string. Molly always seemed to carry these. With a stick she grubs about in a neighbouring patch of ground which once had been cultivated, but which has for years been allowed to run wild, and is now tenanted by weeds and a stray currant bush or so. Here she finds what she re-quires—worms, and in a few minutes she is once more hang-ing her head over the rotten flooring of the sluice. He joins her, and when his eyes become accustomed to the light he can see numerous little heads peeping from holes in the mud, chinks in the walls, and round posts, indicating that goodly eels must be lurking there—perhaps this is the Blue Beard's chamber of eel-land. Molly had tried the game before ; she knew which were the best holes to try near ; the artful way

in which she allows the scriggling worm to drift with the
sluggish tide, not over the hole, but just near enough to
tempt its occupant, is interesting in the extreme to an onlooker,
more especially to one whose soul is full to overflowing with
a lurking desire for sport of any kind. One after another
does Molly lure forth those slimy lurkers in the mud-holes
until there is a goodly array upon the bank. How she held
them and extracted the hooks was always a mystery. It
looked so easy, so simple, so quick, and yet when attempted
by a novice insurmountable difficulties seem to invariably
arise. But the scene changes.

Now she is quietly pacing beside a main drain which leads
to the mill. Her sharp little eyes do not leave a yard unexplored; soon she halts, beckons him to her side, and points
quietly to a sheltered nook where several dykes intersect the
marshland. He looks, he sees nothing—naught but the water-
lilies and the sedges. Looking more into the shadows, as
directed, and straining his eyes the harder, he becomes aware
of an inanimate log-like form lying near the bank in a cool
bower of water-lilies, where the sun is unable to penetrate,
and where what little stream there is eddies round. He does
not require to be told that it is a pike, but at that early age
he does require to be told how to catch it.

It is Molly who gives the first lesson in snaring. A boot-
lace and a broken oar are the implements used, and yet with
this ungainly gear she has landed the fish he would never
have seen, a $5\frac{1}{2}$ lb. jack, upon the bank in less than five minutes
from her first discovery.

Suchlike and similar scenes flash before him. With Molly
as his companion he finds the best runs and the best swims
anywhere within five miles of her home. She knows to a
minute when the tide will turn, when the fish will be on the
feed, and what is the best bait to use. She is the recognised
authority; she is reverenced accordingly.

He sees himself at flight time, as the mist rises from the
marshes, shrouding in an impenetrable veil all objects on his
own level, but which does not prevent him discerning wild-

fowl that pass overhead within shot; or crouching, for what poor shelter a marsh gateway can give against a howling blast, waiting and waiting with a certain knowledge that he will be successful in obtaining shots, because Molly has stationed him *and she knows* the flight of the fowl.

He sees himself threading treacherous rotten swamps, steering from point to point, and at every point being successful in gaining a shot at snipe, all under Molly's direction.

He sees himself again in her company, gathering plovers and redshanks' eggs, which she can find with ease, but at which he is comparatively blind. She it is who can tell by the flight of the birds not only where the nest is situated, but also the number of eggs it contains, and whether they are fresh or sat upon.

He sees himself gathering mushrooms upon the marshes in quantities, more than enough to satisfy his wants, whilst his guide, philosopher and friend is hard by.

In his early sporting days this Amazon princess of the marshes was a friend worth knowing; there Molly, a modern Trilby, domineered as the Svengali of his existence.

He sees himself later, after years have passed over his head, revisiting the old haunts, as summer comes round, and taking it easy in his own lackadaisical kind of way; and as he welcomes the marshman's daughter he does so as an old friend, and feels that it is but yesterday that he exchanged confidences in the osier-bed, although Fate has ordained that his path in life shall lie in a diverse direction to hers.

Half awake and half asleep, he hears the lap of the wavelets against the freeboard of the wherry, and lulled by the soothing sound he dreams on and sees Molly, now in all the glory of womanhood, beloved as of yore by all who know her, and looked up to with the deepest affection by a younger generation of brothers and sisters, who worship the very ground she walks upon. And well they may, for who but Molly, his sporting little Molly of days gone by, could tend them with such care and see to their creature comforts in the manner that she does? Who could take her place in that happy, bright, but small homestead, under the lea of the marsh wall, and who but she could get through the varied and strenuous labours of the day which she betakes upon herself.

As his senses sink deeper into oblivion he sees her courted and wedded to a man after her own heart, with little counterparts of her own sweet self surrounding her, and as the years roll on he sees her sitting over her own fireside, with grandchildren prattling at her knee, while she is amusing them with the tale of how she first initiated her little gentleman lover into the intricate mysteries of successfully hunting fowl, and taking fish on the lonely stretches of the marshland, and how they plighted their troth in the damp recesses of an osierbed, which, although *he* may have forgotten, *she* never will nor can.

Thus does he dream. Ah well, let him dream on, for—

"If we but dream, and
  waking may give pain,
Oh, do not wake, but let
  us dream again."

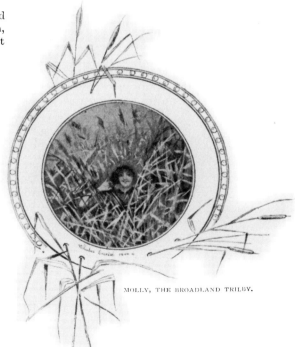

MOLLY, THE BROADLAND TRILBY.

# CHAPTER XVI

### HICKLING DISTRICT

THE reader will doubtless remember mention having been previously made of the River Thurne, better known in the locality as the Hundred Stream.* This river, [at one time, formed direct communication with the sea near Horsey Gap, but its waters now run away at Great Yarmouth. From a sporting point of view a visit to this locality will be found far more to one's taste than to the other rivers named. The rands generally hold snipe, the reed beds waterfowl, and the amount of birds daily to be seen on the wing causes " hope to spring eternal in the sportsman's breast," although perhaps his bag may not be a heavy one.

NAVIGATING THE SHALLOWS.

The rands from Thurnemouth to the entrance to Womack Broad, especially in the month of November, are favourite grounds for snipe, but the fishing is poor.

Womack Broad has little of interest except to the artist or the botanist, and the river from this point to Potter Heigham Bridge is narrow and more like a canal. The water in the river is very shallow, and a boat drawing more

* This name is very common in Broadland. No doubt it arises from the old Baronial divisions of a county, when a Hundred was supposed to contain one hundred families or freemen.

than three feet may at times have to wait for higher water before navigation can be continued.

At Potter Heigham boats may be hired. About half a mile from the bridge is the "Falgate Inn," where there is good accommodation, although it is some distance from the river. Its signboard is sure to attract the visitor's attention. It consists of a small gate hanging over the door, upon which is inscribed the following verse :—

> "This gate hang high,
> But hinder non :
> Refresh and pay,
> And travel on."

Near the bridge is another good hotel, "The Waterman's Arms," quite recently rebuilt in an up-to-date style, and fitted with most requirements. The further we proceed, the narrower does the river become. About a mile beyond Potter Heigham Bridge is a small dyke to the left, which is the entrance to Heigham Sounds, formerly one of the best waters in Broadland for fish and fowl. Pike have been taken there between 30 lbs. and 50 lbs. in weight, and wildfowl have been seen in bunches of thousands at a time. There is a certain variety of water grass of which pochards are particularly fond, which used to grow on Heigham Sounds, and was very attractive to these fowl, but of late they have failed to put in an appearance, except in comparatively small quantities, which is more probably accounted for by the increase of visitors to these waters than by the scarcity of food.

Beyond Heigham Sounds we pass through another narrow dyke, and immediately emerge upon Hickling Broad. This Broad is the most interesting in the Eastern counties to the naturalist, the fisherman and the sportsman. In extent it ranges between 400 and 500 acres, but in depth it does not average three feet, although a deeper channel has been kept open across its centre to Hickling Staithe on the north end of the broad, marked by a range of posts, without

which it would be impossible for a stranger to reach the
staithe unless he had the assistance of a pilot. There are
one or two small islands in the broad upon which wildfowl
love to plume themselves. The fishing is good provided
one can find the right swims, a great improbability without
local assistance. Boats may be obtained at about one shilling
per day. The shooting is preserved, although it is nothing
like so good as it used to be ; still, fowl of all varieties may
be daily seen.

The annual coot shoot at Hickling was an event eagerly
looked forward to by everyone who owned a gun within
ten miles. The slaughter was great and the shooting wild,
reckless and dangerous. To give a brief outline, the shooters
are divided into two parties, those on the land and those on
the water ; those on the land choose a certain bay or part of
the broad which they surround, whilst those on the water
form the boats in well-organised lines and drive the birds
towards the bay. When the birds are encircled the shooters
take no pains to conceal themselves, and the birds, finding
themselves hemmed in on all sides, and realising the trap into
which they have fallen, take to wing and escape as best they
can, by running the gauntlet through the hottest of hot
serenades. The numbers of the slain are counted by
hundreds, but of late years the custom of holding public
shoots has been discontinued, or, when it has been
arranged, it has been kept so secret that only those living
in the immediate neighbourhood have been able to participate in it.

Before the Norfolk and Suffolk Fisheries Act * came into
force the pike at Hickling were netted and the number of fish
then taken seems to us now as incredible, whereas considering
how the fish have been preserved during the past ten years,
one might almost be inclined to think the water was in-
sufficient to hold them.

Had the Broads Protection Society of London won their
case concerning the public rights on Hickling Broad, the

* *See* Appendix.

shooting and fishing on this water, as well as other broads in East Anglia, would have been free to all comers, as they doubtless were some years ago.

Going back only twenty years, we find there were very few villages in Broadland that did not possess several professional sportsmen who derived their living from the fish and fowl they obtained with their nets and guns, but now one rarely meets with one of these old-day sportsmen ; in fact, it is doubtful if there exists a man in Broadland who obtains his living solely by this means.

For small boats Hickling Broad is a beautiful sailing ground, although it is not patronised so much as one would think, A very amusing incident happened during a recent regatta. It was blowing a stiff breeze at the time, and one of the small balanced lug-sail boats upset, throwing its occupants into the water. Before the crew could recover themselves the boat drifted away beyond their reach, and they were left standing on a hard bottom up to their armpits in water. As they were unable to swim they did not feel inclined to follow their boat, but were content to remain on *terra firma* until rescued by another boat.

In the winter time this broad is one of the first to freeze and excellent skating is afforded. Not only is ordinary skating indulged in, but a square sail, about six feet by three feet, is brought into use, with the assistance of which the skater can navigate the broad with remarkable ease. Should a breeze be blowing he will in all probability travel at a greater speed than he desires, but it is excellent sport, and well worthy of a trial.

Ice boats, too, find favour at Hickling, where there is ample scope to indulge in the exciting sport of ice yachting. November is the month for snipe, and the shooting round Hickling Broad is always good. Some of the largest bags of snipe in Norfolk have been obtained here.

To moor to one of the small islands before mentioned and explore the many bays and ramifications of this water, to visit the village, neighbouring local celebrities and places of interest, is well worthy of the time expended.

Now and again these visits will be returned and many a shout of laughter with revelry by night will break the usual stillness around, disturb the waterfowl in their nocturnal repast, and astonish the peaceful water-voles which may have taken up a summer residence upon the islands.

Whenever it was our good fortune to be able to entice any of the local residents on board the *Warrior*, after they had been entertained with the best on board the conversation was certain to lead up to local anecdote, strange experiences and queer reminiscences, in the hope that the visitor or visitors would unfold some of their own. In fact, our crew persistently plotted, by cunningly-devised stratagem, to endeavour to "trot our visitors out," so to speak—and it seldom failed.

One night when the stars were twinkling over the wastes of Hickling Water, and not a breath stirred the slender reed stems, the crew were reclining on the hatchway-deck taking coffee after dinner, at which a local divine, whose keenness for sport was only equalled by his love for old port and Havannah cigars, had been entertained. He was a real good sporting parson, one of those whom everyone would respect and be only too proud to remember. There were many such to be found in the precincts of Broadland in years gone by, but nowadays they seem to be few and far between.

We had laughed immoderately at dinner over his tales, his anecdotes, and his illustrations of " broad Norfolk dialect "; now that we were in the presence of the beauty of the night we were inclined to be indolent and romantic. But the reverend gentleman was one of those who are quite irrepressible. "By Jove," he exclaimed after a silence of some minutes, "why, you are moored at the exact spot where poor Tom found out to his cost that a water-kennel could not be looked upon as a gigantic success."

Naturally he was questioned further on such a remark, and after making himself comfortable against the sail of the wherry he proceeded to spin the following yarn :—

### RATTING AT A WATER-KENNEL, OR A NIGHT WITH A DRUNKARD

It was in the fifties; the winter sun was sinking to rest behind the low stretch of reed-covered swamps which formed our horizon, flooding the heavens with a crimson glow and beautifying Nature in a manner that would have tantalised the landscape painter beyond comprehension. The surface of the vast expanse of water which covered Hickling Broad was as smooth as a sheet of plate glass, and undisturbed except where broken by a rising fish or a dipping bird.

We were reclining in the stern sheets of the —— ; she was a comfortable house-boat, although rough and ready in her construction. Built of good oak timbers, clinched with copper fastenings, she had weathered many a gale at sea, where she had formerly done duty as a lifeboat. But a cabin had been added, with other doubtful improvements, and she formed the winter residence of a sporting Bohemian of eccentric and intemperate habits.

Poor Tom! He has long since joined the great majority. His was a short, sad existence, and all foresaw too plainly how the end would be; but he did good in a way, although he would never admit it, and he was very annoyed when it was brought home to him.

He was one of those "who do good by stealth and blush to find it fame."

In Broadland we see many like Tom ——. They visit us periodically, as butterflies, here to-day, and gone to-morrow; they rarely last three seasons, and considering the pace they go, it is wonderful they can hold out as long as they do.

His fortune might have been anything from £15,000 to £30,000. The actual amount mattered little to him, he lived on the capital, disregarding the interest. Everyone who was poor and needy, or out of luck, was welcome to come; they all met with a kind reception, and they would not go away empty handed.

One of the last fads of his short life was shooting, and he

N

had hired the rights to shoot as far as the eye can reach from here (by daylight, of course), and in order that he might live on the spot he had an extraordinary house-boat especially built for his own accommodation. She was fairly comfortable, but her owner had evinced a sudden craze for dogs—the log-book registered no less than seven of them—which with the skipper, a man, a boy, and myself (a guest), formed the full complement of the crew.

I can remember the particular night to which I refer as though it were but yesterday evening. We were moored on the identical spot that we now are, but then it was wilder and perhaps more picturesque. The house-boat lay half in the reeds and half out, whilst a plankway, similar to the one you have, led onto the island, which, as you see, is small and compact.

Around us in all directions whistled wild birds of every description, but on such an evening flighting was out of the question, nor could we have approached any fowl in our punt had they pitched upon the glassy surface of the water near enough to us.

Silently I sat and smoked, and watched my friend as the liquor mounted to his head and he passed though the varying stages of inebriation. Hours had I lectured him upon the madness of his infatuation for the bottle. It was useless. He was of age, his own master, and argument only made him the more stubborn and wilful in his manner, and deepened the draught of his all-too-frequent potations.

He had risen from his berth about 2 p.m., and breakfasted upon a whisky-and-soda, with part of a sea-biscuit and a salt herring. For half an hour he had been, as he said, very seedy and in need of a pick-me-up, which meant several more whiskies-and-sodas; this brought him to the merry stage. At half-past three he expressed a desire for a little excitement, and as no shooting was to be had on account of the weather, he rowed to Hickling Staithe to endeavour to purchase some rats to which he wanted to break his dogs. In procuring any live rats he failed, but he returned with a boatload of rat-traps, which he insisted in setting all over the island, well baited with various luxuries from our larder. His idea was that if he could get a rat alive we could have great fun with several of the younger dogs. I failed to see the force of the joke, and so expressed myself, but he beseeched me to have patience and I should not be disappointed. Little did I anticipate what was in store for me.

The sun sank to rest without a rat being caught, and our host in the cabin had progressed from the merry to the argumentative, thence to the hostile, and now to the maudlin and drowsy state; he hardly knew the water from the whisky bottle, and swearing to himself he crawled into his berth to sleep himself sufficiently sober to begin another carouse. I smoked a last pipe on deck listening to the water-birds and watching the reflection of the stars upon the broad before I sought my own berth, and was lulled to sleep by the rustling reeds, which a slight breeze from the sea had set in motion.

"Sir, wake up, there is a rat in the trap," said John, the waterman, who was bo'sun's mate and bo'sun combined, and who was acting upon his overnight instructions. "There's a whater—rapping—on the—strap—where, when, which, who, what's matter—"

"There's a rat in the trap, sir;" and he shook the skipper again and again. "Oh, is there?" and half asleep, half awake, he tumbled out of his berth, wildly halloaing his seven dogs from all parts of the ship where they had stowed themselves away as best they could, and scrambling up the companion ladder in a short and airy *robe de chambre*, he toed the plankway for the shore. Not having slept off all the fumes from his overnight carouse, he was much too unsteady to successfully negotiate the single plank, and a mighty splash, accompanied with a big, far-sounding exclamation, broke the silent echoes of the night, whilst the dogs barked and whined, and John, the boy and myself hurried to the rescue.

The cold water acted as a partial steadier to my friend, and as he crawled out from the reeds he inquired the whereabouts of the rat. Its squeals soon located it, and once more the dogs were cheered on to the death. But it was not to be an uneventful one.

Tom, dripping with water, mud and weeds, whilst searching in the grass, aided only by the light of the stars, inadvertently placed his naked toes into an unsprung trap, which instantly closed on them, and immediately "the air went blue for miles." Six of the dogs, worked up to a pitch of no little excitement, had followed their master, some into the water, some on to the land, and two of them were likewise caught in the halo of traps with which the island was bedecked, and these unhappy canines added their doleful music to the general uproar.

John, as is usual with almost all Broadland watermen, instead of going to his master's assistance made tracks to secure the quarry, and I saw his outline fumbling about in the grass after the rat, utterly regardless of the misery around him. In the dark he put his hand on to the vicious rodent before he saw it. Naturally it bit him, and he in his rage made a blind stroke at it with a stretcher, in order to retaliate and to do it to death, which he believed to be the object in view. But, unluckily for him, a retriever was standing by looking on, and John hit the retriever instead of the rat. Poor John! he got *some more* teeth marks in a part of his body which politeness forbids me to name.

All this time my skipper was swearing at everybody and everything, and to make matters worse, after he had extracted himself from the trap, he attempted to release one of his favourite dogs, bidding the boy to do a similar act of kindness to another.

Before I could interfere both the master and the boy were badly bitten by the dogs, who were goaded almost to madness by the pain they suffered, and a fresh outburst of agony rent the air.

Had a native heard it in the distance, and I will vouchsafe to say that anyone could have done so two miles away at least, he would have thought that some of the inmates of Bedlam were loose, or that murder was being committed.

Callous though it may seem, I was unable to repress my mirth, and, indeed, there was some excuse for me as it was one of the most comical spectacles that the human brain can imagine.

The climax was reached when I assisted my wounded skipper on board and into the cabin, and when he realised the fact that the puppy (number seven), either from fear, or urgent necessity, had converted his best slippers into a temporary night convenience.

Much as he loved his dogs, he was bound to admit that to form a kennel on board a small houseboat was a mistake; there was a place for everything, and everything should be in its place, which rule especially applied to the whisky bottle. Muttering anathemas against the so-called joys of living, he reached out an unsteady hand to grasp it, and soon his woes were forgotten in the delirium of an over-heated brain.

Two hours later we carried him to his berth, raving at imaginary snakes and scorpions crawling everywhere, at dogs which mocked him with fiery eyes and lolling tongues and refused to touch the rats which he believed were sucking his very heart's blood from him.

\* \* \* \* \* \* \* \*

I will draw a veil over the scene that followed, it was an awful night, one not likely to be forgotten for the remainder of my life.

" TIM."

## CHAPTER XVII

### HORSEY DISTRICT

A DAB-CHICK
*(Mergus Minor).*

FROM Hickling Broad there is a good excursion to Horsey Mere in the dinghy. A course must be steered over Heigham Sounds and up the narrow and shallow dyke which connects the two stretches of water.

Horsey Mere was at one time celebrated for pike, but is now so overgrown with weeds that the fishing has become almost a dead letter. Shooting was also good, but at the present day it has fallen off wonderfully on account of the number of boats which go backwards and forwards, and little or nothing is to be obtained.

There is a small cut to the north of the mere, which runs to Sea Palling and Lessingham, past Calthorpe Broad, but this district is only of interest to the botanist or to the seeker after moths and butterflies.

Another small dyke leads from Horsey Mere back to the River Thurne, touching the river close to the entrance to Martham Broad; a private water, the fishing on which is not very good, and the same may be said of the shooting.

On Heigham Sounds, and in the neighbourhood of Hickling,

some very good perch may be caught ; in fact, Hickling Broad and Heigham Sounds hold an enormous amount of coarse fish of all descriptions, and good sport is certain if only the right places can be found. The district is also celebrated for rare birds, but as those who shoot them are seldom well versed in ornithology, many valuable specimens are lost and never heard of.

There is a wildness attached to this neighbourhood which is most attractive. On either hand, as far as the eye can see, a vast expanse of water, swamp and marshland stretches away into the distance ; to the north a range of white-capped sand-hills shuts out the German Ocean from the marshland, and if these sand-hills are visited, and the visitor climbs to the summit of one of them, he will wonder why the gales do not break down the thin barrier and flood the whole of the surrounding country. Most of the land is out of cultivation, or is cultivated so badly that one is unable to distinguish whether an attempt has been made to till it or not, but it affords some excellent rough shooting for those whose tastes lie in that direction. Quarters can be obtained in the villages with little or no difficulty. A large acreage should be hired, the rental of which is not great, but the shooter must have plenty of time on his hands, as big bags cannot be obtained without hard work and plenty of it.

The shooting round the wilds of Hickling Broad is fascinating in that it is so different to any other shooting which one is accustomed to. To give some idea of the sport obtained, the following extract has been taken from a diary of the author's.

"Starting early in the morning from an old-world village in the Flegg district, where the only building worthy of note was the church, which, like many other churches thereabouts, was dedicated to the Virgin Saint (it was decorated and fitted up in a manner far beyond the requirements of the district, having also a large tower and well-hung belfry), we cross the churchyard, hunting on our way the rank herbage and nettles, overgrowing many a rustic grave, in search of game.

"The churchyards in Norfolk seem to be the favourite resorts for game of all description, and are rarely drawn blank. Many a dozen rabbits have been shot standing on the graves of ancestors and turning over the bunnies as they dodge in and out of the grassy mounds and as they round the corners of the tombstones, being bolted by ferrets; but on this occasion we were tramping uncertain ground, accompanied by a spaniel and a retriever.

"The visit to the churchyard in question was not unproductive, for a cock pheasant and two rabbits were obtained before leaving its sacred precincts.

"Negotiating a broken-down hedge which divided the churchyard from a thickly-cropped clover ley, 'we spread ourselves out together there'—to use a Norfolk colloquialism —and take all before us *en route* for the marshes.

"The leaves of the grass are wet with the rapidly-thawing rime of last night's frost, which the rays of the rising sun is fast dissolving, and it is too early yet for the birds to have taken refuge in the cover of the roots. Several coveys rise just out of gunshot, but four English birds squat on seeing us approach, and when flushed present an easy target; three of them fall to the four shots whilst a hare is bagged almost immediately afterwards.

"Three stubbles lying between us and the marshes we carefully walk, and whilst so engaged are successful in downing two brace of birds with another rabbit, at the same time we drive all before us in the direction we are going.

"Where the uplands join the marshland, being separated by a grown-up dyke, a long tract of osier bed had been planted, and through this we sent the beaters, doubling it ourselves. For 150 yards we walk without seeing life of any kind, then a hare is observed stealing away far in front. Whilst attention is thus drawn, another hare, which breaks cover behind, is almost lost; had it not been for the dogs puss would certainly have escaped, but she is added to the bag and the beaters proceed.

"At the far end of the osiers flourished a nice clump of trees with good undergrowth; surrounding it as best we can we send in the beaters and dogs. The sport this covert affords is excellent while it lasts, but is over all too soon. On counting up the spoil we find we have added two and a half brace of pheasants, three hares and four rabbits to the bag.

"Having carefully concealed the game in the osier bed, and covered it over with sticks and stones, we start to beat the marshes, a long stretch of which lie before us as far as the eye can see.

"These marshes are what are commonly known in Norfolk as litter marshes. They are favoured by game and water-fowl, and the shooting they afford is very pretty. In extent they average about five or six acres each, more or less. On all sides they are bounded by deep dykes, the bottoms of which seem unfathomable, and they are intersected throughout by smaller drains. In the district where we were shooting the drainage at the time was anything but good, and the marshes were mostly flooded. Some were completely covered by water, others had large pools standing on them here and there, whilst all the dykes were full to the overflowing.

"Walking the first marsh down wind (the best way for snipe), we bag a leash of birds, a hare and two snipe, one of which is a jack. This is a good beginning, and we can hardly expect to keep up such an average.

"When about midway over the marshes we came to a patch which looked bare because there were no rush clumps for some ten or fifteen yards, and that portion of the marsh, comparatively speaking, was as smooth as the putting-green on a golf link. Our friend startled a hare from the rushes, which dodged in and out the clumps in such a manner that he could not get a satisfactory shot at her. As she crossed this open space she flushed a jack snipe, and with a smartness which met with warm approbation he very neatly killed both of them by an almost simultaneously-fired right and left, both the bird and the hare falling together within a yard of each other.

"On going to pick up the game, a picture worthy of the brush of Landseer, unfolded itself before us. The warm colouring of fur and feather was shown up prominently against a background of green swarth, and the still deeper verdure of the rush clumps beyond. The retriever (in whom there must have been a dash of setter blood) stood to point, his reflection mirrored on the calm surface of a pool of water on the marsh, whilst the sun's rays gave light and shade to complete the beauty of the group.

"The next three marshes we visited were almost exactly similar to the first, with the exception that they were devoid of game. The long rushes grew as high as our knees, in some places so thick that we could with difficulty force a way through them. In other places there were large pools of water which we had to circumvent or else wade through, whilst twice, on arriving at the end of a marsh, our steps had to be retraced about a quarter of a mile before we could get round the boundary dykes.

"There is little difference in these marshes, and a description of others will cause repetition. The game found consisted of an occasional hare, a few snipe and here and there a covey of birds, whilst many of them were drawn blank. The sport was as uncertain as it was attractive, for we never knew what target would next be offered.

"Birds which are very rare in most counties in England are not infrequently met with here, and the most curious rights and lefts are recorded by local gunners, which inquiry on the spot will soon elicit. Amongst them may be included stork, bittern, pheasant, partridges, and all specie of wildfowl —avocet, ruffs, reeves, etc. Ground game, too, find their way to these marshes, but the exceptional height of the water on the day in question had driven them back to the uplands.

"We are now a mile or more from the osier beds before referred to, and we find the farmer has been cultivating some of the marshes, let us hope to his advantage. Coming to a bean stubble in close proximity to a barley stubble, upon both of which part of the crop has been left, presumably because it was not worth garnering, we take advantage of the neglect, as it is more than probable it affords cover to birds, although not protection.

" We carefully walk both the stubbles, and add to the bag considerably by so doing, picking up in all three hares and seven partridges. Several more marshes had been ploughed, but here we find nothing except one or two snipe, which spring from the bare land a hundred yards or more away.

" Now we arrive at an oasis upon this desert of marshland —a small clump of trees, covering in all about a quarter of an acre, with a scant undergrowth of elder bushes and nettles. We do not expect to find much here, but at the same time we brush it with great care, although we only add one wood - pigeon and a water - hen to the bag by the effort.

" Next we cross several fine marshes, which give better pasture than any we have yet visited. They are unproductive of game, and for nearly an hour we do not get the opportunity of firing a single shot.

" Leaving the marshes we come to a stretch of osier beds and swamps, overgrown with tall rushes, reeds and water-weeds lying near to the River Thurne. Posting ourselves at opportune stands for commanding the most likely places that game may break cover from, we give our canine companions full liberty to hunt at their pleasure. Whilst thus posted, and intently watching the ends of the osier bed, which immediately adjoins the reed swamps, a large otter comes from the former, and before we are fully able to make sure of its identity it has disappeared beneath the surface of the water. Loud are our lamentations, but had we shot and killed the spaniel the lamentations would have been louder. Vainly do we hunt for almost an hour, trying to drive the otter into a place where we can obtain a shot at him, but in this broadland swamp he defies our efforts, and we are compelled to turn towards fresh hunting grounds without catching another glimpse of him. Not only did this clump harbour the otter, but many birds seemed to have taken up their abode there. We bagged three water-hens and a cock pheasant, but twice that number managed to escape, two of them sorely injured.

" Hailing a boat propelled by a friendly marshman, we punt some way down stream, and are landed upon the river wall adjoining a large dyke running to a drainage mill, at which point we proceed to partake of a well-earned lunch.

" It is a curious country. All around is as flat as the Netherlands ; nothing breaks the line of the horizon except a slight upheaval of the uplands of the Flegg district to the eastward, and in the neighbourhood of Hickling Broad, far away to the westward, a dark clump of woodland stands out boldly against the sky. Elsewhere the marshland fades away into the blue haze of distance.

" Reclining at length upon the wooden boards which cover the sluice, and are warm from the rays of the sun, we discuss our sandwiches and whisky, and enjoy a lazy smoke. After half an hour's rest we proceed again, and beat out several more osier beds, in which only one solitary hare is found ; but on nearing the end of the last osier bed a large flock of pee-wits cross overhead, rather high up ; however, we fire four barrels into their midst and gather three birds. The peewits seem to be the advent of further sport, and although the land looks anything but inviting, from a shooting point of view, we are fortunate in securing some excellent fun for the next three-quarters of an hour.

" Crossing a couple of fine marshes we have several shots at snipe, and in passing over the dam,* to visit the marshes on the other side, fall in with two small coveys of birds, which we hunt round and round the marshes until we have accounted for nearly all their number. Why the birds laid as they did so late in the season was a mystery, unless it was because they had for a long time been left undisturbed.

* A marshland roadway.

" From a secluded little pond or pulk-hole in a marsh, which had been excavated near to the river wall, we bag a duck and mallard, whilst the retriever, in spite of all our shouting, makes off on a small excursion on his own and returns in about twenty minutes from a thick reed bed with a wounded pochard, evidently shot by some flight shooter no considerable time before.

" A Norwegian crow, which was rash enough to croak over our friend's head, meets with an untimely end, but we leave it where it falls, in the middle of a freshly-ploughed field, thinking it may be of some use to the farmer at a future period to frighten other marauders from his seed corn.

" Being now some distance from home, and as the evening is advancing, we think it best to turn our steps in that direction. We therefore make for the river wall, and find ourselves well within sight of that vast sheet of water, Hickling Broad. Many a small lot of fowl can we see circling round the creeks and bays, but although we waste a cartridge in the hope of disturbing some that may happen to be in the immediate neighbourhood, which we hope may come within shot of us, concealed as we are for the moment in a dense mass of reeds and rushes, we are disappointed ; none appear, and after waiting a few minutes we proceed on our way homewards along the top of the wall. In the next 200 yards we twice kill snipe as they are flying over the reeds round the edge of Heigham Sounds, but although we spend upwards of half an hour trying to retrieve them, we are compelled to abandon the hope, and afterwards refuse to shoot several birds which we might have killed on account of the difficulty in obtaining them should we have been successful in our shots.

" The sun is now setting, and the crimson flush which lights up the whole sky foretells of coming wind and stormy weather. There is a nice breeze blowing, and several large flocks of peewits can be seen winging their way from one favourite feeding place to another.

" We are picking our steps across a wet, rough marsh, when suddenly, with a whisk and a whirl, a little knot of birds pass, almost touching the ground, in a manner which in the uncertain light might lead a superstitious person to think of the visitation of some evil spirit or goblin, said to inhabit these parts by those living in the more remote regions, to whom the teaching of the School Board has been but hearsay. It proved to be a bunch of golden plover, but we were so astonished at the suddenness of their coming and going that they escaped without a shot being fired at them.

"Although we keep a constant lookout from this moment until we once more touch the uplands, never a shot do we get.

"The author was now strongly in favour of staying for the flight, but his friend had had enough of it, and enthusiastically argues that the comfort of a roomy saddle-bagged chair drawn close to a warm fireside, in company with a bottle of generous port and Kentish cobs as additional allurement, require some beating. The attractions of each proposition are duly considered, and finally it is decided to toss up and abide by the result. His friend wins, and in triumph leads the way by a short cut through the fields towards the hospitable roof that gave us shelter, and, be it said to his credit, he had in no way under-estimated the tempting lures held out on the bleak borders of marshland to attract us on like a Will-o'-the-Wisp over the fatal bogs, but with this difference: the latter practically exist only in the imagination, whereas the former were taken by us in the enjoyment of sweet reality."

FROZEN OUT.

BURGH ST PETERS.

# CHAPTER XVIII

### THE WAVENEY VALLEY

FOR the purpose of convenience, and in order that no confusion may arise regarding the various districts open to the visitor, a return is once more made to Oulton Broad, and after re-victualling the ship the voyage of discovery is continued up the Waveney or the Beccles River.

For the first two or three miles Oulton Dyke is retraced as far as the sharp turn which forms the outlet of the Beccles River and leads to Burgh Staithe.

The church tower of Burgh St Peter may be kept for a long time in view, rising, as it does, from a narrow spit of up-land on the right-hand bank of the stream. This is one of the most extraordinary towers in England. It looks as if it consisted of square blocks of masonry placed one on top of the other, diminishing in size the higher they go. The interior of the church is quaint and worth visiting, being a typical Broadland place of worship.

The church is quite close to Burgh St Peter's Staithe, where boats may be hired, and good baskets of roach and bream are occasionally taken.

A little further up the reach is Carlton Colville steam drainage mill—a well-known landmark. Three-quarters of a mile beyond this, in the corner of a sharp bend of the river which leads up to the seven-mile carr, is a large reed-bed on the left-hand rand, which is worth beating out, provided one has a dog to do it with. Many are the ducks, mallard, rail and moorhen that it has given shelter to in past days, whilst it is seldom drawn blank in the present.

This neighbourhood is also fair for bream. Rounding the bend before mentioned we come to the seven-mile carr, a very good fishing station for all kinds of coarse fish. It was here that a London angler (about 1890) hooked and landed a seven-pound salmon trout when fishing for perch, and he was perhaps as much surprised as the fish itself. Pike can nearly always be taken in this reach, and it is a pretty place to anchor for a short visit.

Leaving the carr, the river winds away more southerly, towards Barnby Mill. To the left lies Barnby Broad. At one time this broad must have been of considerable size, but lately it has grown up to an alarming extent. Before the Great Eastern Railway made a junction at Barnby, the water harboured fowl of all descriptions, but now their numbers have materially decreased. However, it is not an uncommon thing to see some hundreds on the wing together during the month of November. Snipe and water-birds are numerous at times, but they confine themselves entirely to the hovers in the secluded recesses of the broad. The shooting is, of course, preserved, but there is a long marsh wall bounding the broad to the westward, about a quarter of a mile from the water, and here a few villagers collect at flighting time. Barnby Broad also contains pike, and one hundred pounds in weight has not been an uncommon bag. A large number of otters also find a home in the innermost swamps surrounding the open water. They are very difficult to exterminate, and to hunt them with a pack is impossible. In fact, the only chance one has of routing them from their lairs, and at the same time following them with any success at all, is during the winter when a hard frost has blocked the water and frozen the swamps; then a hunt can be organised with a scratch pack of hounds, which, however, is generally more a matter for amusement than a danger to the quarry.

Between Barnby Water Mill and Oulton Broad lies Carlton Level, a stretch of treeless marshes, where little is to be found except peewits and an occasional mallard. In years gone by, before steam drained the marshes, they were often flooded, and large and numerous flocks of wildfowl, geese and waders afforded excellent sport. For several winters in

FISHROW OR OULTON DYKE.

succession a gaggle of geese frequented these marshes, and defied the efforts and ingenuity of all the local gunners. At that time many rare birds were bagged. One instance is recorded of a stilted plover seen flying low over the marshes, but the gunner, in his excessive eagerness to secure the prize, missed the bird altogether. In recent years the landowners have at great expense put down steam drainage, and wildfowl shooting seems to be practically a "thing of the past." A few years ago the rands beside the river yielded a fair amount of waterhens; even these are now scarce, and nothing can be obtained by the sporting tourist except an exceptional snipe from the rands, a few lapwing as they cross the river, and, very rarely, a duck at flight, or in the early morning.

Leaving Barnby Mill there is a straight run up the North Cove reach, past the Staithe, to Worlingham steam mill. The shooting is all preserved.

Shortly after passing Worlingham steam mill the Aldeby railway bridge blocks the navigation, and one often has to wait a good while before the dilatory attendants trouble themselves to open it. The river here winds about considerably.

In the neighbourhood of Aldeby railway bridge are situated some good snipe marshes, but they are claimed to be private property, and the sporting rights over them are let.

Sayers' Grove, sometimes called Gunner's Hills, is a beautiful sylvan retreat, and one of the most charming spots for a picnic that can be found anywhere in the Waveney Valley.

Arriving at Beccles, the mast must be lowered in order to quant under an ancient Roman bridge of solid stone masonry situated about fifty yards to the east of the modern railway bridge, which is also a fixture.

Beccles is a very quiet, old-fashioned country town, with good railway accommodation to London, or to the fashionable East-coast watering-places. Many think it the best centre from which to start on a Broadland cruise. There is excellent fishing to be obtained both below and above the bridges, and plenty of boats can be hired at reasonable rates. The principal hotel, located in the centre of the town, is "The King's Head." 'The White Lion" is comfortable. There is, besides, the Railway Hotel near the station (the headquarters of the local angling club), the Waveney Hotel adjoining the river, and many other small inns. The stream runs through the town at a considerable pace, and the water is generally as clear as crystal, whilst both perch and roach can at all times be seen darting in and out the weeds waving from the bottom of the stream.

The old curiosity shop near the river may be interesting to some, at all events it is worthy of note. The rates are practically nil, on account of the large revenue obtained from the marshes belonging to the town.

Above bridges the river narrows considerably, the rands by degrees disappear, and the banks become firmer the further we proceed.

A few miles up Dunborough Woods are passed, and Geldeston Lock, which is a charming place to stay at for a few days' quiet enjoyment, is reached.

The river water is so clear that everything on the bottom can be seen, whilst to laze on the bank, smoking, watching the fish swimming in and out of the forest of aquatic vegetation, and hoping that they will be attracted by the dainty lure provided for their special edification, is a pastime which, to the worried business man, should offer a paradise of contentment.

When the coming mists arise and the cattle are heard lowing o'er the lee it is pleasant to drop into the old-fashioned kitchen of the Lock House and yarn with the lock keeper. It is a post which for years has been handed down from father to son, and it carries with it many of the cares of the upper Waveney navigation. The present family are men slow of speech and good listeners, but, draw them out, they will arouse your interest and tell much that is curious and instructive. With pride the head of the family will take you to his inner parlour, which is kept more for appearances than use, where he will exhibit the perch of 5 lbs. 2 ozs. taken by one of his own name from the depths of the sluice pool, the $2\frac{1}{2}$ lb. lampreys and the $14\frac{1}{2}$ lb. trout, all of which have been caught in the same place. He will tell you of gigantic eels, pike and bream, and narrate tale after tale concerning fish and fishing that will at once stamp him as a worthy candidate for the honours of any Piscatorial Society. They must be heard to be believed.

A few yards beyond the lock one cannot fail to notice the puzzle stone, which some intelligent governing body is apparently responsible for. It is a source of much curiosity, and many a bet is wagered upon its meaning. It is a square block of masonry standing on the river bank, having the following inscription upon its face :—

> " This stone is laid upon the foundation of the old mill and over the piece of plank described by Mr Thomas in his award, ten inches below the upper side of which plank is watermark, and three feet below the bottom of this stone."

The wayfarer reads and goes on his journey up stream bewildered at its hidden meaning. But one's attention is soon diverted by the tortuous windings of the river to Ellingham Lock, where a crowbar must be borrowed from the obliging miller (none being provided), and the quant used more freely than watermen appreciate. Soon afterwards the tower of Bungay Church is seen rising from the trees on the horizon.

Bungay Lock, which lies very near to some large maltings, is another difficult part of the river to negotiate, as no crowbar is provided and the lock gates are sadly deficient in more respects than one.

Half a mile further and a landing-staithe is reached where one can moor for the night, progress being barred by the scarcity of water in the river and the abundance of mud and vegetation which chokes up the stream. The ruins of Mettingham Castle are about a mile away to the southward, whilst the ruins of Bungay Castle are located in the centre of the town; the latter are not so well preserved nor kept up as are the former. The keep and gateway at Mettingham are very fine. From Beccles to Bungay the fishing is about on a par with that from Beccles to Oulton, and at all times of the year good baskets may be taken.

At Bungay an extensive common adjoins the town, on which the local Derby annually takes place. The racing is divided into a two days' meeting, and is well patronised by the owners of some good horses.

Although the river runs through Causton, Homersfield and Mendham to Harleston, it can hardly be called navigable, and the sport obtainable upon it is not sufficient to merit attention; besides, so strictly is the ground preserved through

which the river passes, that were one to follow his own
inclinations he would, most assuredly, get into trouble sooner
or later, without gaining sufficient recompense for the risks
incurred.

On the return journey to Beccles we could not resist
lingering another night at Geldeston Lock, where at times
one hears many an anecdote pertaining to the district and
well flavoured with local colouring. On this occasion an
intelligent gamekeeper, evidently a recent comer to the
parish, treated our crew to a discourse dealing with the hire
of shooting rights over parish lands.

"The Parish No-man's land" he designated it, and as
his remarks were by no means devoid of interest, they are
now (without his permission) reproduced as nearly in accordance with his own wording as a roughly-written diary and
a vivid memory will permit.

### A Broadland Poor's Marsh

Few indeed are the parishes of Broadland that have no
poor's marsh. In these days of local government the parish
councillors are eloquent and declaim upon the gross iniquities
of their predecessors, who have (so they affirm), for genera-
tions, allowed the parson and the squire to pitch away the
rights of the poor working man, and allowed the poor's lands
to run to rack and ruin, if indeed they can be located at all.
With the poor's marshes in the various parishes it is just
the same. The arrogant bootmaker, suddenly lifted from the
obscurity of the cobbler's bench to the shining light of the
chairmanship of the P. C., thumps his darkened fist upon the
table in order the more to emphasise his remarks, and asks, in
stentorian tones of his colleagues of that most self-esteemed
body—"If they consider it right?—If the laws of justice
have not been violated?—If their birthright has not been
frittered away and stolen from them by the wicked man of
the parish (viz., the squire), who has dared to store up
money. That *man*" (he proclaims) "has for years hired the

poor's marsh, and what for? Why, to allow the drains to grow up and the marsh to be constantly under water, so that he may shoot a few snipe for his amusement at odd times. But now that the parish has its affairs in its own hands the squire will be no longer able to hire the poor's marsh for whatever sum he likes to pay. No! He'll have to pay a thumping big rent or the parish won't let him have it at all, and the old women will no longer have to go to bed to keep warm, as they will have their Christmas dole of coals from the greatly increased rents produced."

Such an oration is greeted with a storm of cheers, and the enlightened and learned fellow-members of that almighty body solemnly, and with one accord, answer, in deep, guttural tones, "Down with slavery, tyranny and despots." And they fall asleep whilst the despised vicar of the parish mildly remonstrates and attempts to rebut slanderous insinuations by a prolonged and detailed reference to the parish records which hardly one of the council understands—or believes if he does.

But to tell you about the poor's marsh of the parish I belong to. It is an overgrown waste of swamp, reeds and water. Its crop is used for litter and is sold by auction, realising but a few shillings. The sporting rights (snipe) are similarly dealt with, but then as every member of the community who owns a gun, or who can borrow one from a neighbour, claims the privilege of an equal right with the lessee, which it is needless to say he (the lessee) strongly resents, rows are frequent, and the shooting is not always as good as one not-in-the-know would perhaps be led to anticipate.

Our poor's marsh (I will call it " ours " by way of designation) is located on an island surrounded by a dyke named the hundred drain. It is semi-circular in shape, and there is another piece of marshland jutting into it which a landowner in our village is presumptuous enough to claim as his own; but that matters little, as whoever has, or who ever thinks he has, the right to go over our poor's marsh always beats this marsh at the same time, and if the purchaser of the litter on our poor's marsh finds a better bottom of litter on this marsh he generally appropriates it to his own use. Between this marsh and our poor's marsh runs a big dyke, but it is quite grown up with tall reeds, the stubbs of which give a good foothold and facilitate invasions whether with scythe or gun.

In the most secluded nooks of this over-grown waterway a small colony of reed pheasants or bearded tits took up their abode, and I watched them on many an occasion and for many an hour at a time until an unfortunate episode, alike to myself and to the birds, gave a clue to their value to one nicknamed "Snookey," a ne'er-do-weel, a loafer at the village pub, and an ubiquitous prowler with a long single-barrelled, muzzle-loading gun of ancient date and pattern.

How it came about, happened as follows :—

It was a lovely day in February, the sun was hot and the birds were flitting through the yellow reed stems, lively and musical, whistling their sweet silvery notes, which can only be likened to the tinkling of fairy bells. As the colony moved so did I, and with my glasses to my eyes I wandered on un-heedingly. Suddenly, to my consternation, I walked into a mud-hole, and as I floundered about waist deep in the slime I gave vent to a prolonged and heartfelt exclamation commenc-ing with D, which can be expressed in three letters, and is by no means unfamiliar to English conversation. Snookey was at the time doing a prowl round the other marsh, which, according to him, " if it wasn't part of our poor's marsh, ought to have been." He heard the involuntary remark, which, in his limited vocabulary, he evidently mistook for a term of en-dearment or of salutation. Splashing through the belt of reeds which divided us he was quickly with me and soon helped to extract me from the unpleasant predicament in which I was placed.

One thing led to another, and in a weak moment I blurted out the reason of my mishap. " Well," says Snookey, " I hev often heered them things a-kicking up a hulla-ba-loo in the

reeds, but I niver heered as how they was nawthing out o'
the common. I'll hev a better look at 'em next time I cum
across 'em." And so he did. Within three weeks he had shot
the last one, and sold them all to a London naturalist at
7s. 6d. a pair. It was a small gold mine for Snookey; he did
no more work until the summer took him yachting, where
unlimited beer and baccy, with good pay and very little
to do, were inducements which he could never resist. I
always curse that mud-hole and my too long tongue, which
let out the secret and caused a colony of these most interesting and rare little ornaments of Broadland to be
decimated.

But if Snookey preferred personal pecuniary advantages
to any general future ornithological benefits to Broadland, he
was always a willing companion on either mere or marsh,
especially when a full stone jar was on board and there
was the chance of a stray shilling at the end of the day.
Snookey was likewise an authority on the weather as well
as on the habits of fish and fowl. He was great at plover
egging, and our poor's marsh was no bad hunting-ground in
this respect. True, it could not compete with the Fens proper,
Thetford Heath or the Thurne Level of the twenties and the
thirties, when a linen basket could easily be filled with eggs,
but a dozen or so at a time was a fair average for our poor's
marsh, provided one only hit the time right and did not
follow in the footsteps of someone else who had risen earlier
and watched for the opportunity.

Not only plover, but redshanks, snipe, rails, moorhens,
wild ducks, coots, and a variety of smaller birds, all frequent our marsh during the breeding season, and their
eggs can soon be found by anyone having the necessary
knowledge.

As the season advances and August draws near the excitement of an all-night sitting on the confines of the marsh
is eagerly looked forward to by our local wildfowlers, but
of late years the number of the shooters has exceeded the
number of the ducks. The year's crop of flappers from our

marsh are all shot within the first week, including the home-bred red-shank, snipe, coot and moorhens.

Our marsh has little to encourage a visitor who is bent on killing something before November, when the migratory snipe and duck arrive. Then it is an elysium if it is only caught at the right moment, and many a hundred ounces of shot have I distributed over its surface.

A peculiar feature of our marsh is a moving bog. This is situated near the entrance gate, and Nature seems to have placed it there out of sheer cussedness, as a trap for the unwary, whether man or beast. Often have I been caught, more often have I seen my friends caught, or oftener, perhaps, have I assisted in extracting some unfortunate bullock that has been bemired in its slimy embrace. Through the centre of this bog runs a narrow pathway of firm ground, which enables the artful joker to lure his less cautious friends into the very rottenest places before they are even aware of the existence of the mud trap.

Besides this our poor's marsh is rich in flora, and the botanist comes miles to be able to splash about in the surrounding fleets and shallows. Nor are we free from the entomologist, who chases the swallow-tail butterfly with a rashness which he afterwards regrets, as I did in the case of the *Calamophilus biarmicus*.

If the beaming faces of the scientific gentlemen (whom I often wished further) are any guide to the satisfaction they derive from their frequent visits to our poor's marsh, that little plot of land, despised by the many, should be preserved from the ruthless hand of the drain digger, who sweeps away its glories once and for ever. So water-bound is our marsh that little good can come from draining, which destroys its shooting value, but every year sees a new lessee attracted by the fame of the locality, and every spring sees him looking out for some other marsh not quite so frequented by the public.

Yes! our poor's marsh is a place to be proud of. It keeps the parish alive to its importance, although it does not add

materially to the pieces in the parish chest. Many a pitched
battle has been fought in the past over a club shot on the
marsh itself, and many a pitched battle will be fought in the
future in the parish room when discussing how to handle our
property.

IN THE REED SWAMPS.

# CHAPTER XIX

## THE YARE VALLEY

THE " WAVENEY QUEEN."

THE Yare or Norwich River empties itself at Great Yarmouth and may be reached with equal, if not greater, convenience from Oulton Broad than elsewhere. Taking the latter for choice, the reaches to the railway bridge over the river at Herringfleet Hills, near Haddiscoe, and St Olaves railway stations have been already described in Chapter VI.

With a fair wind an easy run of three miles is made as far as Haddiscoe Cut, which, should there be a head wind, it is advisable to tow; a good path will be found all the way along the north bank. A horse can be obtained at either end of the cut, and the distance is worth the small expenditure.

219

Whilst quietly drifting up the cut large flocks of plover are generally seen shifting from one part of the marshes to another, disturbed, no doubt, by marshmen or prowling gunners; and it may not be altogether out of place to say a few words concerning these birds which in Broadland are always with us.

Possibly no other birds frequenting the district afford so much sport or profit to the marshman as plover. The lapwing, peewit, green plover, hornpie, or wipe, as it is called, is most common. There are also grey and golden plover, whilst in certain localities the Norfolk plover, or thick-knee, is by no means rare. Golden plover visit Broadland during the autumn and winter months in large quantities, and are shot by all lovers of the gun, either for market or private consumption. Like snipe they are "here to-day and gone to-morrow," so they must be followed immediately they are known to have arrived in the neighbourhood, or they may be off before a shot can be obtained at them.

A stalking-horse may be used on these birds with great success, no matter whether it be the artificial or the real animal.

At flight time they are often shot, but as it is their custom to either fly very high in the air or very near to the ground, not nearly so many are bagged as otherwise might be the case.

When flying overhead at a considerable height, golden plover might often be taken for starlings were it not for the peculiar habit they have of forming themselves into the shape of a V. It is a habit shooters soon notice, and one which wild geese also adopt. Should one be out with a gun and a flock of golden plover passes overhead, do not be discouraged by reason of the height the birds happen to be in the air, but wait until they are nearly overhead, then discharge one barrel in the air so the shot scatters in the thick of them, and they will often all drop to within a yard of the surface of the ground in a most extraordinary manner, as though they had all been hit, but they continue their flight. If the shooter handles his gun smartly he will be enabled to slip in another cartridge and put in a right and left before the birds have gone out of range.

An amusing instance of this once happened. A marsh-man's boy went out to the evening flight with an old Martini-Henry rifle converted into a muzzle-loading shot - gun, and during the evening an enormous flock of plover flew over him. The birds were quite 100 yards high, yet he fired, and to his unbounded delight they all apparently fell to the ground. In great excitement he danced upon the marsh, shouting, " I've killed the lot ! I've killed the lot !" But when they continued their flight his face was a picture.

During the earliest part of a severe frost hundreds of these birds may be seen on the salt-marshes round the coast, before they finally betake themselves to more southern climes.

Grey plover migrate to Broadland and the East Coast regularly every autumn, about the first week in October. When first over they are very tame, and one can approach within shooting distance without much difficulty ; but as the season advances they mass themselves into flocks and become exceedingly wild and shy. A shore shooter may walk until he drops without getting a fair chance at them, or even picking up a few stragglers, unless he is assisted by a frost.

But the bird which in Broadland affords so much sport is the common plover or lapwing. In years gone by, when East Anglia could not produce a sufficient quantity of wheat to feed the population, when the uplands were almost all heath and warren and the marshland was a swampy fen, these birds must have lived here in countless thousands, but now, as year by year less heath and warren are to be found and the marsh-lands are drained more and more, so do these birds decrease in number.

In the early spring the common plover nest in all parts of Broadland, on the marshes, in the fen, on open fields on the uplands, and especially upon the warrens and the large tracts of heath. They scrab a small hole in the ground and lay four eggs, in colour and markings exactly resembling the surroundings of the nest. These eggs are collected by fenmen and others, and find a ready sale in the market. Seventy years ago a single egger would take from 100 to 200 dozens of eggs during a season from the marshes round Potter Heigham, Acle, St Bennet's Abbey, or any such neighbourhood as Thetford Heath ; and the local gamekeepers and dealers in Norwich and Yarmouth were in the habit of sending between 500 and 1000 eggs per week to the London markets. But nowadays these records have dwindled considerably, and although there is a good supply of eggs during the spring, the eggers find nothing like the quantity demanded.

Searching for plovers' eggs is one of the most interesting pursuits that can be imagined, and the difficulty of finding the eggs with anything like success can hardly be believed, yet to an old hand it is as simple as picking up hens' eggs. So clever are some of the old fenmen and plover-eggers that when rowing up a marsh dyke they will, to your astonishment, inform you there is a plover's nest situated in a certain spot on the marsh, the number of eggs there are in it, and how many days these eggs have been laid. Should you throw doubt upon their assertions they will stop the boat, guide you straight to the nest, and on breaking one of the eggs confirm what they had previously told you. Apparently the egger draws his conclusions from the manner in which the birds conduct themselves, whilst the experience gained from many years' practice completes the rest.

A novice at the art may walk about a field in which there are many nests and yet not be able to find one for an hour or more, unless, perchance, he puts his foot on the eggs and so discovers it ; but a man accustomed to the work sees the nest immediately, and can tell in what condition the eggs are, and so be able to judge whether to gather them or allow them to remain to hatch.

At the close of the breeding season both old and young birds betake themselves to the low meadows, especially those which are fairly moist. Here they remain until the autumn. During October and November they are joined by migratory birds from other countries. The first frost drives them to the coast, when they depart almost immediately for the south. During August and September they afford good sport to flight shooters, who are always out after them with more or less success.

When October comes they collect in larger flocks and great numbers are sometimes taken by netting. The most favourite place for netting is a small island in the midst of a flooded marsh. The meshes of the nets are coloured the same as their probable surroundings, and the pattern used is the ordinary clap-net—known to all bird-catchers—with the exception that one net only is used instead of two. Round the edge of the net stuffed peewits are set, and near the end nearest the fowler one or more live peewits are anchored down upon a small board which, working on a pivot sunk into the ground, can be raised at the will of the string-puller some little height into the air. The decoy-birds are all placed head to wind and the net is pegged down accordingly, so that when it is pulled over it will catch the birds as they are settling amongst the decoys. The poles of the net are about ten feet long, and the art of making a big haul is to allow the straggling part of the flock of birds to pass and not to pull the net over until the thickest part of the flock can be reached.

Green plover are killed from the artificial stalking-horse or by using a live horse or pony which will stand fire, but when they have been shot at once or twice in this manner the game is played out.

Another plan is to drive a horse and cart into the field where they are, as sometimes one can get within range by driving or riding round them, gradually decreasing the distance until sufficiently near to shoot.

All plover are easily called. Not only do they reply to their particular whistle, but they also are attracted by it in such a manner that an easy shot is often offered and the birds secured.

They undoubtedly do good to the land, and certainly should be classed with the farmers' friends.

Of late years many people have stated their belief that these birds will soon be exterminated, but if they saw the quantity that at present frequent East Anglia, and if they knew how capable these birds are of looking after "number one," their fears would be allayed. Drainage has done more to drive plover away than the egger or the shooter, and with the innovation of the steam-driven turbine it seems as if the day was not distant when they may be added to the list of the rare birds of Broadland.

At the north end of the cut lies the village of Reedham. At even-tide, when the sun is setting in the marshes and the dew is rising, the village presents a picture which can only be described as truly magnificent. There is a touch of that peculiar local quaintness which one sees in Norfolk and nowhere else in the United Kingdom.

Many times have artists depicted various scenes from Broadland in the London galleries, and one wonders why Reedham has not been chosen more frequently than has been the case. Passing through at midday, one is not struck so much by its beauty, for it is only at sunrise, or at sunset, that it can be fully observed.

The river from Reedham to the Dicky Works, on the western extremity of Breydon Water, so far as sport is concerned, is similar to the first part of the North River, and that part of the Waveney from St Olaves' Suspension Bridge to "The Dicky Works." Thus, to comment on the run from Reedham to Yarmouth would only be repeating what has been written in a previous chapter. Passing silently by the miscellaneous collection of houses, maltings and buildings erected along the river bank, with the flowing tide under us, we take a more southern course and traverse the centre of the Yare Valley, with its great expanse of marshes reaching far away on either hand.

About a quarter of a mile from the village a ferry is situated, where there is a large flat-bottomed square ferry-boat used for the conveyance of cattle, horses and carts over the river. It is worked by means of a chain, similar to the one at Horning Ferry, but Reedham Ferry has not such picturesque surroundings as Horning.

A hundred yards beyond the ferry, on the south bank of the river, is a public-house, where in days gone by large quantities of contraband goods were landed for distribution over the surrounding country. Half an hour spent in the tap-room with a few gratuitous quarts of ale will bring forth curious anecdotes, interesting to those whose tastes lie in that direction.

Reedham always has been celebrated for its bream fishing, not only on account of the quantity to be caught, but also for their quality and size. Early morning is the best time to fish, also when the heat in the summer is so intense that the shallower waters of the Broads are unproductive. Ledger tackle is generally used on account of the current, which is very strong, except, of course, at the turn of the tide.

About a mile above the village of Reedham, on the left-hand bank, the visitor will notice a curiously-shaped cross, somewhat after the style of those met with in Ireland, and he will no doubt puzzle his brains to ascertain why such a monument should have been erected in such a bleak and uninviting spot. This landmark is called Hardly Cross, and it defines the boundary of the jurisdiction of the Norwich Corporation and the Great Yarmouth Port and Haven Commissioners.

At this point the River Chet, a small winding stream communicating with the country town of Loddon, joins the Yare. Although wherries navigate this so-called river, they have difficulty in finding a place where they can turn round before arriving at Loddon should they desire to do so, and if two of them meet, passing would be most awkward, if not impossible. The fishing is not worth mentioning, and the same may be said of the shooting, because the river runs through private grounds and is strictly preserved. The land belongs to the Beauchamp family, on whose estate

P

a thousand head of pheasants a day is not an unusual bag
for several days in succession when the coverts are shot.
From Hardly Cross there is little of interest in the river
until Cantley is reached, which is a celebrated station for
anglers and yachtsmen.

At Cantley Red House excellent accommodation may be
obtained and boats and all other requisites to sport hired with
very little trouble. One of the most celebrated swims in the
neighbourhood is known as "Crow's Hole," which can be
pointed out to the angler from the end of the quay. The
river here is broad and deep, and there are some magnificent
reaches for sailing.

Cantley may almost be looked upon as the headquarters
of the Yare Sailing Club, which has for some time been the
largest sailing club in the world, and which holds most of its
race meetings here.

Leaving Cantley the river takes a sweep in a south-
westerly direction, then winds away north-west to the entrance
of Buckenham and Hassingham Broads. Both of these broads
are private and they afford a sanctuary and retreat for wildfowl; being only shot occasionally, the fowl never seem to
desert them, and they thus help to keep the district well
supplied. Buckenham Broad is so shallow that the fishing on
it is not reliable; there are, however, a few good pike, and
bream.

Proceeding up the river, the three entrances to Rockland
Broad are passed. The fishing on this broad is public
and at times good sport may be obtained, although the water is
somewhat over fished. From Buckenham Broad to Brundall
the river lies almost due northwest, and is bounded on the
north by rough-bottomed swamps very favourable to game
and wildfowl. The swamps are dotted here and there with
pulk-holes both large and small, in which lurk solitary pike
and quantities of waterfowl of all descriptions. Enormous
bags of snipe have been made on these marshes in years past,
and a one-time owner of the property, a gentleman who
distinguished himself, *inter alia*, by breaking the Bank at

Monte Carlo, asserts he once shot no less than 1200 with his own gun during a season. This shooting is preserved, and there is but little chance for a stranger to hire it.

Some years ago the shooting on the river was worthy of consideration, especially in the early part of August, but now the birds seem to be aware of the fact that any part of the river is dangerous ground, and they rarely give a chance to the shooter. Large bags of moorhen, with a few snipe and duck thrown in, might then have been obtained by hunting the rands with a good dog, but now "the game is not worth the candle."

The fishing, on the other hand, is very good, and in the autumn large catches of pike are made by spinning in the river, taking advantage of favourable winds and tides. By way of example, two gentlemen landed no less than sixty-three fish in one day, most of which, however, they returned to the water on account of their diminutive size.

At Buckenham boats may be obtained at the inn for a shilling a day and upwards; this is within easy rowing distance of Rockland Broad, whilst there are several good swims in the immediate neighbourhood. The inn is about half a mile from Buckenham railway station on the line from Lowestoft and from Yarmouth to Norwich, and the accommodation is all an angler can desire. The best place for roach will be found near the entrance to a running sluice or mill stream, but it is advisable to take a boatman who can and who will point out the swims, and by his local knowledge and anecdote he will amply compensate the small additional outlay which his presence entails.

Brundall is another celebrated angler's resort, and any amount of boats, of all sizes and description, may be hired here, but the best fishing-boats are to be obtained at Coldham Hall. At Brundall the Yare Hotel, adjoining the station, offers fair accommodation. Several boat-builders have their headquarters at Brundall, as it is one of the favourite yachting centres, and many racing craft are built here.

Coldham Hall is situated on the other side of the river, half a mile from the station; it is a large, roomy and favourite riverside inn, with good accommodation and picturesque surroundings. The boats are let at one shilling to two shillings and sixpence per day, and all kinds of bait can be obtained. It lies contiguous to Surlingham Broad, another public water noted for its roach and pike, but it is advisable to obtain permission to fish it, although apparently the right is claimed.

The river winds considerably at this point, and from Coldham Hall to the west entrance of Surlingham Broad it forms a horse-shoe, entirely surrounding a stretch of marshes about fifty acres in extent, which during the winter months are flooded and afford safe skating. Once or twice during a good season race meetings are organised, and a large concourse of people collect to watch the contests. The skating is managed by a local man, who provides cloak-rooms and other accommodation, whilst the charge is sixpence and a shilling per head, which includes ferrying and re-ferrying from and to Brundall Station.

Continuing to the ancient city of Norwich the river is most picturesque. Woods run from the uplands to the very edge of the water, beautiful little nooks and grown-up dykes are met with almost every hundred yards, and houses nestling amongst the trees make one envious of their occupants. The shooting on the river is not worthy of consideration, but to those fortunate enough to be invited to the parties organised to shoot the land on either side the sport is exceptionally good, which can easily be imagined by the visitor who notices the large number of pheasants constantly crossing and re-crossing the stream.

From Brundall to Bramerton Woods End the water offers good fishing of all kinds, but before reaching this point Surlingham Ferry, situated on a neck of firm land, and surrounded by a thick clump of tall willow and other trees, is passed on the left. The house affords all necessary creature comforts, and invites one to linger in its vicinity. There are a few boats which are good, but the visitor must not expect to get shooting unless he hires it. Surlingham Ferry is some distance from any railway station, but it can be reached by road or water. Thence to Bramerton Woods End are many good bream swims.

Bramerton Woods End is "the Richmond" of Norwich, and on Sundays is always crowded with citizens who have been brought out by river steamers at the rate of sixpence per head. There are extensive tea-gardens attached to the hotel, which is a modern building with large rooms. It is situate on the side of some hills, high for Norfolk, which are well wooded, and the neighbourhood around is very pretty. Sailing is unsatisfactory on account of the trees, but there is plenty of life on the river, which, if it disturbs the angler, may lend an interest to those who find sport dull. About a mile beyond Bramerton the Postwick Hills rise from the north banks; this is a favourite place for picnicking, and is held in high esteem by the residents of Norwich.

A straight reach due west runs to Crown Point, and on the way are several objects of interest. Thorpe Asylum on the right, and the Devil's House on the left bank, which latter peculiar and interesting structure would have long since fallen down had it not from time to time been bolstered up. A little beyond the Devil's House, rising from a well-wooded hill, is the tower of Whittlingham Church, with the statues of a few dilapidated apostles guarding its ivy-clad ruins.

At the bend of the river, under the hills of Crown Point, the scenery is more attractive, though no sport can be obtained. One cannot pass without being attracted by the gamekeeper's cottage, nestling as it does in the deep recesses of the well-wooded hills, surrounded by flowers, overrun with creepers, and forming a sylvan retreat the prettiest imaginable.

A small arm of the river runs past this cottage, which is preserved, and it is said that good pike are occasionally taken from its waters.

At Thorpe Village the river has been diverted from its bed and a cut made about a quarter of a mile in length, so that the railway (which passes twice over the old river) may not interfere with the traffic. On the edge of the water-way round the old bend of the river lies the village, said to be the prettiest village in England. There may be much truth in this statement, although there are many other villages quite as pretty, if not prettier. Near the railway bridge boat-yards are located, at each of which boats may be hired; situated as they are so near to Norwich, the hiring price is a little more than elsewhere. There are several inns, mostly adjoining the river, their gardens being pictur-esquely laid out, and accordingly attracting many visitors. At "Thorpe Gardens" boats are to let, as also at Hart's, Field's, and Dale's boat-yards. Another pretty little house in Thorpe Village is the "King's Head," but it is not so much frequented as the "Gardens."

Passing the second railway bridge, Trowse Eye, or, as it is sometimes called, Trowse Hythe, is reached, where in the early part of the summer large quantities of bream collect and good bags are often made.

The river here divides itself into two parts, the northern-most branch being the Wensum, and running through the city, the other being the Yare, which runs as far as Lakenhem then winds away due west, whilst another branch, taking a southerly course, is named the Tese or Tas.

Following the Wensum, the largest of the three streams we have named, we go by the gigantic mustard and starch works of Messrs. J. J. Colman & Co., Ltd., and passing under several bridges, arrive in sleepy, quiet Norwich.

At the Foundry Bridge, near Thorpe Central Railway Station, are good moorings, which will be found to be in the heart of the quaint old city.

The upper reaches of the river can be explored with a dinghy by making little trips for the purpose, sometimes returning to Norwich by rail, and sometimes sleeping out at riverside inns.

By no means the least attractive is that small portion of the river which winds in and out between old buildings, under bridges and past ruined watch-towers, which cannot fail to be objects of great interest to an observant tourist.

The upper parts of this river can only be explored by rowing boats, which can, however, be hired at various places at cheap rates.

The Wensum, arising somewhere near Whissonsett, flows through Fakenham, Raynham, Ryburg, North Elmham, Bylaugh, Lyng, Attlebridge, Taverham, Drayton, Costessey, and on to the New Mills at Norwich.

The fishing between Norwich and Hellesdon produces good roach and dace, and the fish are better than those taken from the river below Norwich, on account of the greater purity of the stream.

At Hellesdon a large flour mill intercepts the course of the river, and permission must be obtained from the owner to pull one's boat overland round the mills in order to navigate the river above.

Under the Ringland Hills excellent sport may be found with roach, bream and pike, but permission to fish must be sought from the local proprietress.

At Attlebridge trout are taken, not in large quantities, but the fishing, considering the stream, shows a fair amount of sport; leave has to be obtained, and the sport is well worthy of consideration.

The Yare from Lakenham to Intwood and Earlham affords a good quantity of roach and pike, but the latter do not run to any great size.

The Tese, or Tas, which winds through Caistor and Dunston to Tasburgh, is little more than a large dyke, but trout are sometimes caught, although the sport they show is poor on account of the sluggishness of the stream.

Shooting is quite out of the question on these upper reaches as the river-bed belongs to the adjoining landowners on either side.

Not wishing to experience possible annoyance from an

over-curious and idle crowd on the public quay by mooring near Foundry Bridge, the wherry was laid-to for the night under the trees on the south bank of the stream at Trowse Eye, in company with other craft. Amongst these were the well-known fleet of Colonel Leathes, always recognisable from afar by their prettily-trimmed red-and-white striped awnings.

After dinner the popular colonel honoured us with a visit and through the rings of Havannah smoke he unfolded to an attentive and admiring audience the triumphs of fifty years ago, when Captain King's meadow (opposite) was yearly thronged with the aristocracy of the county to cheer on the local oarsmen to victory against all comers; when the feats of George Knights of Wymondham and others were renowned throughout England, and how fifty-mile rowing matches were the rule rather than the exception.

A request for a yarn to enter in the ship's log-book was immediately responded to as follows :—

COLONEL H. M. LEATHES ON CRUISE.

"You must know that years ago the yachting men of the county formed a private cruising club, which was probably the origin of the yacht clubs of the present day. What charming days those were with the cruising club! What yarns at night! What music! How delicious the early morning plunge overboard all together at a given signal into the clear limpid stream! the chaff, the fun! But I fear we sometimes carried our jokes too far, and that our amusement was somewhat one-sided. The story I will tell is an instance of this, and comes back vividly to my memory, although it happened many years ago. I will call it—

### TOPER'S TRIAL.

"In 1862 we got up a North River cruise with several yachts belonging to the cruising club, under Commodore R——. The start was made from Cantley, if I remember rightly, and the following day saw the little fleet all safely moored for the night at Acle Bridge. On board one of the yachts was an old waterman, engaged to work the craft, who had turned up very 'rusty,' he grumbled at this and at that, until he ended by saying 'he should go home again.' Of course this meant throwing part of the fleet more or less into a dilemma and obliging the owner of this particular yacht to go back to Yarmouth to engage a fresh hand. As our time was limited it was suggested that the old man should be patted on the back and cajoled into changing his mind, and to remain with us until we had reached a part of the river where it would be no easy matter for him to desert the ship or find his way back to the bosom of his family.

"The old waterman was always known on the stream by the name of 'The Toper.' It had apparently originated from his inordinate love of something stronger than water. Toper had, on the occasion of his mutiny, taken as much as was good for him, and had consequently become quarrelsome, but at last he was calmed down, and, little expecting what was in store for him, he sailed on with us from day to day, until we finally reached Coltishall Lock, quite away, in those days, from the reach of railways, and many miles from his home at Yarmouth.

"Some wicked unknown person, on the morning of our reaching Coltishall, had placed three tiers of gunpowder in Toper's filled pipe, which he afterwards replaced in his forecastle, and knowing also the peculiarity of his victim in being addicted to the habit of wearing no stockings, he had stuffed his shoes with mustard and cayenne. Not long after-

wards I observed old Toper very fidgety, then I saw him take
off his shoes, examine his feet, and with his pocket-knife
carefully scrape them, muttering to himself, and finally he
put both naked feet in the river. Finding ere long the
beneficial effect of this process, he brought out his pipe,
searched for a lucifer, and rubbing it on the leg of his
trousers, lit his pipe. In another instant there was a big puff
of smoke, and Toper was looking green dragons, and talking
in language more forcible than elegant, which caused me to
retire below.

THE LAST OF THE CRUISING FLEETS UNDER COMMODORE H. M. LEATHES.

"That afternoon all Coltishall was warned that if they
wanted to see any fun they should come down to the fleet at
8 p.m. and hear the proceedings of a district court-martial.

"After dinner the cloth was removed from the pleasure
wherry's cabin (we had fitted up a wherry wherein we could
all meet each evening to dine together), and the commodore
took the chair. Counsel for the prosecution was an old
dragoon officer; counsel for the defence, a member of the Cape
Parliament; the other members of the court were constituted
not according to Cocker, and the tribunal was very mixed.
A crowd had gathered on the bank and the time for fun
arrived when Toper, who was wondering at the concourse of

people, found himself suddenly seized and marched down the gangway into the presence of the recently-elected judge. The old man highly disapproved of the proceedings, and vainly endeavoured to gain the deck ; but at last, finding this an utter impossibility, he stood calmly awaiting the next *dénouement*.

" The hatches were raised round the wherry's hold, so that people on the bank could see perfectly all that went on ; and when quiet had at last been obtained, the proceedings began.

" ' Oyez ! Oyez ! You of the name of Toper stand forth,' said the judge, in grave tones. ' I deeply regret to see a man of your years ' (he was seventy years old that very day) ' brought before me upon so serious a charge. You have committed one of the gravest offences it has ever been my lot to try. I shall content myself with but few remarks upon the subject at present, simply reading to you the charge upon which you are brought before this honourable court, and I have only to add that I feel certain a most impartial and thorough investigation will take place. At the proper time you will be allowed, on your own behalf, to make such remarks as you may deem necessary ; in the meantime your case is in able hands, and I am sure that the learned counsel for the defence will conduct it in such manner as will reflect the highest honour on—on that member of the cruising fleet who has at the last hour accepted the brief on your behalf. Prisoner at the bar, you, of the name of " Toper," stand charged with the terrible crime of not having saluted the commodore's flag in the middle of last night as you came to your moorings. What have you of the name of " Toper " to say in answer to the charge? Are you guilty, or not guilty ? '

" ' If you please, sur, I ain't fond of this 'ere 'umbug. This wery arternoon someone calling hisself a gentleman 'as made a three-decker o' my pipe, and burnt my toes with mustard and kaianne pepper ! I calls it a shame and a insult on grey hairs, I does, and that's all I're got to say on the matter.'

"These irrelevant remarks by Toper were severely censured by the judge and the trial proceeded. The speeches of counsel I forget, but I know they convulsed everyone with laughter; so much so that in the end even old Toper himself couldn't help joining in the fun. At last the case was ended and the prisoner found guilty, but in consideration of his great age he was strongly recommended to mercy.

"'Prisoner at the bar, you have been found guilty, I deeply regret to say, by the unanimous verdict of the jury. I

THE GIPSY LIFE OF BROADLAND.

will not comment upon the enormity of your crime. Your conscience must have already told you the heinousness of your sin. It only remains for me now to pass upon you the sentence of this honourable court, which is, that you be turned adrift, on your return down the stream, on Hickling Broad [several hundred acres of water] in a jolly-boat, without oars, without mast, without sails, without a rudder, without meat, without drink, and lastly, without clothes—in fact, in a state of nudity, in an empty boat! But the jury recommended you to mercy on account of your great age, and as it is ever the prerogative of justice to lean towards the side of

mercy, I have considerable pleasure, under all the circumstances of the case, in mitigating the severe punishment I have
already awarded by allowing you a paper shirt, collar and a
pair of braces! Remove the prisoner.' So ended the great
trial at Coltishall Lock.

"By the time 'Toper' had finished his cruise with us
there was not a happier man in the fleet. And when we ended
our voyage a purse was made up for the old man, and he left
us declaring 'he never sailed with such a nice merry lot of
gents in all his life.' His latter statement might have had a
double meaning as the practical jokes played upon the old
man were innumerable."

THE LARBOARD WATCH.

LATEENERS RACING ON WROXHAM BROAD.

## CHAPTER XX

### YACHTS AND YACHTING DURING THE PAST, 1800 TO 1880

AMONGST the sports of Broadland, boat-sailing and yachting stand pre-eminent. It is a sport in which all can indulge, from the millionaire in his luxurious steam yacht to the guttersnipe in a washtub; there is plenty of room for everybody without being obliged to rub shoulders against undesirable company.

In Broadland are some 200 miles of waterway open to the Bohemian tourist, and a grand total of over 4000 acres of open water—made up from the combined area of the various broads and lagoons. The normal range of tide is trifling, and there is no swiftly-running stream to contend against, except near Great Yarmouth, which renders these

238

inland waters ideal cruising grounds. Access to the sea is gained at Great Yarmouth and Lowestoft, from either of which ports vessels of no mean burden can enter or depart.

The launching of the first pleasure boat or yacht upon the waters of Broadland cannot be traced, but several veterans of the Norfolk and Suffolk Yacht Club can, through their forbears, prove the existence of regattas upon Wroxham and Oulton Broads during the past hundred years. In those days they were called " water frolics," and the craft were very different in shape and rig to the present up-to-date racing machines.

A hundred years ago it was the custom of certain residents in Bloaterville (Great Yarmouth) and the neighbouring village of Caistor to betake themselves to the river once a year to see the boats sail past on their way to Wroxham Regatta. To-day that custom is still followed, although there are daily, throughout the yachting season, so many visitors on the river bank that the slight increase on the occasion in question is hardly noticeable.

From 1800 to 1850 the improvement of Broadland pleasure-craft was slight, but during 1850 to 1870 a development of speed, appearance and comfort became marked. This was materially increased in the following ten years, and as each year succeeded the other, new craft made their appearance. Boat-builders' yards sprang up, and boat-racing became the all-absorbing sport of the summer months.

To what degree this pastime has taken hold of the natives and visitors of Broadland can now be seen.

The first boat of any prominence at all remembered was the old *Maria*, built by Mr Brown of Great Yarmouth, in the spring of 1834, for a Mr Plowman of Normandstone, near Lowestoft; " heart of oak " was the material selected, and each plank was critically examined before being passed, which probably accounts for her marvellous preservation.

At the death of Mr Plowman the *Maria* passed into the hands of Mr Gilbert of Cantley by reason of his marriage with Miss Plowman, but he did not own her long.

In the year 1837 she was purchased by Sir Jacob Preston,

Bart., of Beeston Hall, near Barton Broad, and she remained in his possession until the date of his death, 1894. From the commencement of her new ownership she entered upon a very successful racing career, her first winning bracket being secured at Wroxham water frolic, when she beat the *Leviathan, Louisa,* and several others which had previously made their names famous.

Between 1837 and 1840 the reputation of the *Maria* as a crack local racing yacht was enviable and she was considered the fastest boat afloat. This was once pretty clearly demonstrated at Wroxham Regatta, where the *Maria* attended as usual

THE " MARIA " ON BARTON BROAD.

to compete for the open cup advertised by the committee to be sailed for; but as all the other yachts present refused to cross the starting-line on the ground of the absurdity of attempting to lower her ever-victorious colours, her owner withdrew her name from the race and the cup was sailed for by the other boats. After a very exciting race the cup was won by and presented to the *Hornet,* but the crew engaged to sail the *Maria* were so exasperated at being done out of their extra prize money, they boarded the *Hornet,* and a free fight ensued, in which the man who held the cup was knocked overboard —cup and all.

An obliging diver appeared on the scene, and in consideration of the sum of half-a-sovereign recovered the lost trophy, with which, safely stowed away in her lockers, the *Hornet* got up sail and made all haste towards Yarmouth. When the crew of the *Maria* heard of this their anger rekindled, and they also crowded on every stitch of canvas possible, with a view to overtaking the *Hornet* and renewing hostilities, but the latter boat had obtained such a good start that she was never overtaken, although she received some little damage from a few volleys of stones which the partizans of the *Maria* hurled at her when passing Horning Village on Sir Jacob Preston's estate. In those happy days of yore sport on the Broads hardly seems to have been confined to yacht-racing pure and simple.

The chief antagonists of the *Maria* were the *Red Rover* and the *Pearl*, both very much larger vessels; the smaller boats refused to enter against her on the ground that it was useless for them to do so.

In 1839 the *Maria* beat the *Red Rover* at Oulton Broad, at Wroxham in 1842 (including the *Pearl*), at Great Yarmouth in 1843, and again at Wroxham on a later date. The *Red Rover* was known throughout England as a racer. She was the winner of over 120 cups, and will be more particularly referred to later.

After 1850 the *Maria* was not regularly raced, but she attended all regattas, and so good was the workmanship and material expended on her that her only repairs worthy of the name for fifty years consisted of a new stem, two or three planks, and one new suite of sails. In 1897 her absence from Wroxham Regatta was commented upon for the first time in sixty years, yet in spite of all her wear and tear she was considered as good and as sound as ever.

The *Maria* being lateen - rigged, her mainmast was stepped just abaft the midship section, and it is a fact well worthy of notice that when her lines were taken off in 1885 her displacement was found to be in accordance with the then latest theory of Mr Colin Archer as to what is the best form for speed.

It is remarkable to be able to record that in 1887 the

Q

*Maria* was raced quite in her old form, upon Barton Broad, by Sir Jacob Preston and his son Mr T. Preston. She again beat everything in her class, although she was sailing with the same crew, the same sails, and nearly all her original gear of fifty years previously; the only additions that could be traced were a new garboard strake and some new spars.

At his death (1894), it is rumoured that Sir Jacob Preston left by will a provision sufficient to preserve this veteran yacht in good order and up-keep for all time.

The old *Sylph*, belonging to Colonel Harvey of Thorpe, near Norwich, was another great antagonist to the *Maria*, but, the patriarch of all Broadland boats was undoubtedly the *Augusta*, built in 1755 or thereabouts. Colonel H. M. Leathes of Herringfleet Hall states that she retained practically all her old material up to 1867, and that he last saw her about 1885 in a dyke at Buckenham Ferry, where she was affording a home to an artist who was living in her for the winter. She would then be 130 years old.

Another wonderful racer was the *Enchantress*, built about 1850, by Mr Green of Wroxham, to replace his old craft, the *Widgeon*. She was at first lateen-rigged, measuring nineteen feet on the ram, with a counter seven feet long, beam, nine feet, and draught of water four feet; her foreyard was sixty feet. In 1867 she was bought by Mr O. Diver of Great Yarmouth; six feet were added to her bows, she was converted into a ten-ton cutter, and her racing days received new life, which were continued with more or less success for some years. At the present day she may be met with labouring along under the management of tourist crews. What an ignominious ending to a proud career!

In the forties the fastest racing craft of Broadland were lateeners, which invariably beat the so-called cutters, and by the rules of racing they were compelled to grant a time allowance.

Prominent amongst the lateens may be mentioned the following:— Sir Jacob Preston's *Maria*; Mr Thornton's

*Naverino* of Beccles; Mr Bonfellow's (of Normandstone, near Lowestoft), *Coriander;* the *Leander* of Bungay; Messrs Morgan's *Phœnix* of Norwich; Mr Green's *Widgeon;* Mr W. Everitt's (of North Cove Hall, near Beccles), *Hornet;* Colonel Wilson's *Atalanta* and Mr Webster's *Lotus,* both of Beccles: Admiral Preston's *Novelty,* but this latter boat was really a nondescript rig and she was subsequently altered to a yawl. There were, of course, many others that unfortunately cannot be called to memory.

During the forties there were but few cutters built. The most prominent were Mr T. T. Berney's *Meteor* of Morton (this gentleman was a great supporter of sport in the country, and, it may be added, he was one of the first to start yacht-racing in these waters), Sir William Beauchamp Proctor's *Pearl* of Hardley, near Loddon, and Mr Burrough's *Wallace* of Norwich, and Captain Coster's *Red Lancer.* The latter boat was originally named the *Kestrel,* but she was renamed by her new owner, who altered and re-rigged her; but eventually she was sold to that great Norwich celebrity, Mr W. Butcher, who gave her back her original name.

At this time Colonel Harvey of Thorpe Lodge, a good all-round sportsman, was one of the great supporters of the water frolics, and was often to be seen on the deck of the *Augusta, Maria, Phœnix, Queen Mab,* or his own boat, the *Sylph.* The *Waterwitch,* a sixteen-foot boat, belonging to Mr Robert Etheridge of Thorpe, was one of the startling successes among racers, and the commodious barge, *Rob Roy,* is worthy of mention, if only for the fact that she was the forerunner of a large class of boats of which more hereafter.

The *Waterwitch* was a lateen, designed and built by Mr Etheridge in the year 1818, which date is identified by her subsequent owner Mr P. E. Hansell, who narrates how an old shipwright at Etheridge's. boathouses was wont to fix all subsequent events from the origin of her launching—" Ter *Worterwitch* wor lornched the daay Painter " [the celebrated Norfolk pugilist] " fought the Black on Mussel 'eath " [Mousehold Heath, near Norwich].

The greatest water frolic of the Norwich folk during the forties was held at Thorpe Gardens, where the county families and all other the nobility and gentry, as the announcements described them, would assemble and crowd with their families towards Captain King's meadow to seek sport, music and seclusion (!) for the moderate outlay of half-a-crown. But these gatherings were held too far up stream to encourage much sailing, and the sport was mostly confined to rowing matches.

In the fifties the cutters became more fashionable, and the time allowance given by the lateen-rigged grew shorter and shorter, until it was taken off altogether and both lateens and cutters sailed on even terms.

Prominent amongst the racing cutters may be mentioned the *Kestrel*, belonging to Mr W. Butcher of Norwich, and three boats from Aylesham (Dr Morton's *Oberon*, Mr Smith's *Daphne*, and Mr Scott's *Sphinx**); Mr Frances's *Venus* of Beccles; Mr Blyth's *Long Looked for Come at Last* of Great Yarmouth; Mr T. M. Read's *Belvidere* of Norwich, and Mr Tomlinson's *Vindex* of Great Yarmouth.

From 1840 to 1860 the ideal model of a racing boat may perhaps be characteristically described as "a cod's head bow with a mackerel tail"; the floor was flat, long and very much hollowed out below the water-line. Dead wood and forefoot were believed to hold boats up to windward, which theory did not explode until the nineties. An observer would not fail to notice that if one of these old models was taken, the dead wood cut away and the hull elongated from the water-line, the result would very nearly approach an up-to-date racing model; the difference not being so great as one would imagine.

With regard to rig, the so-called cutters were rigged as sloops, having a long gaff and an over-large mainsail and jib, foresails not being practical.

The lateens were rigged very differently. A short foremast, stepped right in the eyes of the boat with a rake for'ard, supported an enormous lateen foresail, the foreyard of which

* Pronounced by local watermen *Spinax* (?).

WROXHAM REGATTA, 1868

(from an old Painting).

ranged from eighteen feet to fifty-six feet, whilst the mizzen-mast was rigged with another lateen sail or a large gaff-mizzen—equal to the mainsail of any similar-sized boat.

In the fifties the lateeners were divided into three classes, fourteen feet, sixteen feet and nineteen feet on ram—from outside stem to sternpost—but later in the sixties Mr W. S. Everitt built a lateener twenty-one feet in length, rigged with a foreyard of sixty-three feet, six and a half inches diameter at the sling. So long was this yard that a sliding gunter had to be fitted to it for reefing purposes. Lateeners were wonders to sail near the wind, and were very handy in the narrow, tortuous waterways, although their sails were cumbersome to hoist, to cover up and to reef. In running before the wind it was not unusual to meet with mishap, as in the narrow rivers it was almost impossible to ease the sails in a squall, and occasionally a boat would run down head foremost. Apart from this a lateen foresail was an ideal sail to back a craft off the mud with.

During this decade three prominent boats put in an appearance—Mr Green's *Enchantress* (nineteen feet); Mr Crow's *Elizabeth* (sixteen feet), of Horning, and Mr Blake Humphrey's *Miranda* (nineteen feet) of Wroxham.

Even in those days (the early forties) there were cranks as well as smart craft, and the former will perhaps be sufficiently dealt with if two of them are mentioned.

Lieutenant Kisby, R.N., introduced the first, a boat called the *Bermuda*. She was a craft with little freeboard, plenty of sheer, and a long single mast raking aft which carried a three-cornered sail running up her mast on hoops, and an ordinary jib for'ard. She was fairly fast although she did not do what was expected of her by her owner, and eventually sank into oblivion.

The second was introduced by Captain Preston of Lowestoft, and appropriately named the *Experiment*, a follower of his former boat, the *Novelty*. She had no timbers at all but was built by moulding a hull of very thin planking, which was plastered over with canvas and tar; when dry another casing of wood was laid over the first one diagonally and covered with another casing of canvas and tar. This casing process was repeated again and again until, it is said, no less than three barrels of tar were used in her construction. But misfortune followed in her wake, for, when launched, she started leaking, and on account of her curious build it was impossible to discover the whereabouts of the leak ; and she was never of much use as a racer, nor indeed for anything else, as she was rigged with two lug sails, the cloths of one of them being alternately blue and white, and of the other alternately red and white, she was one of the most conspicuous of craft at Broadland water frolics.

An amusing incident once happened in connection with these sails. Early in the season, shortly after fitting out, the captain came cruising up the course, when suddenly a gust of wind converted his sails to rags, or rather blew out all the coloured part of them (which the dye had rotted), leaving only the white stripes hanging gridiron fashion upon his yards. So far as is known this is the first instance on record in the annals of Broadland yachting where the theory of a practical use of sails upon a racing boat, with holes in them to let the wind through, has been tried.

In 1858 the-cutter yacht, *Belvidere*, was built by Harrod of Great Yarmouth for Mr T. M. Read. She proved a most decided success from the date of her launch, beating the lateeners *Enchantress, Vampire* and *Elizabeth* continually. She also added more renown to her name by leading such yachts as the *Kestrel* and *Argonaut* (an eighteen-tonner) round a full course, and passing the winning post ahead on her merits, they being all larger than herself. The *Belvidere* continued to be the fastest vessel of her size from 1858 to 1872, winning a great number of prizes; during the latter half of this period she was owned by Mr W. Clabburn of Thorpe.

In 1885 she passed into the hands of Mr Harvey-George of Gorlestone, and was altered, raised and renamed the *Cynthia*. She was twenty-four feet long on the ram, and measured nine tons. Being a deeper-bodied yacht than the racers of her time her accommodation was much superior to others.

On summarising it will be found that from 1840 to 1850 racing craft consisted almost entirely of lateeners and large cutters, but from 1850 to 1855 smaller cutters appeared and mixed with the lateen, accepting a time allowance of half a minute per foot.

About 1855 the establishment of a club was attempted, which was called "The Amateur Yacht Club," but it fell to

THE ELEVEN-TONNERS STARTING FROM FIXED MOORINGS, WITH JIBS DOWN, ON OULTON BROAD.

pieces after a life of only three months, owing to the originators spending all the subscribed funds on the opening cruise (?).

During the years 1855 to 1859 cutters separated more or less from lateeners, and in 1859, what is now known as the Royal Norfolk and Suffolk Yacht Club sprang into existence and boats became classified by tonnage.

The origin of this club, of which the Prince of Wales was patron, is interesting. Prior to its inauguration (1859), racing craft were measured and time allowance was calculated upon the ram, which was the measurement from the top of the stem to the top of the sternpost, every other latitude being allowed free and unhampered. Consequently boats favoured excessive beam and absurdly long overhanging sterns and counter-sterns; so much so, that the helmsman sometimes appeared to be forward of amidships.

With the growing popularity of racing another evil became apparent to yachtsmen. There was no means of con-trolling the behaviour of watermen, who were necessary to the full enjoyment of the sport. So flagrant were the offences of the more turbulent of this body of men that matters were brought to a crisis after the water frolic on Burgh Flats in 1858, when the crews of two racing yachts boarded one another, lashed their craft together and fought out their differences to the bitter end.

After this certain gentlemen well-known in Broadland called together a meeting at the Maid's Head Hotel, Norwich, at which the following (*inter alia*) were present :—Mr R. N. Burroughs, Mr B. Branford, Mr F. Brown, Mr F. Dowson, Mr W. Jecks, Mr W. Everitt, Mr W. Mann, Mr H. Morgan, Mr J. B. Morgan, Mr W. S. Everitt, Mr W. Millard, Dr R. K. Morton, Mr T. M. Read and Colonel Wilson.

At this meeting, held on the 9th April 1859, existing grievances were discussed, and a club was formed which hoped to exercise some sort of control at future regattas ; the proposed name was subject-matter for much discussion, but eventually the present title without its prefix was agreed upon, and by way of compliment to the Suffolk members, who were in the minority, Colonel Wilson was elected the first Commodore of the club, Mr C. W. Millard was appointed Secretary, and Mr H. Morgan, Treasurer. Rules were discussed and framed, flags chosen, and a sum of thirty pounds subscribed in the room to purchase a club challenge cup—in order that history might not repeat itself.

The Committee consisted of the following yachtsmen— : Mr W. Jecks (Norwich), Mr H. P. Green (Norwich), Mr A. J. N. Chamberlin (Wroxham), Mr W. Henry Scott (Aylsham), Mr

T. M. Read.     W. S. Everitt.     H. Morgan.

SOME MEMBERS OF THE ROYAL NORFOLK AND SUFFOLK YACHT CLUB, INCLUDING THREE OF ITS FOUNDERS.

W. Frederick Green (Wroxham), and the Officers of the Club. The entrance fee was three guineas and the annual subscription one.

With influential men at its back the club became a success from the first, and within a few days of its inauguration upwards of sixty members were enrolled upon its books at an annual subscription of a guinea each.

The burgee originally chosen had a white ground with a blue margin and a red Maltese cross in its centre ; but it was changed to a white ground with the Prince of Wales feathers upon receiving the Royal Patronage, which was on the 16th of February 1867.

As an ensign the club selected a white flag with the Jack in the corner and a large Prince of Wales feathers in the fly. The Royal Yacht Squadron at once took exception to it on the ground that it resembled the white ensign which they were the only club entitled to fly.   Major H. M. Leathes was one of the members deputed by the club to interview the authorities, but Captain Beauchamp Seymour (afterwards Lord Alcester) insisted on the flag being disused, which was followed by an order from the Admiralty.

A red ensign was next selected with the Prince of Wales Feathers, which produced a further order from the Admiralty to strike out the Royal feathers from the fly : eventually a red ensign, with the alteration above alluded to, was passed and the burgee was at the same time altered from a white to a red ground.

One of the first steps the club took was to alter the rules of measurement to the tonnage system based upon length and width, no shifting ballast and limited crews. This was advocated by Mr T. M. Read and successfully carried into effect.   Next the Committee assumed to themselves power to suspend or excommunicate any waterman or other person from sailing in any club race upon just and sufficient cause shown.

Three annual fixtures were decided upon as follows :— Cantley in June, Wroxham in July, and Oulton in August.

After the club was formed the yachts were at first divided into two classes. Class I., Cutters. Class II., Lateeners. Most of the meetings were confined to two races daily, and in Class I. the smaller yachts were allowed to compete on the usual time allowance. The course was about six to eight miles, and the prizes offered were more valuable, although it can hardly be said they were less coveted than they are now.

The inauguration meeting of the new club was held at Cantley on the 16th June 1859, and a course of eight miles marked out. The events of the day were divided into two races. The entries for the first included the following yachts :—

| NAME OF YACHT. | RIG. | TONNAGE. | OWNER. |
|---|---|---|---|
| *Argonaut* | Cutter * | 9 | Mr E. S. Trafford |
| *Belvidere* | Cutter | 9 | Mr T. M. Read |
| *Kestrel* | Cutter | 12 | Mr W. Butcher |
| *Sphinx* | Cutter | 7 | Mr W. H. Scott |
| *Tantivy* | Cutter | 6 | Mr J. B. Morgan |
| *Oberon* | Cutter | 5 | Mr R. K. Morton |
| *Clara* | Cutter | 3 | Mr F. P. Smith |
| *Union* | Cutter | 3 | Mr A. J. N. Chamberlin |
| *Little John* | Cutter | 1 | Mr S. Young |
| *Enchantress* | Lateen or Fore and Mizzen | 6 | Mr H. P. Green |
| *Maud* | Do. | 10 | Mr J. R. Asher |
| *Atalanta* | Do. | 7 | Col. G. Wilson |
| *Osprey* | Do. | 6 | Mr E. Swatman |
| *Ida* | Do. | 4 | Mr A. Master |
| *Amateur* | Do. | 6 | Mr F. Brown |

A considerable amount of interest was centred in this race by reason of the new rules and measurements introduced, and because it was not definitely known which class (cutter or lateen) under the new *régime* was likely to hold the supremacy. The new allowance on measurement was a minute

* The term cutter is a local misnomer, as these yachts were sloop rigged.

per ton, irrespective of the distance sailed, and the *Enchantress* had many partizans, who increased in number when it was found to be blowing half a gale on the morning of the race.

A most spirited contest ensued, and the times of the leading boats were as follows :—

|  | hr. | mins. | secs. |
|---|---|---|---|
| *Belvidere* | 1 | 38 | 3 |
| *Oberon* | 1 | 42 | 15 |
| *Kestrel* | 1 | 42 | 40 |
| *Tantivy* | 1 | 46 | 40 |

The result of this race was an acknowledged victory for the cutters and heralded the decline of lateens. Several mishaps befell the competing yachts, which perhaps should be recorded, as, had all gone well, the *Oberon* would undoubtedly have won the race. She was disqualified on account of her breaking the rule as to the limitation of her crew, whilst the two three-ton cutters, the *Clara* and the *Union*, carried away part of their rigging, which compelled them to retire.

The second race, which was confined to foresail and mizzen-rigged yachts, was sailed over the same course, and the following were entered :—

| *Osprey* | Mr E. Swatman. |
|---|---|
| *Maud* | Mr J. R. Asher. |
| *Atalanta* | Col. G. Wilson. |
| *Amateur* | Mr F. Brown. |
| *Ida* | Mr A. Master. |

The *Ida*, for some reason or other, did not start and the race finished as follows :—

|  | hrs. | mins. | secs. |
|---|---|---|---|
| *Osprey* | 4 | 0 | 47 |
| *Atalanta* | 4 | 5 | 34 |
| *Amateur* | 4 | 11 | 10 |
| *Maud* | Not timed. | | |

Other regattas followed, and each centre organised its own meetings as well, so that yacht-racing became firmly established as one of the leading sports of Broadland. During the seventies the mòst exciting and perhaps the best matches were between the ten-ton boats, such as the *Elaine, Alarm, Lethe, Firefly, Maud, Scud*, etc., and the owners of these craft enjoyed the dual pleasure of being able to live in comfort aboard.

The *Hilda* was a boat built by Major H. M. Leathes of Herringfleet Hall for sea and river work, also with a view to racing. She had enormous spars and carried a large spread of canvas, but in so far as racing was con-

cerned proved herself somewhat of a disappointment. The *Lake Lily*, another of Major Leathes's numerous craft, was originally a ship's boat. On being washed ashore at Great Yarmouth she was sold by auction for 30s., Major Leathes buying her afterwards for £3. He had her fitted up for river work, with

" HILDA."   " LAKE LILY."

tent cabin and many ingenious contrivances, which increased her value some twentyfold.

## COMMODORES OF THE CLUB.

### SINCE ITS INSTITUTION IN 1859.

| DATE. | NAME. | YACHT. | RESIDENCE. |
|---|---|---|---|
| 1859 | Colonel Wilson | *Atalanta* | Beccles |
| 1860 | E. S. Trafford, Esq. | *Argonaut* | Wroxham |
| 1861 | W. H. Scott, Esq. | *Sphinx* | Aylsham |
| 1862 | Fred Brown, Esq. | *Amateur* | Norwich |
| 1863 | R. J. H. Harvey, Esq. | *Myth* | Brundall |

| DATE. | NAME. | YACHT. | RESIDENCE. |
|-------|-------|--------|-----------|
| 1864-5 | W. H. Clabburn, Esq. | *Belvidere* | Thorpe |
| 1866-8 | Major H. M. Leathes | *Waveney Queen* | Herringfleet |
| 1869 | P. E. Hansell, Esq. | *Glance* | Thorpe |
| 1870 | J. Tomlinson, Esq. | *Vindex* | Gt. Yarmouth |
| 1871 | J. B. Morgan, Esq. | *Scud* | Norwich |
| 1872 | H. E. Buxton, Esq. | *Curlew* | Gt. Yarmouth |
| 1873 | F. G. Foster, Esq. | *Spray* | Norwich |
| 1874 | B. V. Winch, Esq. | *Alarm* | Norwich |
| 1875 | Henry Morgan, Esq. | *Firefly* | Norwich |
| 1876 | Col. H. M. Leathes | *Waveney Queen* | Herringfleet |
| 1877 | Joseph Stanley, Esq. | *Zoe* | Norwich |
| 1878 | J. J. Colman, Esq., M.P. | *Wanderer I.* | Norwich |
| 1879 | J. P. Hall, Esq. | *Alarm* | Gt. Yarmouth |
| 1880-1 | E. Birkbeck, Esq. M.P. | *Florence* | Horstead |
| 1882 | B. V. Winch, Esq. | *Arrow* | Norwich |
| 1883 | W. Cooper-Brown, Esq. | *Kiama* | Haynford |
| 1884 | T. M. Read, Esq. | *Zephyr* | Norwich |
| 1885-7 | Sir Charles Harvey, Bart. | { *Midge* Swallow } | Rainthorpe Hall |
| 1888-9 | John Lee Barber, Esq. | *Wanderer II.* | Lowestoft |
| 1890 | Sir E. Birkbeck, Bt. | *Florence* | Horstead |
| 1891 | W. Cooper-Brown, Esq. | *Kiama* | Thorpe, Norwich |
| 1892 | Sir R. Palmer, Bart. | *Keenaghmore* | Maidenhead |
| 1893 | Wm. Cadge, Esq. | *Phantom* | Norwich |
| 1894-5 | Lt.-Cl. Preston, R.A. | *Phœnix* | Fishley |
| 1896-9 | T. M. Read, Esq. | *Bella Donna* and *Meneen* | Norwich |
| 1900-2 | R. J. Colman, Esq. | *Castanet* and *Tugela* | Norwich |

The starting of the Norfolk and Suffolk Yacht Club gave a great stimulus to racing, and new yachts soon began to show themselves. *Wanderer I.* was one of the most prominent. Originally she was a fourteen-tonner built by James Hastings of Great Yarmouth for Mr Jecks, but she soon afterwards changed hands, becoming the property of Mr J. Lee Barber, who raced her with considerable success for many years. Eventually she was again sold to Mr J. J. Colman of Norwich, who twice lengthened her in the bows until her ton measurement was increased from fourteen to twenty tons or thereabout. After this lengthening she never raced on fresh waters, although she occasionally competed in the Road-steads against such boats as the *Red Rover*, *Kiama* and the *Frederica*—a visiting yacht belonging to Mr Pochin.

"WANDERER I."     "LETHE."

The *Lethe* (subsequently re-named the *Foe*) was another good boat in her day. She was owned by Mr Joseph Stanley of Norwich.

In 1860 Mr Samuel Nightingale bought the *Red Rover*, which had not then been regularly raced for several years. He altered, refitted and improved her every year, and she was very soon the acknowledged crack of the Norfolk and Suffolk Yacht Club, which proud position she retained until 1885, when, owing to the health of her owner, she was withdrawn from the racing world. To give some idea of her alterations it may be mentioned that she grew from about fourteen to twenty tons between the years 1861 and 1883. In 1888 she was broken up and the materials sold.

Without doubt the *Red Rover* was accountable for the increased tonnage amongst local yachts, to prove which may be called to mind the *Argonaut*, eighteen tons ; the *Alabama* (afterwards renamed the *Water Lily*) fourteen tons, owned by Mr F. Green ; the *Little Yankee*, fourteen tons, which was built at Cowes ; the *Emerald*, a schooner of eighteen tons belonging to Sir Thomas Beauchamp, Bart. ; the *Kitten*, twelve tons, which was built by Harvey of Wivenhoe, was a great success at sea but a total failure on inland waterways, and was owned by Mr Clabburn of Norwich ; the *Eva Mary*, eighteen tons, belonging to Sir Harry Bullard ; *Waveney Queen*, a yawl of twenty-four tons, owned by Major H. M. Leathes ; *Marguerite*, five tons, owned by Mr Ket Thompson ; *Zephyr*, fifteen tons, belonging to Mr T. M. Read ; *Rover*, sixteen tons (Mr T. H. Palmer) ; *Vampire*, ten tons, (Mr W. S. Everitt) ; *Amateur*, six tons, built by Etteridge of Thorpe (Mr F. Brown) ; *Wanderer I.* (Mr W. Jecks) ; *Vixen*, nine tons, and the *Atalanta* (Colonel Wilson) ; *Sphinx*, five tons (Mr W. H. Scott) ; the *Myth*, nine tons, a half decker (Mr R. J. H. Harvey, afterwards Sir Robert Harvey, Bart.) ; and the *Glance*, eleven tons (Mr P. E. Hansel).

These yachts soon proved to be too big for river racing, and their size began to diminish in favour of ten-tonners, whilst the larger yachts degenerated into cruisers.

In 1861 Mr Ket Thompson introduced an American " centre-board " yacht as a new class of racing craft in the five-ton *Marguerite ;* she was Una-rigged, under-canvassed and alto-gether too small to compete successfully with other boats of her time. A considerable local outcry was also raised against the fairness of this innovation. Soon after her appearance the centre board was removed in favour of a deep lead keel, a long counter was added, and her name changed to the *Fleur de Lys*, under which she won many races until the year 1870. In 1862 another attempt to introduce the centre board was

R

made by the then High Sheriff of the county, Mr R. J. H. Harvey (afterwards Sir Robert Harvey, Bart.), who purchased the *Myth*, a yacht of nine tons built by Ratsey of Cowes. She was considerably altered (in order that she might pass

the club rules) as follows: —a moderate counter, the sliding centre plate taken out, her keel fixed and an enormous spread of canvas added. In light weather she was a success and beat the *Red Rover*. This boat was the forerunner of a class that held the sway until 1883, having as their chief characteristic a flat floor and deep lead keel; the *Lethe, Zoe, Elaine, Alarm, Phantom, Maud, Firefly, Gem* and *Witch* may be mentioned as boats of this type.

These yachts were all large compared with the modern craft which frequent Broadland at the present day, and for ten or fifteen years the *Red Rover* (S. Nightingale) reigned supreme. Elated at her success at home, she, in 1863, ventured to the Thames, where she entered for the Seventy

THE "MAUD."

Guinea Wedding Cup, presented the year H.R.H. the Prince of Wales was married, which was won by the *Octoroon*. The *Red Rover*, being unfortunate in carrying away her crosstrees, did not show up at the finish. But later, at Hunstanton, in a light wind, she (the *Red Rover*) beat all the Northern boats with the greatest of ease, thus proving herself to be equally as good at sea as she was upon the rivers and lagoons of Broadland.

The year following the *Red Rover* was converted from a clincher into a carvel-built vessel, which improved her speed.

During the sixties, cutters (by reason of the new measurement) grew longer, narrower and more wall-sided, freeboard was lowered, and in bad weather their decks became very wet and uncomfortable.

In 1862 the fashion changed somewhat to increased beam and reduced tonnage. Mr D. Hatcher built the *Queen* for Colonel Whitbread of Rushmere, near Ipswich; she was a sea-going vessel, fifteen tons, drawing eight and a half feet of water, with high freeboard, and soon became noted as a racer. The following yachts were also prominent during that year: —In the cutter class, the *Kestrel*, twelve tons (Mr W. Butcher); *Wanderer I.*, fourteen tons (Mr J. Lee Barber); *Union*, three tons (Mr A. J. N. Chamberlin); *Wallace* (Mr G. Y. Collinson); *Isabella* (Mr C. H. Chamberlin); *Maude*, one ton (Mr F. G. Foster); *Foam* (Mr F. Frere); *Phœnix* (Mr T. S. Jackson); *Oberon*, five tons (Mr R. K. Morton); *Bittern*, seven tons (Messrs J. B. & H. Morgan); *Red Rover*, fourteen tons (Mr S. Nightingale); *Rover*, sixteen tons (Mr T. H. Palmer); *Flirt*, two tons (Mr J. Playford); *Belvidere*, nine tons (Mr T. M. Read); *Augusta*, six tons (Mr B. Russell); *Sphinx* (Mr W. H. Scott); *Phœnix*, four tons (Mr W. Stewart); *Daphne* and *Clara* (Mr F. P. Smith); *Argonaut* (Mr E. S. Trafford); *Marguerite* (Mr H. K. Tomlinson); *Medora* (Mr J. Tomlinson); and the *Fairy* (Mr W. S. Young). The *Sylph*, a schooner of 107 tons, was owned by Mr W. H. Trafford.

In the lateen class:—

*Ripple* (Mr W. B. Bramford); *Amateur* (Mr F. Brown); *Brenda* (Mr J. Day); *Vampire*, ten tons (Mr W. S. Everitt); *Merlin*, four tons (Mr J. Foster); *Enchantress*, six tons (Mr H. P. Green); *Merlin*, four tons (Mr A. J. Hubbard); and the *Ariel* (Mr W. Mann).

In 1862 the total membership of the Norfolk and Suffolk Yacht Club was about ninety all told. As the club grew and prospered the water frolics of old gave place to well-organised regattas, at which the racing was watched with much interest and the sailing regulated by strict rules, which were rigorously enforced. It may not be considered out of place if a word is here added regarding the most important of these gatherings which was annually held near Great Yarmouth.

This greatest of all water frolics of olden times was a day

THE OLD TYPE OF SIXTEEN-FOOTERS RACING ON BURGH FLATS.

to be remembered, not so much by reason of the sailing capabilities of the boats which competed, as for the reminiscence of individual adventure. Everybody looked upon it as a duty they owed to society to get more or less elevated *in spirits* towards the close of the day, from those in highest authority to the lowest of the low.

Burgh Water Frolic, now a fixture of the past, was annually held, from time immemorial, upon Burgh Flats at the westernmost end of Breydon Water. It was a gathering which everybody in the district attended, and was looked forward to from one year to another with great expectation.

Until the sixties it was customary for the Mayor and Corporation of the Borough of Great Yarmouth to attend the meeting in state, and a special wherry was chartered some weeks beforehand, in order that it might be repainted and decorated in honour of the occasion. Sitting in the midst of a profusion of bunting and gaudy colours, the Borough fathers contemplated the aquatic contests, imbibing the while choice wines and consuming other delicacies which were provided at the expense of the Mayor for the time being.

Of course a band of music was in attendance, and they too were allotted a special craft, generally one of the roomy boats which were used for ferrying fish from the fishing-smacks in the roadsteads to the beach—all fish used to be landed on the beach in those days. This boat was also painted in many colours and highly decorated.

After a few hours spent watching the races, the dignified councillors, with the Corporation officials at their head, proceeded in state to the " Burgh Cage " (a meadow upon which the cement works now stand), under the shadow of the walls of the ancient Roman fortress, there to partake of a generous lunch, from which the majority of those who sat down returned in a less dignified manner than they went.

No wonder that the country folks, the town folks, and everybody who owned, or could borrow, a boat made their way to Burgh Water Frolic when it received such patronage ; and the attendance was favoured, in that the town and neighbourhood made the date a general holiday, giving their *employés* a day's leave of grace—sometimes with a day's pay to boot.

After lunch, which, as might be expected, was usually somewhat prolonged, the whole flotilla of boats made their way as best they could to Cobholm Island, and moored along the shores just below the Knole Point, in order to witness aquatic sports, followed in the evening by a grand display of fireworks, at which all Yarmouth was present.

A curious coincidence happened to the author's father in

connection with one of these frolics, which is worthy of repetition.

The morning fixed for the frolic proved a very blustering one, and when it blows on Breydon Water navigation is no joke, especially in one of the old style of boats, with their straight, deep sterns, cut-away bows and mass of deadwood for'ard. Well, to get along with the yarn. The Mayor and city dignitaries arrived, the banks were thronged with people, the waters were crowded with craft of all kinds, and the band was duly moored in the most conspicuous position just off the course, in a boat gaudily got up in the usual style.

THE "MARS."

During the first race for the big yachts, the wind was blowing half a gale and the band was compelled to play for all they were worth to make themselves heard at all. Whilst they were thus straining at their instruments, one of the larger yachts, which was over-canvassed, got the upper hand of her helmsman and ran away. Despite all the efforts of her crew she touched the mud and instantly shot up into the wind, running stem on into the band-boat, upsetting her and precipitating the musician crew into the water.

Great commotion ensued and a number of boats put off to the rescue, but the most ludicrous sight of all was to see the big drum sailing merrily away to leeward, towards the " Dicky works," over the Breydon Flats, with a ship's boat and a gunning punt in chase manned by amateur crews in the form of a couple of mud-bedrabbled bandsmen.

Fortunately, no one was much the worse for the mishap, but several of the instruments were lost, and now follows the remarkable part of the story. Just twenty years afterwards the author's father, who had seen all that is above related, was yachting on Breydon Water on the anniversary of that particular day, and seeing a man trawling for fish, he rowed over to him in the dinghy in the hope of making a suitable purchase for the morrow's breakfast. What was his astonishment when the man, in place of fish, produced a cornet that he had just taken out of his net, which he was able to identify as belonging to Tom Cosgrove, the leader of the band, who was upset at the Burgh Water Frolic

" WAVENEY QUEEN."

that very day, and almost at that very hour, just twenty years previously.

With the establishment of the Yacht Club and numerous annual fixtures or regattas at which yacht-racing and not feasting was the main object of the gathering, the term " water frolic " rapidly died into disuse, and soon became almost forgotten ; now only a native of the remoter parts, and he an old one, would understand the meaning of the expression.

Among the most prominent of sea-going yachts owned by a Broadlander may be mentioned the *Mars,* purchased in 1881 by Mr J. J. Colman, M.P., from Mr R. E. Burroughs. She was built at Lymington in 1873 by G. Inman & Son, and registered 41 T.M.

The first ocean yacht race of the Norfolk and Suffolk Yacht Club (it was from Harwich to Lowestoft), came off on Saturday, 29th June 1867, and terminatad in favour of Mr S. Nightingale's *Red Rover.* The event was fixed for the previous Thursday, but was postponed in consequence of the unfavourable character of the weather, which was so rough that it would have been dangerous for the competing yachts to put to sea. The breeze continued to blow the whole of Thursday and Friday, but on Saturday morning the wind veered round to the south-east ; and as this was just what the yachts wanted, it was determined, though the sea still ran pretty high, that the race should be at once brought to an issue. No objection was offered by any one of the competitors, and it was accordingly at an early hour in the morning the fleet assembled round the Bell buoy off Harwich.

The competing craft were four in number—the *Waveney Queen,* seventeen tons (afterwards enlarged to twenty-four tons and turned into a yawl), Colonel Leathes', then the commodore of the club; *Red Rover,* cutter, fourteen tons (afterwards enlarged to eighteen tons), Mr S. Nightingale of Yarmouth; the *Water Lily,* fourteen tons, Mr H. P. Greene of Wroxham; and the *Ariel,* schooner, twelve tons, Mr T. M. Read of Yarmouth. After some slight delay the yachts were arranged in line by the commodore, and exactly at 9.30 a.m. a start was effected. The *Red Rover* at once took the lead, followed by the *Ariel,* with the *Waveney Queen* and *Water Lily* astern. About ten o'clock the wind freshened to a smart breeze, whilst the yachts were carrying the largest spread of canvas possible. At half-past eleven the Lowestoft Ness was sighted, and

*Galatea.*        *Tara.*

THE START.

*Galatea.*        *Tara.*

THE FINISH.

in the following order the yachts entered Lowestoft Harbour : —

|  | Hrs. | Mins. | Secs. |
|---|---|---|---|
| *Red Rover* | 1 | 50 | 29 |
| *Ariel* | 1 | 56 | 36 |
| *Waveney Queen* | 2 | 2 | 31 |
| *Water Lily* | 2 | 6 | 45 |

The first yacht accomplished the run, a distance of forty-seven miles, in 4 hrs., 20 mins., 29 secs., and the last in 4 hrs. 51 mins., 45 secs.; and as fully two hours had elapsed before Orford Ness was rounded, some idea of the pace may be formed from the fact that the remaining thirty miles were performed in less than two and a half hours, which, for yachts of small tonnage on a neap tide, must be pronounced as most successful. It must also be remembered that these yachts were built, with the exception of the *Ariel*, for the navigation of inland waters; the time allowance of the latter was only three minutes, and she lost the race by seven seconds.

It was intended at Harwich that eight yachts, competing for a prize of their own, should accompany the Norfolk and Suffolk yachts to Lowestoft, but the unfavourable weather which prevailed on the Thursday prevented this arrangement being carried out.

In looking at the photograph of the *Waveney Queen* one cannot fail to note the enormous spars she carried. Her jib was forty-four feet on the foot, whilst from the peak of the gaff to the deck was no less than seventy-four feet, which gives some idea of her vast spread of canvas. She beat the *Red Rover* at sea, August 31, 1888.

Speaking generally, the East Anglian Coast is not a good one for yachting. There is a lack of good harbours of refuge, and a labyrinth of sandbanks from the mouth of the Thames to the Humber, which combine to render yachtsmen very chary of eastern waters, so that with the exception of the Harwich Regatta week, first-class yachts are rarely seen within sight of land, or passing up and down channel. Amongst many of the local sandbanks there is also a dangerous " set " in the currents, which requires to be known and allowed for when coasting, and it is always advisable under these circumstances to make a sea passage by day, if possible from port to port, and not to depend too much upon the chart and bearings.   However, this makes good seamen, careful navigators, and it teaches those who go in practically for yachting how to handle their craft under difficult circumstances.

THE " WASP."

In running northwards from the mouth of the Thames and passing " down swin " (by far the safest passage), about forty miles takes one safely into the fine, and at all times accessible, harbour of Harwich.   The next stretch away to the northward is a constant dodge in and out of sandbanks the whole way to Lowestoft, and when once there, the harbour is not to be approached with ease at all times of the tide.   The deepest channel to enter Lowestoft Harbour is found immediately under the south pier-head, whilst care must be taken, if a strong ebb tide be running, that the yacht is not suddenly shot up into collision with the south pier. Once fairly into this port, perfect safety is reached and there are twelve feet of water at all times of tide.

Yarmouth Harbour should never be attempted under any circumstances unless well-known ; even then it is advisable to take a pilot to moorings when going any distance up the river. Better still to engage a steam tug both going in and out of this very dangerous bar harbour. One curious point also to remember on entering the port of Great Yarmouth is the height of water over the bar, which does not assume the maximum and minimum at exact high and low-water time of tides, but some two hours afterwards. From Yarmouth there really is no refuge worthy of the name of "harbour" until the Humber is reached, although that river is by no means an easy one to navigate even partially.

About 1865 lateeners disappeared from the Broadland racing world, and from 1870 to 1880 the cutters grew bigger and bigger, but a smaller class was also recognised. The classes were then divided as follows :—Class I., over ten tons ; Class II., under ten tons and over six tons ; Class III., under six tons.

Among other boats of the time (1870 to 1880) can be re-membered the *Vindex* (Mr J. Tomlinson) ; the *Scud* (Mr J. B. Morgan) ; *Curlew* (Mr H. E. Buxton) ; *Alarm* (Mr B. V. Winch) ; *Spray* (Mr F. G. Foster) ; *Firefly* (Mr H. Morgan) ; *Zoe* (Mr J. Stanley) ; *Wanderer I.* (Mr J. J. Colman) ; *Florence* (Mr E. Birkbeck) ; *Bittern, Belvidere II., Kiama* (Mr W. Cooper-Brown) ; *Zephyr* (Mr T. M. Read) ; *Midge* and the *Swallow* (Sir C. Harvey, Bart.) ; and many others.

The *Wasp* was a ten-ton cutter built about this period by Mr Henry Kelt Thompson in his barn at Brooke, upon lines taken from the *Marguerite*, and proved to be fairly successful in her class.

About 1874 or 1875 a few private matches were organised for lug-sail and open boats as these crafts began to be fairly

numerous on the waterways; this originated the idea of forming another club to encourage *amateur yacht-sailing*, as the
Norfolk and Suffolk Yacht Club refused to recognise any
boat under four tons. Also the Norfolk and Suffolk Yacht
Club employed professionals to steer and sail their boats
when racing, which, as the number of yachting men increased,
was taken exception to, not only on the ground of sport but
also of expense.

In the early part of 1876, Mr L. E. Bolingbroke of
Norwich, who had been a great supporter of yachting interests
in every shape and form, convened a meeting at Thompson's
boathouse, King
Street, Norwich, at
which Messrs B. V.
Winch, J. Youngs, C.
Dicks, R. Buttle, H.
Osborne, W. Dicks,
E. Willgrass and
others were present.
After some con-
siderable discussion
a club was formed
called the *Yare
Sailing Club*, for
the purpose of en-
couraging smaller

THE "KIAMA."

classes and amateur sailing. Mr B. V. Winch was elected
President, and Mr L. E. Bolingbroke Hon. Secretary. The
club faithfully carried out its intentions, and so well
has it prospered that it was in the Jubilee year of 1897
the largest sailing club in the world, having a membership
which numbered nearly 600.

In 1880 Mr Bolingbroke married, and having other more
important duties to attend to, he relinquished his office to the
Rev. G. P. Buck, who, after being secretary for several years,
was succeeded by Mr H. Kett, and in turn by Mr F. S. Culley,
the present secretary.

## COMMODORES OF THE CLUB

### SINCE ITS FORMATION IN 1876.

| DATE. | NAME. | YACHT. | RESIDENCE. |
|---|---|---|---|
| 1876-8 | B. V. Winch, Esq. | *Alarm* | Norwich |
| 1879 | J. Chamberlin, Esq. | *Para* | Catton |
| 1880-3 | B. V. Winch, Esq. | *Arrow* | Norwich |
| 1884 | G. Beauchamp, Esq. | *Lolypop* | Langley |
| 1885 | G. C. Davies, Esq. | *Swan* | Norwich |
| 1886 | E. Tillyard, Esq. | *Trixie* | Norwich |
| 1887-8 | J. J. Colman, Esq., M.P. | *Mars* | Norwich |
| 1889-91 | F. Bullard, Esq. | *Gitana* | Catton |
| 1892-3 | Col. H. E. Preston | *Phœnix* | Ryde |
| 1894-9 | E. J. Poyser, Esq. | *Ianthe* | Beccles |
| 1900 | H. C. Bolingbroke, Esq. | *Elf* | Norwich |
| 1901 | G. E. Preston, Esq. | *Empress of India* | Wroxham |
| 1902 | Col. P. E. Back | *Wild Duck* | Oulton Broad |

The subscription was only five shillings per annum and every amateur yachtsman eligible to become a member. The regattas held by this club at once became and still are the events of the season, so far as yachting in Broadland is concerned, and at the Acle August fixture it is usual to see yachts and boats of all rigs moored to the river bank on both sides, and as near to one another as they can conveniently get, for a mile and upwards, which shows the popularity of the club.

The burgee has a blue ground with a yellow cross.

In 1898 an innovation was introduced into the club, which necessitated a reorganisation of its rules and constitution. After much debate it was determined to have a large and adequately-fitted houseboat on board of which members could obtain meals, accommodation for the night, and any other convenience they might require. The boat was built by Messrs Collins of Wroxham, upon solid lines, for a registered syndicate of certain supporters of the club, who took shares at one pound each, and the boat was let to the club at a rental producing about five per cent to the share-holders. In consequence of this happy addition the sub-scription to the club was raised to ten shillings per annum, and the scheme proved itself a great success in every way.

During the eighties boat-builders became more prominent,

THE " RAMBLER."

and visitors, who came to spend the summer season at Lowestoft, Great Yarmouth, Cromer and Southwold, penetrated to the broads in considerable numbers. In con-sequence the demand for boats increased and a new industry, " boat-letting," was established in Broadland.

About this period (1880) Messrs Press Brothers of North Walsham conceived the idea of raising the hatches of a trading wherry and filling the vacancy with glass windows, partitioning off her hold into several cabins and upholstering the interior with some idea of comfort. This example was immediately followed by others, with additions and improvements. These pleasure wherries are now let by the week, including the services of two men, at prices varying from ten to twenty guineas per week.

The first wherry fitted permanently for pleasure cruising was built by Mr Fred Farr of Beccles, about 1840, but these craft did not come into general use, nor become popular, before 1880.

Before 1880 yachts were almost all private and very few of them could be hired by strangers, but with the sudden popularity of the broads the various yacht-letters collected small fleets, which, during the all-too-short season they let to their advantage.

The idea of the pleasure wherry suggested a new craft to the waterways, namely, barge-yachts. The first of these was the *Lotus*, built by Mr T. Branford of Great Yarmouth; she was followed by the *Helen* (Mr Burleigh of Halesworth) and the *Kiama* (Mr W. Cooper-Brown), now owned by Mr Vernon D. Wilcock and still one of the best afloat, and many, many

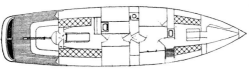

BELOW-DECK PLAN OF THE "RAMBLER."

others, including the *Rambler* of Oulton Broad (Messrs W. S. Parker and J. Colman); *Thyrza* (Mr A. Weldon); *Keenaghmore*, twenty-six tons (Sir R. Palmer, Bart.); *Ianthe*, twenty-four tons (Mr E. J. Poyser); *Waveney*, fifty-five tons (Mr J. T. Poyser) now Mr F. Dowson of Norwich; *Heron*, twenty tons (Mr C. G. T. Treherne); and the *Spider*, twenty-four tons (Mr J. R. R. Godfrey).

Amongst the early pleasure wherries, which were fitted with all the comforts and luxuries that any ordinary tourist to Broadland could reasonably require, may be included— the *Leisure Hour*, belonging to Mr G. Grimsell of Reedham;

the *Waveney Queen*, Mr Fred Miller of Oulton Broad; the *Dorothy*, Mr F. J. Lacey of Norwich; the *Claudian*, Mr G. Smith of Wroxham; the *Chloe*, Mr R. H. Dobson of London; the *Warrior*, Mr Hugh Johnson of Oulton Broad; the *Gladys*, Mr H. W. Newman of London; the *Industry*, Mr W. E. Holt of Great Yarmouth, and the *Woinora*, Mr J. Womersley of Norwich.

Amongst the more modern pleasure wherries and those which have been most magnificently fitted up, regardless of expense, may be mentioned the twenty-six-ton *Empress of India*, built for Mr G. E. Preston of Wroxham in 1896; the forty-ton *Gaviota*, belonging to Col. H. E. Preston of Ryde, and the thirty-ton *Victoria*, belonging to Mr W. G. Jones of Brixton.

A FRIEND IN NEED.
(The *Alda*)

S

WHERRIES RACING ON WROXHAM BROAD.

# CHAPTER XXI

### YACHTS AND YACHTING DURING THE PRESENT, 1880 TO 1900

IN 1882 several yachts of the small four-ton class were built on an entirely new model, namely, with greater depth of body, displacement and freeboard, yet at the same time with less beam. The *Dolly*, built by Messrs Hastings of Great Yarmouth for Mr Morgan, was an extreme type in this respect, but the *Trixie*, built by Mr Brighton of Southtown, Great Yarmouth, for Mr E. Tillyard, was a beautiful boat, and for several years carried all before her. She was about twenty-four feet six inches on the water-line, six feet six inch beam, with a draught of three feet nine inches. Another boat, the eleven-ton *Mocking Bird*, built for Mr Prescott Westcar, from designs by Mr Dixon Kemp, raced at the Isle of Wight with success but was an utter failure here ; she was rigged as a Una. In 1883 the *Constance*, another Una-rigged boat, proved a failure. In 1885 Mr

Brighton turned out the *Kingfisher* for Mr J. E. Crisp of Beccles, a fast and powerful boat of ten tons. She was longer, narrower, deeper-bodied and had more freeboard than the other yachts of her day; and considering the great turn of speed she showed when once given the chance to race, the pity is that she was so seldom allowed to face the starter.

In 1886 two new twelve-ton yachts put in an appearance—*Wanderer II.*, built by Mr Brighton for Mr J. Lee Barber,

THE "RETORT."

and the *Firebrand*, built by Messrs Page & Chambers of Lowestoft for Mr Fred Last. Both yachts had the new-fashioned fiddle bows designed for ocean racing and carried an enormous spread of canvas. No expense was spared on either boat, and competition for the local prizes was very keen; but the *Wanderer* soon proved her superiority not only in Broadland but also at race meetings held at sea under the auspices of the Royal Harwich Yacht Club.

In 1887 the *Retort* was launched from the yard of Messrs Page & Chambers with a view to lowering the laurels of

*Wanderer II.*, but her owner, Mr F. Last, was again disappointed. However, two years later, the pluck and determination of Mr Last was deservedly rewarded by the *Corona*.

About the year 1887 a small syndicate was privately formed for the purpose of building suitable club premises at Lowestoft. A site was acquired from the Great Eastern Railway Company overlooking the yacht basin and the south pier, on which a commodious bungalow club-house was erected, and the members of the club then numbered about 250.

In the early part of 1883 the inhabitants of that very much go-ahead little borough and seaside resort, Great Yarmouth, determined to have a Yacht Club of their own, and at the instigation of Mr H. Harvey George and Mr F. Danby Palmer a meeting was called at the Town Hall for the purpose of promoting it.

This meeting (Mr H. Harvey George in the chair) was held on the 16th day of March 1883, and almost every one of any importance in the town attended. The past revels of Burgh Water Frolic, before alluded to in these pages, were re-awakened, and amidst much enthusiasm the club was formed, the first committee including the following gentlemen :—Mr H. Blake, Mr H. R. Harmer, Mr F. Danby Palmer, Mr W. H. Stanley, Mr R. E. Dowson, Mr. J. Mack, Mr T. Morgan, Mr A. A. Steward, Mr W. S. Chamberlain, Mr. H. Bond, Mr T. M. Baker, Mr G. F. Crane, Mr J. P. Hall, Mr. J. Hall, Mr S. Lacon, Mr Oswald Diver, Mr C. Diver, Mr F. Burton, Mr W. Teasdael. Mr F. Carpenter, Mr W. Barnard Mr W. Brighton, Mr J. H. Bly, Mr Isaac Preston, Mr J. Mack, Mr F. Mack, Mr J. Hastings.

The first commodore of the club was Sir Edward Birkbeck, Bart., and the secretary, Mr H. Harvey George. The burgee is red and blue with semi-lion passant with fish's tail.

The first regatta was held on Breydon Water on the 14th June 1883. On the 14th September 1888, through the kind offices of Sir R. P. Beauchamp, Bart., a twenty-pound challenge cup was obtained—partially purchased by subscription amongst the members. It is sailed for over a twelve-mile course with a time allowance of fifteen seconds for every three inches or part of three inches, L. W. L.

In 1890 the honorary secretary, Mr H. Harvey George, after having fairly set the club upon its legs, resigned, and the club was again fortunate in securing the services of the present honorary secretary, who has done great things towards its success. Mr G. H. Lovewell Blake for a number of years had been a well-known figure on the waters of Broadland, and when he devoted his energies to the further promotion of the Great Yarmouth Yacht Club, that institution soon grew into an important factor in the annals of local yacht racing.

THE "SAYONARA."

In 1893 the subscription of the club was reduced from ten shillings and sixpence per annum to five shillings, which was a move in the right direction, as was proved by the large increase of members. In 1890 the members numbered seventy; at the time of writing there are 240 duly enrolled.

In the year 1897 a more ambitious venture was undertaken by one of the keenest and best amateur yachtsmen in the club, Mr Ralph G. Watling, the then rear commodore. He worked energetically, not only amongst the members of the club, but amongst all those interested in boat sailing in East Anglia. As a result of his efforts, cordially backed up by the officers of his club, amongst whom may well be mentioned

Mr E. P. Buckworth, the owner of the *Sayonara*, one of the smartest cruisers of her day, then commodore, a very handsome gold Jubilee Challenge Cup of the value of 100 guineas was purchased. It was won at the first race, held on 23rd August 1897, on Breydon Water by the *Vixen*. It was hoped that this cup might be the means of stimulating still further the interest in yacht-racing in Broadland and also cause strange boats to visit the waters in greater numbers than heretofore.

The club holds four permanent annual fixtures, and the list of commodores includes the following names:—

### COMMODORES OF THE CLUB

Since its Institution in 1883.

| Date. | Name. | Yacht. | Residence. |
|---|---|---|---|
| 1883-4 | Sir E. Birkbeck, Bart. | *Florence* | Horstead Hall |
| 1885 | W. Burdett-Coutts, Esq. | ...... | ...... |
| 1886 | Sir H. W. Tylor, M.P. | ...... | ...... |
| 1887 | F. Danby Palmer, Esq. | *Lady of the Bure* | Gt. Yarmouth |
| 1888 | Sir R. P. Beauchamp, Bart. | *Lolypop* | Langley Park |
| 1889-93 | F. Danby Palmer, Esq. | *Lady of the Bure* | Gt. Yarmouth |
| 1894 | N. R. Suffling, Esq. | ...... | Gt. Yarmouth |
| 1895 | W. E. Worship, Esq. | *Zoe* | Gt. Ormesby |
| 1896 | F. Danby Palmer, Esq. | *Lady of the Bure* | Gt. Yarmouth |
| 1897 | E. P. Buckworth, Esq. | *Sayonara* | Crostwick Old Hall |
| 1898 | R. P. Chamberlin, Esq. | *White Wings* | Gt. Yarmouth |
| 1899 | R. Watling, Esq. | *Checkmate* (*p.o.*) | Gt. Yarmouth |
| 1900 | G. H. Lovewell Blake, Esq. | *Daphne* | Gt. Yarmouth |
| 1901 | E. P. Buckworth, Esq. | *Sayonara* | Crostwick Old Hall |
| 1902 | R. F. Boileau, Esq. | ...... | Ketteringham Park |

The nineties were accountable for a great change in yachting circles. Until that period yachts had been almost invariably steered by professional watermen, who wrangled amongst themselves, and were accountable for numerous collisions, and charged the owner of the boat an absurdly high sum for steering her to victory ; in fact, it was not uncommon

" WANDERER II."

to receive a bill for the remuneration of the crew which far exceeded the amount of the first prize.

On account of this unsatisfactory state of affairs the yacht clubs brought in rules that in all club races the boats must be steered by amateurs or be liable to disqualification. Mr F. Green and Mr W. S. Everitt tried to introduce this rule in 1860 but without success, and had not racing become so expensive, by reason of the extortions of the professional crews, its introduction might have been postponed for several more years.

Again, it was not until 1890 that Broadlanders were beaten in their own waters by a strange boat (the *Mystery*), but her stay was of the shortest and not long enough to give local talent a fair chance.

Reverting again to racing (1880 to 1890), Mr Brighton, first of Bungay, then of Southtown, Great Yarmouth, was the foremost designer and boat-builder; for years he swept the decks without a recognised opponent. His best boats were the *Trixie* (Mr E. Tillyard), three tons; *Wanderer II.* (Mr J. Lee Barber), nine tons; *Lolypop* (Sir Reginald Beauchamp); *Kingfisher* (Mr J. E. Crisp) and the *Isabel* (Mr W. Smith), both about seven tons, although they were debarred from racing by their respective owners.

*Wanderer II.* was built by Brighton of Southtown, Great Yarmouth, for Mr J. Lee Barber. She was nine tons Thames measurement, constructed of yellow pine, which after cedar is the best wood for a racing yacht, and cost her owner nearly £100 per ton before she was completed. She was one of the last successful straight - keeled yachts which have been gradually displaced by the fin-keeled and cut-away-stem type; what she would have done had she been modernised it is difficult to conjecture, as she was always an extraordinarily fast boat. During her first season in Broadland she was placed first thirteen times out of fourteen starts, whilst at Lowestoft, Great Yarmouth, Harwich and other marine regattas, she also distinguished herself. For beauty in lines it was difficult to find her equal, and after an ever-victorious racing career she entered the cruising class.

In 1899 she was sold, and has left for the waters of the Onwell.

In 1889 he (Brighton) designed the *Greyhound* for Mr J. P. Hall, which was certainly one of the most successful of all his successful boats.

Other boats of the time worthy of note were the *Gypsy*, owned and built by Mr T. Morgan; and the *Falcon*, built by Mr J. Hastings, and owned by Mr N. Suffling, of Great Yarmouth; the *Ada* (Mr A. Watling); *Terrier* (Mr H. Osborne); *Mosquito* (Mr H. Reynolds); *Imp* (Mr T. Morgan, afterwards Dr A. Marshall); *Flash* (Mr R. G. Bateley); *Castanet* (Mr R. J. Colman); *Silver Star* (Mr C. W. Barton); *Prairie Flower* (Mr W. G. Everitt); and the *Odd Trick* (Mr E. Morse).

The nineties saw the decline of the large cutters, and so unpopular did the river fixtures of the Norfolk and Suffolk Yacht Club become, as compared with those of the Yare Sailing Club, that it was difficult to get sufficient entries to make a race at all. Few new boats were built, and had it not been for the energy of Messrs F. & C. Last, who seemed determined to have a yacht capable of beating the *Wanderer II.*, the classes of the club would have had to be

"CASTANET."

altered. The two gentlemen named built several nine-ton craft, which always came in second, until the *Corona* (called by yokels, *Crowner—Anglicè, Coroner*), built for them by Mr C. Peed of Oulton Broad, and altered by Messrs Page & Chambers of Lowestoft, *at last* turned the tables.

About 1890 the racing machine, *Gossip*, was designed and built by Mr George Mollett of Brundall. She was as quaint a looking craft as one could well meet with and looked like a raft raised upon two pontoons. She was a double-hulled boat drawing less than a foot of water, and her middle was hollowed out so that when she rested upon an even keel an undivided waterline extended all round her. In sailing she ran over the water rather than cut through it, and as she carried 450 feet of sail area it is no wonder she left everything else behind. She was very simply rigged with a large lug-foresail and a small mizzen, whilst her stability was assisted by a sliding centre-plate of three feet to four feet exposed area. Her rough measurements were L.W.L., seventeen feet; beam, seven feet; depth, two feet.

After winning her first race at Oulton Broad on a Whit Monday, she was offered for sale for thirty pounds but purchasers were shy as they did not altogether appreciate her appearance and preferred a safer ship to sail in. She was however sold a few days afterwards, and her new owner, during her first racing season, won prizes equal in value to more than double the purchase money.

This boat was the forerunner of a class of racing machines which exercised full sway upon the waters of Broadland for the next seven years. These boats have no comfort even for sailing, much less for cruising; everything is sacrificed for speed.

The *Castanet*, a bluff-bowed, spoon-shaped vessel, with a broad stern and small keel was Mr Mollett's next success (1892), but her owner (Mr Russell J. Colman) was unable to hold the Challenge Cup at his pleasure more than one season, for in 1893 the *Challenge* (Mr W. Stewart) showed herself a much faster boat.

The *Castanet* was built by George Mollett of Brundall for Mr R. J. Colman, and was at the time the most advanced type of racing boat of her class. During her first season she started fourteen times, securing twelve prizes, eight firsts and four seconds; in her second season she won eleven prizes out of fourteen starts. As a cruiser is not only comfortable, but exceedingly handy, a great consideration in the narrow waterways. Her chief competitors included the *Greyhound, Ada, Gossip, Silver Star, Ino* and *Challenge*.

Another fast boat was the *Bubble* (Mr W. Stewart), but she was soon sold to go abroad (Russia), and raced but very little.

*Talisman I.* was designed by Mr Walter Stewart (who was also responsible for the *Odd Trick, Bubble, Challenge, Sticklebat,* and many other boats) for Mr R. Lee Barber, who built her himself in 1894 for the modest initial outlay of about £30. She was the first seen in Broadland of the flat-bottomed unballasted type, and won for her lucky owner, the first year she was launched, between £70 and £80 in money prizes, besides numerous cups and specials. In length she was twenty-five feet over all, her beam was seven feet, and she drew only three inches of water, except when her seven-foot dagger plate was lowered. For racing, she was what is termed "a hard weather boat," going well only when a stiff breeze was blowing; a haystack could sail past her in light weather. Among other good points she was never known to capsize, although many times was she waterlogged. In 1895 her sporting owner sent her over to the Riviera, where she won several races against well-known boats, but the sea was found to be too choppy for her when there was any quantity of wind. Whilst here, she proved how excellently safe she was, as on one occasion her crew started from Nice with a light wind aft which gradually increased in violence until all sails had to be taken in, and the frail boat was driven helplessly before the wind many miles out to sea. To bring her to the wind, or to attempt to make the land was impossible, whilst her luckless occupants were kept fully occupied baling out the water with a pail and handcup. This from a boat, the total depth of which from deck to keel was only fourteen inches was no easy task, and as fast as the water was ejected more found its way in. Eventually Bandol, near Toulon, and nearly seventy miles from Nice, was reached after a most exciting time. In 1897 the *Talisman I.* was sold to a Russian who took her away to the Danube.

*Talisman II.* was also designed by Mr W. Stewart, and built by Smith of Oxford for Mr R. Lee Barber upon lines

"TALISMAN I."

somewhat similar to those of her predecessor. She was another very successful boat when there was a good, stiff, racing breeze, but practically useless during calm weather. In 1900 she was sold to Mr T. H. Thomas of Lynn, who continued to race her and won many prizes.

The *Zingara*, built by Mr George Mollett for Mr Fred Bullard, won several prizes in 1894, as did the *Silver Star* (Mr C. W. Barton, afterwards Mr G. M. Chamberlin), but in 1895 the *Bream* (Mr J. W. Waters) appeared. This boat was another machine. She was built privately at Acle and held

" TALISMAN II."

the Yare Challenge Cup until 1897, when two new boats built by Mr Linton Hope of the Thames alternately beat everything, namely, the *Checkmate* (Messrs Watling, Sikes

& Mayall) for the first part of the season and the *Dream* (Mr A. S. Cope) for the latter part.

Prior to the appearance of the last boats named, Messrs G. M. Chamberlin and Russell J. Colman bought the *Bodagh*, which was a very pretty and fast boat; besides, she had the recommendation of being more in the nature of a yacht, but her reign lasted only until the advent of the *Checkmate*.

Another great success was the *Vixen*, designed by her owner, Mr F. H. Chambers, and built by Messrs Press Bros. of Wroxham. She won more prizes than any other boat of her class; but she changed hands several times, being bought by that excellent all-round sportsman, Mr G. M. Chamberlin, afterwards by Mr E. J. Theobald, subsequently by the Rev H. Rogers.

During the nineties dinghys received official recognition and prizes were offered for them. This was soon followed by a rule to define what was to be considered a dinghy.

As soon as this class was formed it became very popular and many enthusiasts built new boats every year.

The best boats in this class were built by Mr George Mollett of Brundall and Mr R. Collins of Wroxham. Amongst the dinghys which have been prominent at times may be mentioned the *Gladys* and the *Britannia* (Mr E. J. Theobald); the *White Seal* (Messrs E. M. & F. Corbett); *Wave* (Mr E. Hicks); *Silver Star* (Mr G. M. Chamberlin); *Mitzie* (Mr F. R. R. Godfrey); *Six and Eight* and *Pick-me-Up* (Mr H. R. Everitt, *the author of this book*); *Jack and Jill* (Dr E. Hewer); *Topsy* (Mr G. Humphrey); the *Romp* and the *Venture* (Rev. H. Rogers); whilst the *Mayfly* (Mr C. F. Howell) proved herself to be by far the fastest of all for two seasons. In 1898 the *Bonnie*, designed by Mr F. H. Chambers, owned by Mr G. M. Chamberlin, and built by H. Press of Wroxham, was champion, winning sixteen first prizes, three seconds and one third out of twenty-one races, besides three special cups; she was a new type of boat, although within the rule, and entirely revolutionised the class. In 1899 several machine dinghys were designed by Mr F. H. Chambers, following the lines of the *Bonnie*, and built by

THE "SILVER STAR."

THE "BONNIE"

THE DINGHY "CASTANET."

THE "VIXEN"

Messrs H. Little & Co., Ltd., of Brundall. They include the *Gipsy* (Captain T. Sergeant) ; *Castanet* (Mr R. J. Colman); and the *Waif* (Messrs E. Hewer, M. Brooks and R. May).

In 1894 the enthusiastic dinghy owners were not satisfied with their lot; they wanted more notice from the yachting world, more races and more boats in their class. So they agitated amongst themselves, and in 1895, at the instigation of Mr E. Hicks and Mr H. Mower, both of Norwich, a meeting was called, and fixed for the 23rd of April, at the Bell Hotel, Norwich, to discuss the situation. Not a large gathering appeared, but it was resolved to form a club for their own special class, which was entitled " The Broads Dinghy Club," its objects being to encourage the building and sailing of small and inexpensive boats, and so to endeavour to bring the class more prominently before the various yachting and sailing clubs.

The subscription was two shillings and sixpence per annum, and the burgee a five-pointed blue star on a white ground. Seven fixtures, dating from April to September, and over every variety of course, were also appointed. At these races points were awarded in accordance with the number of starters, and at the end of the season the prizes were awarded in accordance with the total number of points gained.

The only officer of the club acted in a dual capacity as honorary secretary and treasurer combined. Mr E. Hicks originally held this post, but in 1896 he resigned in favour of Mr H. S. Page.

The length of course sailed in dinghy races is about six miles.

In 1895 the inhabitants of Oulton Broad, or, as it is locally called, " Little England," bestirred themselves for the purpose of establishing a sailing club of their own. As Oulton Broad is one of the largest yachting centres their efforts were successful, and the club now numbers about 200 members. The burgee has a white ground with a blue cross and a red square in its centre.

The object of the club, which is named the Waveney Sailing Club, is to encourage the improvement and sailing of small yachts and boats, but it does not require much insight to get at the reason of its establishment. The Norfolk and Suffolk Club is an exclusive and an expensive club to belong to; besides, it encourages large yachts and is only open to amateurs; the Yare Sailing Club encourages smaller craft, but is only open to amateurs; the Great Yarmouth Club is local and only open to amateurs; but the Waveney Club is open to all, and the professional yachtsman or water-

THE "CHECKMATE."

man can own his half-rater, twenty-five footer, or dinghy, which most probably he has built himself during the long winter evenings, and he is not debarred from entering his boat and racing it. This is the only club offering prizes to professional watermen, and considering the large number of them there are, the club would seem to supply a want that was felt.

At all events, several of the watermen living at Oulton Broad have been induced to save money and possess themselves of a boat for racing purposes, and as the majority of the club's regattas are held on a Saturday afternoon, which is usually a half day with working men, much enjoyment is

T

afforded to them which they would otherwise have to go without. The fixtures of the club are very well attended and the prizes offered compare favourably with other clubs, whilst the roll of membership goes on increasing yearly—at the time of writing it numbers over 200.

The *Unit* is a sixteen-foot half-decked open boat, and belongs to a class especially made by the Waveney Sailing Club. Perhaps this boat redounds more credit to her designer, builder and owner, than any other craft that has ever floated upon Broadland waters. This is not said unadvisedly, as Mr W. S. Parker of Oulton Broad, her owner, is a working man, who for many years was employed upon one of the G. E. R. Company's dredgers in Lowestoft harbour, to which employment he was tied from six in the morning to six at night, yet when the Waveney Sailing Club was inaugurated in 1896, and this particular class was defined, he at once designed the *Unit*, and built her entirely himself during his spare hours, which must have been few, as Mr Parker is a Sabbatarian. The only parts of the boat that were not moulded and fashioned with

THE "UNIT."

his own hands were the iron centre-plate, ropes and necessary ironwork. In her first season she started forty-three times, securing thirty-three firsts, eight seconds and two thirds, forty-three prizes in all (besides specials and challenge cups) out of forty-eight entries. Every year since her sporting owner has entered her in every race possible, and at the time of writing she is still "Cock of the Walk" at Oulton Broad.

The rules of the various clubs it is not necessary to go into, but it may be interesting to give the different classes as they are divided.

## THE ROYAL NORFOLK AND SUFFOLK YACHT CLUB.

### CLASS I.

Yachts exceeding thirty feet linear rating.

### CLASS II.

Yachts over twenty-four feet and not exceeding thirty feet linear rating.

### CLASS III.

Yachts not exceeding twenty-four feet linear rating.

### CLASS IV.

Dinghys as defined in the Yare Sailing Club Rules.

### CRUISERS.

Sailing under Handicap Regulations.

## THE YARE SAILING CLUB.

### CLASS I.

Boats exceeding twenty-four feet and not exceeding thirty feet linear rating, which shall have fixed cabin top and bulkheads, the cabin top to be not less than five feet long and four inches above the deck.

### CLASS II.

Boats exceeding eighteen feet but not exceeding twenty-four feet linear rating.

### CLASS III.

Boats not exceeding eighteen feet linear rating but restricted to twenty-one feet length over all with $\frac{1}{4}$-inch finished planking.

### CLASS IV.

#### DINGHYS.

Boats to be open boats not exceeding fourteen feet in length over all, clench built, 140 feet of canvas to cover whole of sail area, no outside ballast, inside ballast not to exceed three hundredweight, centre plate (exposed) not to exceed four square feet and eighty pounds' weight, and to be of a uniform thickness throughout. Rudder to be ordinary wood rudder to unship. *Outside fixed keel and deadwood together not to exceed three inches in depth, and the gar-*

CLEARING THE COURSE

DINGHIES STARTING.

THE ACLE TO WROXHAM RACE, SHOWING FORTY-THREE STARTERS TO ONE GUN.

"MEMSAHIB."

"PLAYMATE." "CHECKMATE." "DREAM."

"CHALLENGE."    "STICKLEBAT."                    "ZINGARA."

*Club House-Boat.*        *Falcon.*        *Thelma.*        *Sayonara.*

CRUISERS STARTING.

"LADYE."                    "WHITE WINGS."    "BUGLER."

*board strake to show inside the boat.* Draught, exclusive of centre keels, not to exceed fifteen inches with crew and ballast on board. Crew not to exceed two persons.

### A Handicap Class.

#### CRUISERS.

A cruiser shall be defined as follows :—" A yacht or boat that has not sailed in any recognised club race (except handicaps) for at least six months previously to the race for which she has entered as a cruiser." Cruising " yachts" shall have a substantial fixed cabin top and two bulkheads and at least three feet six inches headroom from any part of the platform of the cabin.

## THE GREAT YARMOUTH SAILING CLUB.

### Class I.

Boats exceeding twenty-four feet and not exceeding thirty feet linear rating, and having fixed cabin tops and bulkheads, the cabin top to be not less than five feet long.

### Class II.

Boats above eighteen feet but not exceeding twenty-four feet linear rating.

### Class III.

Boats not exceeding eighteen feet linear rating.

*Cruisers and Dinghys.*

## THE WAVENEY SAILING CLUB.

### Class I.

Boats not exceeding twenty-four feet linear rating.

### Class II.

Boats not exceeding twenty-five feet in length on L.W.L. and beam added. If with overhang one third of same be added for the purpose of computing time allowance.

### Class III.

Open and partly-decked boats not exceeding sixteen feet over all.

RACING ON BREYDON WATER.

"MEMSAHIB."          "CHECKMATE."

"BODAGH."          "VIXEN."

## CLASS IV.

*Bona-fide* cruisers of any rig or tonnage, having fixed cabin top and bulkhead.

## CLASS V.

Dinghys.

## THE BROADS DINGHY CLUB.

For dinghys only as defined in Class IV. of the Yare Sailing Club.

The formula used generally by all the clubs for determining rating is as follows:—

$$R = \frac{L + B + \cdot 75\,G + \cdot 5 \sqrt{S.A.}}{2}$$

In this formula L = length on L.W.L. as now measured. B = greatest beam wherever found. G = underwater girth of the vessel from L.W.L. to L.W.L., taken at ·6 of the loadwater line from its fore end and measured along the actual outline of the vertical cross-section at that station. If the draught forward exceeds the draught at that station, twice such excess be added to G. In the case of centreboard double the extreme depth of the board (when dropped to its full extent below the keel) to be added to G. In taking these measurements all hollows in the fore and aft underwater profile of the vessel to be treated as filled up straight. Bulb or ballasted boards to be measured in the same way as fixed or fin keels. S.A. = sail area as now measured.

## NORFOLK AND SUFFOLK YACHT AND SAILING CLUBS ASSOCIATION.

### FEES FOR MEASURING.

For Yachts not exceeding 24 feet linear rating ... ... £0 10 0
   ,,       ,,    30  ,,    ,,    ... ...    15 0
   ,,  above ,,    30  ,,    ,,    ... ...  1  0 0

In former years water frolics, or, as they are now called, regattas, were comparatively few and far between, but nowadays there are fixtures falling for every week from May to September, and hundreds of pounds are annually offered for competition. But the great event of the year, so far as Broadland yachting it concerned, is what is known as the Wroxham Week. It is usually fixed about the end of July and the early part of August, and means nearly a fortnight's racing. The yachts from the Yare, Wensum and Waveney make for Great Yarmouth and meet at the yachting station on the Saturday, all sailing up on the flood tide to Acle on the Sunday. Monday and Tuesday are fixed for Acle Regatta; Wednesday for the river race from Acle to Wroxham, in which forty to sixty starters cross the line; Thursday and Friday, Wroxham Regatta; Saturday, Wroxham Bridge Regatta; on Sunday the yachts make Coltishall, and on Monday a regatta is held there.

Wroxham being one of the oldest (if not the oldest) fixtures on record, a few words may not be out of place concerning it. That it existed so far back as a hundred years there is ample testimony, whilst it is also well-known that in the fifties Mr Green of Wroxham was one of its most ardent supporters, and each year he entertained largely upon his house-boat. From 1859 to 1879 the Norfolk and Suffolk Yacht Club took up the leading reins, but in consequence of the gradual increase in the size of the boats and the difficulties of access the club retired in favour of a general committee, styling itself the Wroxham Broad Regatta Committee. This committee threw considerable spirit into their work, and with such energetic men as Mr E. T. Ayers (Great Yarmouth) and J. B. Pearce (Norwich) at the head of affairs, its success was assured. Funds were hunted up, fresh blood infused into the management, two days' racing were substituted for one, novelties and innovations yearly introduced, all of which assisted the sport and added to the enjoyment of everyone who attended the fixture, and it has now been worked up to such a pitch that it can compete favourably with other inland regattas held anywhere in our tight little Island.

Pleasure launches have been few and far between in Broadland until quite recently. The *Alda*, owned by Mr J. J. Dawson Paul of Norwich, was in fact the only one really worthy of the name of pleasure launch, and she for many years has been the queen of the small fleet of her class. In the cities and towns mechanics or engineers have perchance fitted up boats of ancient build with engines equally as out-dated as the craft, in which they have navigated the rivers and waterways. Occasionally a steam tender to some large, sea-going

THE " FROLIC."

yacht visiting Lowestoft or Great Yarmouth has penetrated the Broads on a flying visit, but, taken on the whole, launches did not in the past find favour in the eyes of Broadlanders.

The motor craze, however, has now found its way even to these peaceful and secluded haunts, and launches of all shape, size, build and method of propulsion are to be daily met with. The most beautifully fitted and graceful of them all is the *Frolic*, purchased from the Thames in 1900 by Mr J. J. Dawson Paul, but as this class of craft pertains more to reaching or viewing sport than to assisting it, further comment becomes unnecessary.

The following is a return of the more important annual fixtures, with their approximate dates :—

| Date. | | Name of Club. | Place of Meeting. |
|---|---|---|---|
| April | 29 | Broads Dinghy Club | Brundall |
| May | 13 | Broads Dinghy Club | Acle |
| ,, | 15 | Norfolk and Suffolk Yacht Club | Race to Harwich (Marine) |
| ,, | 20 | Yare Sailing Club | Breydon |
| ,, | 25 | Great Yarmouth Yacht Club | Cantley |
| June | 3 | Yare Sailing Club | Cantley |
| ,, | 7 | Oulton Regatta Committee | Oulton Broad |
| ,, | 8 | Waveney Sailing Club | Oulton Broad |
| ,, | 10 | Great Yarmouth Yacht Club | Breydon |
| ,, | 17 | Norfolk and Suffolk Yacht Club | Cantley |
| ,, | 18 | Norfolk and Suffolk Yacht Club | Cantley |
| ,, | 24 | Broads Dinghy Club | Cantley |
| July | 1 | Yare Sailing Club | Cantley |
| ,, | 5 | Norfolk and Suffolk Yacht Club | Yarmouth to Reedham and back |
| ,, | 8 | Broads Dinghy Club | Oulton Broad |
| ,, | 12 | Beccles Town Regatta | Beccles |
| ,, | 13 | Waveney Sailing Club | Beccles |
| ,, | 15 | Yare Sailing Club | Oulton Broad |
| ,, | 16 | Great Yarmouth Yacht Club | Oulton Broad |
| ,, | 22 | Norfolk and Suffolk Yacht Club | Lowestoft (Marine) |
| ,, | 26 | Acle Regatta Committee | Acle |
| ,, | 27 | Yare Sailing Club | Acle |
| ,, | 28 | Yare Sailing Club | Acle to Wroxham |
| ,, | 29 | Wroxham Regatta Committee | Wroxham Broad |
| ,, | 30 | Wroxham Regatta Committee | Wroxham Broad |
| ,, | 31 | Wroxham Bridge Regatta | Wroxham |
| Aug. | 2 | Coltishall Regatta Committee | Coltishall |
| ,, | 5 | Broads Dinghy Club | Wroxham |
| ,, | 7 | Waveney Sailing Club | Oulton Broad |
| ,, | 11 | Horning Regatta Committee | Horning |
| ,, | 12 | Broads Dinghy Club | Acle |
| ,, | 18 | Norfolk and Suffolk Yacht Club | Lowestoft (Marine) |
| ,, | 19 | Lowestoft Town Regatta | Lowestoft (Marine) |
| ,, | 20 | Norfolk and Suffolk Yacht Club | Lowestoft (Marine) |
| ,, | 23 | Barton Regatta Committee | Barton Broad |
| ,, | 26 | Norfolk and Suffolk Yacht Club | Oulton Broad |
| ,, | 27 | Norfolk and Suffolk Yacht Club | Oulton Broad |
| ,, | 28 | Waveney Sailing Club | Oulton to Somerleyton and back |
| ,, | 31 | Potter Heigham Regatta Committee | Potter Heigham |
| Sept. | 2 | Yare Sailing Club | Cantley |
| ,, | 7 | Great Yarmouth Yacht Club | Breydon |
| ,, | 9 | Broads Dinghey Club | Cantley |
| ,, | 16 | Waveney Sailing Club | Oulton Broad |

The before-mentioned are all recognised fixtures and largely attended by those interested in boat sailing, whilst the marine regattas which annually take place at every watering-place on the coast-line have not been included. For example, Harwich, Felixstowe, Southwold, Kessingland, Lowestoft, Gorleston, Great Yarmouth, Caistor, Cromer, Sherringham, Wells and King's Lynn, etc.

THE "WINDFLOWER."

One of the finest sea-going yachts sailing from the port of Lowestoft is the *Windflower* owned by Mr Vernon D. Wilcock; she is about sixty tons register.

Inland on the rivers and broads are numerous local fixtures organised for the purpose of boat sailing and matches, but these minor events have been omitted from the above list as they mostly originate and are organised by mine host of the river-side angling resort or pleasure gardens, and are more particularly for the benefit of himself and his brewers; as examples may be named, Hickling, Horn-

THE CRUISER "WHITE WINGS."

ing Ferry, Stokesby, Martham, Burgh Flats, St Olaves, Reedham, Buckenham, Brundall, Surlingham, Bramerton and Burgh St Peter, etc., yet it must not be overlooked that a great amount of sport is shown.

The introduction of the racing machine to Broadland Waters has been regretted by many, if not by all the most prominent racing men, as in this class everything is sacrificed to speed. The beautiful lines of a racing yacht are enchanged for a wooden dish, and the stability of old is supplanted by a skin about as thick as an ordinary cigar box, which bends about like a basket and cannot be expected to last more than a couple of seasons.

Were it not for the cruisers which sail under handicap regulations we should not, at the present day, have a real yacht at all to look upon at Broadland regattas. The cruiser class is made up of the racers of ten, twenty and thirty years ago, together with a modern type of boat which certain builders are turning out for the express purpose of competing in the class.

FROM THE ONE DESIGN CLASS.

The most prominent boats between 1895 and 1901 were the following: *White Wings*, cutter, eleven tons (Mr R. P. Chamberlin); *Barbara*, sloop, six tons (Mr H. Champion); *Io*, cutter, ten tons (Mr F. Clifton); *Castanet*, cutter, three tons or 25.4 rating (Mr R. J. Colman); *Sayonara*, cutter, five tons (Mr E. P. Buckworth); *Phantom*, cutter, seven tons (Mr. H. M. Cadge); *Bodagh*, lug, 24·3 rating (Mr G. M. Chamberlin, now Mr Lawrence Mills); *Magpie*, lug, two tons (Mr W. P. Barratt); *Ada*, cutter, four tons (Rev. B. G. Barnard-Smith); *Playmate*, cutter, six tons or 29·4 rating (Mr. H. P. Crowe): *Ladye*, sloop, four tons (Mr E. C. Hawkins); *Doreen*, cutter, twenty tons or 38·6 rating (Messrs F. Last and C. H. Last);

*Ino,* sloop (Mr T. N. K. Roberts); *Spindrift,* cutter, eight tons (Mr F. S. Rogers); *Thelma,* cutter, four tons (Mr T. Sergeant), and many others.

With the new century Broadland yachtsmen became advocates of the one design class. Each club brought forward different designs, and although many meetings were held nothing definite could be agreed upon, until a small clique of energetic and enthusiastic sportsmen took the lead by ordering seven boats from a Thames boatbuilder to be built from the same moulds, and costing complete £100 each. Throughout the season they raced at every regatta and many times privately, whilst all the clubs recognised them, although it cannot be recorded that the design of the boats was generally approved either by the clubs or by their individual members. Without doubt they are pretty little boats and wonderfully handy for sailing, but on the other hand it is thought they are open to improvement.

1898 was a great year in the annals of the Norfolk and Suffolk Yacht Club. Since 1867 the members had agitated for an Admiralty Warrant, but unsuccessfully, and hope had been deferred so long that the hearts of most had grown sick and weary. Fortunately for the club its roll of members included the name of the most energetic member of Parliament. the Lowestoft division had ever known, Mr H. S. Foster, M.P. No sooner did he ascertain the goal of their ambitions than the matter was as good as settled. He agitated in all quarters, untied the red tape of the Circumlocution Office, stirred up the sleepy officials, and, strengthened by the strong support of the Patron of the Club, H.R.H. The Prince of Wales, the objections of the Admiralty were overcome and the long-waited-for distinction at last conferred.

THE OLD
CLUB-HOUSE

Geo.J.Skipper,F.R.I.B.A.
& F.W.Skipper
ARCHITECTS,
NORWICH.

NEW CLUB-HOUSE OF THE ROYAL NORFOLK AND SUFFOLK YACHT CLUB.

## COPY OF ADMIRALTY WARRANT.

*By the* Commissioners *for executing the Office of* Lord High
  Admiral *of the United Kingdom of Great Britain and
  Ireland, &c.*

Whereas we deem it expedient that the Members of the Norfolk
and Suffolk Yacht Club, being natural born or naturalised British
Subjects, should be permitted to wear on board their respective
vessels the Red Ensign of Her Majesty's Fleet, with the distinctive
marks of the Club on the fly thereof, viz. : a Crown with the Prince
of Wales' Plume underneath, on the following conditions :—

We do therefore by virtue of the power and authority vested in
us, under the provisions of the 73rd Section of the Merchant
Shipping Act, 1894, hereby Warrant and authorise the Red
Ensign of the Her Majesty's Fleet, with the distinctive marks of the
Norfolk and Suffolk Yacht Club, to be worn on board the respective vessels belonging to the Norfolk and Suffolk Yacht Club
and to Members of such Yacht Club, being natural born or naturalised British Subjects, accordingly, subject to the following conditions :—

1. Every vessel belonging to the Norfolk and Suffolk Yacht
   Club, in order to be eligible to wear the Ensign authorised by this Warrant, shall have been registered as a
   British Vessel in accordance with the Merchant Shipping Act, 1894.

2. The Ensign shall not, without our authority in writing, be
   worn on board any vessel belonging to the Norfolk and
   Suffolk Yacht Club while such vessel is lent, on hire or
   otherwise, to any person not being a Member of the
   Club, or who, being a Member of the Club, is not a
   natural born or naturalised British Subject.

Given under Our Hands and the Seal of the Office of Admiralty
  this Ninth Day of March, 1898.

(Signed)  FRED. G. W. BEDFORD.
  ,,    A. W. MOORE.

By command of their Lordships.
  (Signed)  EVAN MACGREGOR.

On 2nd June the ceremony of hoisting the new colours took place at noon in unpropitious weather, a salute was fired, and all the yachts, and many of the vessels in the harbour, were decked in bunting from stem to stern in honour of the occasion. Had it not been for the excessive enthusiasm, zeal and energy of Mr H. S. Foster, M.P., Mr T. M. Read, the popular commodore, and Mr A. T. Clarkson, the secretary, it is exceedingly doubtful whether the honour would ever have been granted. In the evening a celebration dinner was held at the Royal Hotel, at which the following were present:—

The commodore (Mr T. M. Read) in the chair, the vice-commodore (Rev. H. Rogers) in the vice-chair, the rear-commodore (Mr T. Sergeant), the Earl of Stradbroke, Sir Cuthbert Quilter, Bart., M.P. (vice-commodore of the Royal Harwich Yacht Club), Mr H. S. Foster, M.P., Sir Harry Bullard, M.P., Mr T. H. Tacon, High Sheriff of Suffolk, the Mayor of Beccles, the Inspector-Commander H.M. *Coastguard*, Rev. Canon Lawrence, Rev. B. G. Barnard-Smith, Rev. G. Champion, Sir Charles R. Gilman, Captain F. Barton, Captain Henderson, Dr A. Marshall, Dr Wynne, Colonel T. Wilson, Colonel T. Mayhew and Messrs L. T. Cobbold (Ipswich), A. F. Mayhew C. F. Davey, J. W. Reynolds, T. H. Woods, W. S. Brockley, J. Watson, H. M. Cadge, Gordon Barratt, C. A. Gauntlett, S. A. Allingham, L. T. Clarkson, C. F. Hughes-Hallett, G. J. Grimsdick, F. Bullard, W. E. Holt, W. G. Everitt, C. P. Hart, A. G. Notley, Edward Elliot, L. F. Orde, R. Lee-Barber, H. K. Whiting, B. Preston, W. S. Everitt, W. H. Mann, Gilbert Morse, S. L. Barrett, E. P. Buckworth, A. W. Fenton, C. B. Foster, J. L. Peto, H. R. Everitt, G. M. Chamberlin, A. Savill, C. S. Gilman, R. C. and F. G. Mayhew, A. E. Costerton, Francis D. Longe, Edgar Morse, F. W. Jex Blake, T. P. Angell, E. F. and E. H. Barlow, G. E. Preston, M. B. Byles, F. G. Cotman, G. Sillen, W. Warman, W. W. Cook, etc. It is interesting to note that the company at the hoisting ceremony included three of the founders of the Club, viz., Messrs T.

M. Read (the present commodore), Henry Morgan and W. S. Everitt.

As a natural sequence to this high honour the members grew dissatisfied with their club-house at Lowestoft, and a new scheme was at once put on foot for the promotion of a more commodious and substantial building capable of affording better accommodation, greater comforts, and which would be worthy of a Royal Club.

LOWESTOFT YACHT BASIN AND PIER ON REGATTA DAY.

WINTRY SNAP-SHOTS.

# CHAPTER XXII

## UNDER THE LEE OF THE NORFOLK SANDHILLS

ONE autumn the author was the fortunate recipient of a pressing invitation to stay a week-end with a hospitable divine whose living was situated on the bleak level of marshland, bounded by dunes and sandhills on one side and the meres and lagoons of Broadland on the other. The invite was worded in a manner that could not be refused, and on the appointed day the Great Eastern Railway Company conveyed our few belongings to a small wayside station, leaving a dozen miles or more to be negotiated before the welcome walls of the rectory would come in sight.

Outside the low-roofed shanty, which formed a station of great importance in the eyes of Norfolk yokels, sat our host in a small pony-cart, his genial face beaming with delight on our appearance. The weather was bitterly cold, and after the usual greetings we were glad to settle well down into a big fur-lined coat and suck the pipe of contentment in silence.

At first the road was sheltered by tall trees, and it wound in and out between narrow lanes with high hedgerows and good banks; but by degrees the country became more open, the trees less frequent, and the houses on the wayside fewer, and separated at greater distances. Then we noticed that we had left the upland behind us and had entered a region as flat as the Netherlands. On either hand a broad dyke yawned to receive us should the mare shy as some evil-disposed quadrupeds of this class are often wont to do.

Broken clouds had been chasing each other all day across the sky, and, as soon as the sun had set, rain, sleet and hail alternated. The wind had gradually increased, and was blowing almost a hurricane, north-east by east, full in our faces. When we left the uplands and emerged on to the road over the bleak, unsheltered marsh, we felt its full force and keenness, whilst far away to the eastward, where we knew were located the sandhills which kept the sea from the marshland, lightning flashed at irregular intervals.

The moon did not rise until late, and what few stars managed to struggle through the angry-looking clouds overhead only seemed to intensify the darkness of the fast-gathering night. That drive was an experience. Conversation was too laborious to be pleasant, whilst the sleet and hail cut the face and seemed to chill the very marrow in our bones. Every now and again the dim outline of some gaunt old watermill would suddenly spring up in the path and tower above us, the wind howling and shrieking round its shutters in a manner tending to arouse one's superstitions and to remind one of the erratic ramblings and heroic deeds of Don Quixote de la Mancha.

If the windmills passed reminded us of this insane hero of ancient times our steed did so the more. Like the trusty Rozinante the mare was slow beyond comparison, and stumbled frequently in the deep ruts now full to overflow-ing with slush from recent rain or an uprising tide. The intense darkness added to the difficulties of progression, and an occasional gleam of some reflected light in the waters of broad, soft-bottomed dykes on either side gave warning of what we might expect should the animal take a false turn or play tricks, and, to make matters worse, both the gig-lamps had been extinguished by the boisterous wind. But it is a long lane which has no turning, and at last, when the cold had begun to penetrate our furs, when our toes seemed frost-bitten and we had almost lost hope of getting to our destination that night, we rounded a clump of willows, passed another mill, saw the cheerful lights of two or three cottages, and ten minutes later were warming our toes at the blazing logs of the rectory fire.

Here we found a substitute for the peerless Princess Dulcinea del Toboso in the bright, rosy-cheeked little daughter of our host, a child of seven or eight summers, sweetly attractive in her rural simplicity. She, in company with her brother, an interesting youth of about the same age, danced round us in delight at the prospect of a visitor to that out-of-the-way region, whilst we lost no time in winning their joint affections by producing a large parcel of sweets, which were promptly transferred to a disused tobacco tin (their comfit box), and which were discussed by them for the rest of the evening with huge delight. Our host, all aglow with hospitality, busied himself with the bringing in of the traps and sporting paraphernalia.

In the midst of these responsibilities he suddenly burst in upon us with an anxious inquiry : "How about the bait I told you to bring along ? I can't find it anywhere."

This forgetfulness was most annoying, and we cannot help using strong language. "*Cayó sel rayo!* we have left it behind us."

Thoughtfully he stroked his chin. Inquiringly he looked at us. We could do nothing but look at him. "Well, what is to be done?" he said.

"*Quien sabe*, unless we use artificial," was the reply.

"I must consult John." With that he bounced out of the apartment.

In a few minutes our friend was back again. "It's all right; John is going with the pony the first thing in the morning, and expects to be able to get all the bait you are likely to require."

In a relieved frame of mind he seated himself, crossed his

legs, folded his hands, and gazed benignly at the glowing embers.

For an hour we discussed the prospects of sport, the wildness of the neighbourhood, and the probabilities of the weather. We dined well, in accordance with the customary hospitality of a Norfolk host, and retired in good time to rest.

The morning broke fine, but cold. It was Sunday, and we, drawing the curtains from the window, saw the grey old church with its thatched roof and rounded tower in the immediate foreground of the view. It was a pretty picture. Giant ivy embraced the outer shell of the sacred edifice, climbed some distance up the tower and along the roof. A pheasant was searching for its breakfast in the grass, white with hoar frost, which grew among the silent tombstones ; and a nimble little squirrel busied himself collecting his winter store from under the russet leaves beneath a fruitful oak. Looking upwards we saw a small bunch of wildfowl winging their way eastward, and the cooing of some pigeons told us it was high time we likewise completed our toilet and sought for breakfast.

At ten a.m. the Sunday school class arrived. Half an hour's discourse on the mighty deeds of valour enacted by David sent them away interested and, it is to be hoped, enlightened. At 10.45 our host bethought him of his other duties. The church sexton, clerk, groom, gardener, warren-keeper and general man-of-all-work was absent ; he had gone to forage for bait. A difficulty arose as to who should manipulate the heating apparatus of the church and toll the solitary bell for service. We volunteer and are accepted.

Old maxims often predict truth, more especially so does the one which runs, " Fools rush in where," etc., and before we had been fifteen minutes in the church we repented the rashness of having so suddenly volunteered assistance.

The flue would not draw, the wood would not burn, and when at last, with much persuasion, a small flame was fanned into being, the smoke leaked out in many places and half filled the building. During these operations a starling and two sparrows entered through a hole in the roof to watch operations, but as soon as we had obtained a fair grasp of the solitary bell-rope they departed without staying for service.

It will be a long time before that call-to-prayer will be forgotten. What the majority of the inhabitants of the parish thought we know not and absolutely dare not inquire.

The first intimation that the bell was moving was one tremendous smack of the tongue, which sounded as though it had cracked the metal; this was followed by spasmodic clangs and funeral tolling by way of variety; the harder we tried to get anything like a regular ring the more wildly afflicted the music (?) seemed to be, until in despair we let go the rope to rest a while. But this was not to be, for a few minutes after we had desisted from the effort our friend arrived coughing violently through the smoke and directed that the bell must be kept going *somehow* for ten minutes at least.

This was no joke. It was cold and a trifle damp in the vestry. The place was full of smoke and we were no hands at all at the art of bell-ringing; besides, our host's remarks were not complimentary to our efforts. We—well,

> "In that sacred building there, we did not exactly swear,
> But there are moments—when one wants to be alone."

Soon after this the congregation began to arrive and the opportunity was taken of slipping back to the rectory for an overcoat, the wisdom of which forethought was afterwards appreciated.

There were eleven of us all told to hear the opening words concerning the wicked man and his wrath, and this number was *not* increased as time went on.

Five over-groomed children, the aforesaid Sunday-school class, sat in the front benches. The gardener and a maidservant from the Hall, who, alas! were apparently more interested in each other than in the service, occupied a pew below the rood-screen; a very rosy-cheeked farmer's daughter presided at a small harmonium which at times wandered a trifle by reason of weak notes and want of air; whilst the two children of our host composed the choir.

The service progressed in the usual manner until a hymn was announced, when an incident occurred. The rector had taken a severe chill in driving over the marsh dam the night previously, and one side of his face was now puffed out to an alarming size. It impeded his speech considerably, but that seemed a matter of small import, for he rattled off the service, and all would have gone well *had he not attempted to sing*. But when the harmonium had played several bars of music without any response from the congregation, although the opening lines had been passed, he essayed to lead his flock in the way they should go by singing him-self,—

" Hark ! a thrilling voice is sounding."

The result was ludicrous. Without wishing to appear irreverent one cannot but admit that it was impossible to maintain a serious face. The gardener dug his companion in the ribs with his elbow, whilst she stuffed her pocket-hand-kerchief into her mouth, and soon afterwards they hurriedly left the church.

All unheedingly our good-natured rector sang on, alone and out of tune, with an absolute indifference to the large diminution of his audience. Then he mounted the pulpit to deliver his sermon. It was short and sweet, lasting but ten minutes. It was directed at the children who sat in a row in a pew exactly beneath the pulpit, and when the benediction had been pronounced he solemnly walked to the vestry and the congregation filed out.

This gave us an opportunity of examining the interior of the church, which was interesting indeed. The pews seemed to be hundreds of years old. They were built from solid oak, inches thick, which appeared to have been collected from wreckage from the beach. There were several monuments, and a rood-screen adorned with rough carving, a closer in-

spection of which showed remnants of the gilt and colour of
bygone days. In the wall, worn stone steps led up to the
loft, which had now been taken away, and all around be-
tokened that once the church had been prosperous and well-
endowed. To-day the tide of agricultural depression is
sweeping over it, and it cannot be expected, when the tithe
rent-roll fails to produce fifty pounds a year, that the rector
can keep up its former glories, educate his children and ad-
minister charity with the munificent hand that his heart
desires but his purse denies. In spite of all his troubles and
anxieties to make both ends meet, we found him contented
with his lot, and happy, ever ready to deny himself when he
could benefit others, and holding out the hand of friendship
to all around him.

In this remote corner of England scrupulous doctrines
were neither preached nor practised, and we do not blush to
confess that after luncheon we repaired to the reed-fringed
mere intent on pike. The wind was still north-by-east and
very gusty, but the sun was shining, and we hoped for the
best. So cold was it that we found a sweater, a cardigan
jacket and an overcoat hardly kept us warm, and our fingers
soon lost all sense of touch in handling the wet line.

Round the edges of the mere, dense reed beds smothered
other vegetation, and hardly a tree was in sight except the
little clump which shadowed the church and the houses surrounding it. A small island was situated in the middle of the
water, upon which a fishing hut had been erected, and round
this we fished assiduously for hours. The channel running
along the western shores was also spun over again and again
without a rise, and as the sun dipped into the mists of the
marshes we gave up all hope of getting fish, and directed the
boatman to head our bows for home.

Numbers of wildfowl were on the water; particularly we
noticed teal, mallard, widgeon and pochards, not to mention a
colony of coots, whose spluttering on rising would have disturbed
any fish they passed over. So far as sport with the rod was
concerned, our first afternoon was a blank; but we glanced

over that broad expanse of water and registered a vow that two more days should not pass before some of the mighty pike we were assured that it contained were lured forth. Poling our punt up a narrow channel, through the reeds and sedges, we disjointed the rods, sunk the bait can, and went home.

On the morrow we had arranged to visit the sandhills where the rabbit warren was located. To those who have never shot over sandhills, the experience is a novel and thrilling one. We looked forward to the sport with eagerness and impatience.

During the night it froze hard, and before the sun had had time to melt the hoar frost from the hedgerows, we were afield with beaters and dogs. Taking on our way some of the roughest and foulest stubbles we have ever walked over, we put up covey after covey of partridges (mostly Frenchmen), straggling little bunches of green plover, and an occasional snipe. The air was still and biting, the heavy curtain of white mist had not been entirely dissolved, and weary migrants were observable winging their way inland after a long flight over the German Ocean.

The shyness of the birds kept them well out of harm's way at the outset, but we were driving all before us, and we rejoiced to see them seek the refuge of the marram grass on and under the lee of the sandhills, where we knew we could handle them to advantage. A quarter of a mile on the land side of, and running parallel with, the sandhills was a large dyke with a high wall beside it. This was for drainage purposes, and also to keep the sea water from flooding the marshes in case it broke through the hills. Between this wall and the foreshore lay a waste land covered with rank herbage. At frequent intervals stagnant pools encouraged the growth of the black rush, the evergreen rush, and sedgy spear grass, whilst here and there small patches of sweet grasses extended as smooth and even as the well-kept greens on golf links. These luxuriant feeding-grounds were kept close cropped by the rabbits, which were numerous.

We walked in line and fired to our hearts' content. Every few yards we kicked up a rabbit, sometimes several, but to stop them as they darted through the rank ground growth, over the limited open spaces, or round a tussock of rushes, required some skill. Every fifty yards or so we came upon a hillock or mound, where the rabbits found they could burrow, and they had not omitted to take full advantage of these outlying retreats. We had no ferrets with us, and when they outwitted us by gaining a temporary shelter in these refuge places we did not stop or attempt to unearth them. We had no occasion to do so, for there always seemed plenty more ahead. Having crossed, re-crossed, and well walked many acres of this waste land with shots at partridges, rabbits and plover, we took a beat along the sandhills, where we found the best of the sport we had as yet experienced. Alternately we walked, one on the outskirts of the hills, the other along the tops, with beaters on either side of us.

It was exhilarating, sporting and exciting—exhilarating by reason of the strong air and pure ozone which we inhaled direct from the sea; sporting by reason of the shots we obtained; exciting by the difficulties in progression, and because we had no idea at what quarry our guns might next be directed. In many places the surface of the damp sand had been frozen quite hard, and when one endeavoured to run down what looked like a perpendicular slope, the smooth sand of which we would naturally expect to find soft and yielding, it was a disagreeable surprise to realise it hard as rock, and in consequence to be precipitated from the top to the bottom at a higher rate of velocity than was required or desired. After a couple of tumbles of this description we became more cautious, and when we were again deceived by the outward appearances of a slope, the fall was broken by glissading gracefully down upon the seat of our nether garments.

Some years ago, before starting on a hunting expedition to Norway, we had had a sling fitted to our gun, with other alterations to suit probable requirements, and as we were using the same gun now, we fixed the sling and found it most useful. The sling in no way interferes with the shooting, and by throwing the strap over one shoulder both hands are free, and the gun can be quickly brought up to sight any object required. For some hours we enjoyed the most excellent sport.

When a knoll was approached on which a covey of partridges had been marked down we circumvented it, sending a beater over the marram-clad heights to disturb the birds ; and the shots they afforded as they whirred overhead inland, coupled with the wild nature of the surroundings, gave a thrill of pleasure to success which no ordinary day's sport could produce.

Noon arrived all too quickly, and weary afoot and heavily laden with the spoils of the chase, our faces were turned homewards. Fain would we have continued the work until the light waned and the curlew's weird evening call heralded the coming gloom, but a telegram had unceremoniously summoned our return, and time and trains wait for no man.

After lunch, reluctantly we bade our adieux and were soon retravelling the weary marshland dam, with its dangerous dykes and giant watermills, our faces towards the uplands, which could be but faintly seen on the distant horizon, our backs, alas ! being turned upon those hospitable walls where we fain would but too readily have stayed and seen more of the goodly folks within.

As we bumped along on the uneven road, turning in our mind the experience of the visit and gazing absently at a mirage which glittered in the sunlight over the marsh level, we reflected with satisfaction that we had at least left behind two little souls supremely happy rattling their sweet tin under the lee of the Norfolk sandhills.

# CHAPTER XXIII

ENCH TICKLING

ONE stinging hot afternoon we were sitting in the dinghy drifting idly down a long dyke leading into a secluded broad some distance from the main river, with the sail flapping against the mast and the main-sheet over the gun'ale unfastened and un-heeded. We felt almost too lazy to gaze about us, and when our pipes went out it was really too much trouble to refill them. On emerging from the dyke the boat gradually drew over the broad at a pace not exceeding two miles an hour, and would probably have continued its course until stopped by a reed bed

A QUIET CORNER.

had we not been awakened into action by an angry hail from a rough-looking specimen of humanity in a light punt, who was seemingly drifting like ourselves in among the weeds of a bay more secluded and more quiet-looking than the remainder of the water.

"Now then, why can't yer look out where yer coming to? Ain't the broad big enough, or do yer want to spoil every-body's sport ? "

We informed the gentleman in question that " the intru-sion was quite unintentional on our part ; at the same time

317

we should be obliged if he would kindly state in what way we were annoying him, as we failed to see what sport was possible under the circumstances in which he was placed."

This polite address failed to elicit any reply except a gruff rejoinder to " hold yer blooming slarver* an' mind yer own business."

By no means abashed at his rudeness, and our curiosity being thoroughly aroused, we steered the dinghy into the reeds hard by and pressed our would-be adversary to partake of a drink and a cigarette, adding that we were strangers to those parts eager to learn anything appertaining to sport, and if he could be of service we were not averse to pay him well for his information.

This seemed to ease his mind and he came alongside for the proffered refreshment, which on such a day would require a great tension of forbearance to refuse.

We noticed he had several very fine tench in the bottom of the punt, a brace and a half of which soon changed hands for the modest sum of one shilling. After the third glass of beer, and when his pipe was well alight, he became more confidential. He had caught them with his hands—in other words, he was engaged in the illicit practice of "tench tickling."

As long as the bottled beer lasted we plied him lavishly with it, and not only did he tell of the secrets of his art, but then and there gave ocular proof by several most successful experiments. This was another example which opened our eyes to the secrets of Broadcraft, and which made us reflect again upon the fact that so little is seen or heard of the really genuine primitive methods, devices and engines that always were, and still are, used by the natives in certain parts of these out-of-the-way regions.

When a visitor appears upon the scene, how quickly and deftly are all pike-snares, night-lines, trimmers, liggers, nets and other poaching engines stowed away, and the only too-willing marshman (with visions before him of a week's

* Conversation—*Norfolk Dialect.*

TENCH TICKLING—A POACHER AT WORK.

wages earned in a day) immediately essays to accompany the angler, or whoever he may be, upon his diurnal rambles. Indeed, the native is truly an indispensable acquisition, for who more fitted to manage the boat and impart that local knowledge so necessary to success ? Although the artful old poacher may know full well at the time the bag will be light in proportion to what *his* would be if he were out alone and proceeded to work in *his own peculiar* way.

Of course, the numerous Piscatorial Protection and Angling Associations which are springing up in all fishable waters tend in a great measure to suppress this, yet in the wilder parts, remote from railways, towns and "the madding crowd," there are those who have always gained their subsistence, more or less, from the products of the water and marsh. To them it seems hard indeed that their ordinary course of livelihood should be deemed illegal, and many continue former practices, only under the cloak of stealthiness and cunning, to avoid if possible the avengeful arm of the law.

Netting, which was once carried on to a large extent, and by which means it was not uncommon to obtain several tons of fish in a night, is now completely done away with.

Poachers might still easily evade the water-bailiffs, but they would have great difficulty in disposing of their contraband gains, and the law, besides forfeiting all nets, implements, etc., found thus employed, renders the risks too great for netting to be extensively indulged in. However, they make up for it in a great measure by poaching on the smaller and less-easily-to-be-detected scale, viz., by trimmers, eel-lines (with many hooks), anchored lines, night-lines, and pike-snares, etc., etc., far too numerous to be here detailed, and which necessarily cause a great amount of anxiety and trouble to preservers, for, unless caught red-handed, the delinquents almost invariably delude them by making off, disposing of their implements *en route*. In many cases an apparatus for receiving and sinking their quarry at a moment's notice is carried in their boats, and when at last overtaken, they plead utter innocence and ignorance of the offence with which they are charged.

But we digress—we are not speaking of poachers, but of "tench tickling." This, however, although not illegal everywhere, is so in all navigable rivers in Norfolk and Suffolk (by a bye-law passed in 1890),* and within 400 yards of any navigable river or broad. It is considered as poaching, as it is unsportsmanlike. Still, one interested in country outdoor pursuits generally likes to know all one can about everything connected with the subject, and so accordingly on this, our first opportunity, we were initiated into "the art"—as indeed it may fairly be called. Few places offer equal advantages for "tench tickling" to the secluded and smaller broads of Norfolk. They seem made for it, and every facility is to be found, as will be seen in the following description.

Quoting the Rev. Richard Lubbock in his *Observations on the Fauna of Norfolk*, he says that "tench catching" (as he therein denominates it) orginated with a family of the name of "Hewitt," at Barton, all the members of which were fishermen and gunners. One of them, observing the sluggish nature of this fish, attempted to take them with his hands, and often succeeded. The art has spread, and the system is better understood, so that at this time there are in Norfolk fishermen who, upon *shallow waters*—for in deep nothing can be done thus— prefer their own hands, with a landing-net to be used occasionally, to bow-nets or any other engines. *The day for this occupation cannot be too calm or too hot.* During the heats of summer, but especially at the time of spawning, tench delight in lying near the surface of the water amongst beds of weeds; in such situations they are found in parties varying from four or five to thirty in number. On the very near approach of a boat they strike away, dispersing in different directions, and then the sport of the "tench-tickler" begins. With an eye like a hawk, he perceives where some particular fish has stopped in his flight, which is seldom more than a few yards; his guide in this is the bubble which arises generally where the fish stops. Ap-

---

* *See* Appendix.

X

proaching the place as gently as possible in his boat, which
must be small, light, and at the same time steady in her
bearings, he keeps her motionless with his pole, and, lying
down with his head over the gunwale and his right arm
bared to the shoulder—taking advantage, in his search, of light
and shade—he gently, with his fingers, displaces the weeds,
and endeavours to descry the tench in its retreat. If the
fisherman can see part of the fish, so as to determine which
way the head lies, the certainty of capture is much increased;
if he cannot, immersing his arm, he feels slowly and
cautiously about until he touches it, which, if done gently
on head or body, is generally disregarded by this sluggish
and stupid fish ; but if the tail is the part molested, a dash
away is the usual consequence. Should the tickler succeed in
ascertaining the position of the fish, which, under favourable
circumstances he generally does, he insinuates one hand,
which alone is used, under it, just behind the gills, and raises
it gently, but yet rapidly, towards the surface of the water.
In lifting it over the boat side, which, it need not be said,
should be low, he takes care not to touch the gunwale with
his knuckles, as the very slightest jar makes the captive
flounce and struggle. On being laid down the tench often
remains motionless for full a minute, and then begins apparently to perceive the fraud practised upon it. The
fisherman then, if he " marked " more than one tench when
the shoal dispersed, proceeds to search for it. If not, he
endeavours to start another, by striking his pole against
the side or bottom of the boat—several are generally close
at hand. The concussion moves other fish, when the same
manœuvres are repeated. In this way fifteen or sixteen
good-sized table tench can be taken in a short space of time.
And in the course of a favourable day one good tickler will
easily secure five or six dozen.

However, "tench tickling" does not seem so pusillanimous
a proceeding as " trout tickling," for it is a well-known fact
that the former are very difficult fish to induce to take bait
of any description, and the only period that they are

apparently approachable is when the wheat is in bloom ; then the best bait to use is potato paste.

Since the Norfolk and Suffolk Fisheries Act came into force in 1877* no quantity of tench have been taken, except in private waters, and the rivers and broads now fairly teem with them. They are generally taken (in private waters) with bow-nets, which are prohibited by the before-mentioned Act. The habit which these fish have for exploring lanes and holes in the weed-beds is taken advantage of, and two scythe blades are attached to the end of a long pole, by means of which a narrow lane is cut in the weeds, forming a loop allowing the fish to go in at one end and emerge at the other. In the middle of this lane the bow-nets are sunk and the fish show little hesitation in going into them.

It has been observed that pike draw into the shallows in the month of March, the local term for which is " bushing " ; tench follow their example in June ; whilst eels, on the contrary, migrate, with the tide, the sharp-nosed, or grigs, in the spring, the silver or broad-nosed eels after the first heavy rains in August.

At one time tench were called in Broadland " doctor fish," because it was believed that the slime upon them contained healing powers, and that when other fish were ill they would seek out tench and rub themselves against them in order to get the benefit of their healing slime, but it seems this theory is exploded.

When properly prepared and cooked tench are really excellent eating. After being caught they should be put into a tub of clean water with a constant stream running into it, or into a fish tank, and kept there for a few days and fed upon bread, which causes them to lose the muddy flavour. In transporting, pack them in wet grass.

The epicure should stew them in port wine, when he will find that they are real delicacies, and, if properly cooked, he will in future belie those who deprecate their gastronomic value.

* *See* Appendix.

## CHAPTER XXIV

### PIKE AND PIKE FISHING

GOOD pike fishing in Broadland can be obtained almost anywhere, and worthy of much more attention than strangers are wont to bestow upon it. The best time to indulge in the sport is the early autumn, when the weeds are dying down and the fish are in good condition, with voracious appetites, when they are accustomed to draw out from the shallows in favour of deeper pools and secluded bays. It is the time when the leaves of the sweet chestnut trees have fallen, and our English oaks clothe themselves in a burnt-sienna-coloured mantle and the hoar frost is found upon the blades of grass at breakfast-time.

Then it is that the *Esox lucius* darts from his lair with a rush and a swirl, cleaving the water like a torpedo which causes the reel to hum and the blood to tingle in every vein of the fisherman's body.

Then it is that the fish is full of life and activity, whilst its appetite can scarce be appeased, so much so that it will attempt to gorge other fish its own equal in weight and bulk. At this period of the year nothing seems to come amiss to its palate—rats, frogs, ducks, waterhens and other fowl, whilst instances are on record where bathers have been attacked as well as animals drinking from the stream; even swans, when feeding with their heads under water, are no exception.

A FORECAST OF PROMISE.

In Broadland the owners of private waters are not very obliging in granting permission to pike fishers to invade their waters until after the wildfowl shooting is ended, but there is such a vast expanse of public water where the sport may be indulged in, that the would-be angler need not concern himself on this account. He need only remember the fish are there, ready and waiting to be caught, whilst auspicious weather, coupled with a fair amount of skill, will ensure heavy baskets.

The ways and means of taking pike are legion, and it is to be regretted that as many are taken in the waters of Broadland by poaching devices as are caught legitimately on rod and line. We plead guilty to the soft impeachment, not once, nor twice, but repeatedly; our only excuse is that we have been fishing on private waters and have been exasperated beyond measure by the apparent shyness of the quarry and we have felt compelled to quench by some means or other an insatiable thirst for blood.

In slightly commenting upon a few of these poaching devices, liggers or trimmers should be first mentioned. When these machines were in common vogue, twenty-five or fifty years ago, pieces of brightly-painted wood were used which could be easily seen and retaken, but as they grew into disrepute and became illegal, less prominent and conspicuous floats were adopted, a bundle of rushes being found to answer equally as well, if not better. Again there are the night-lines laid from a reed bed, a bank, or an island. Or the crotched stick-trimmer is brought into play. It is as ingenious as it is deadly, and is fashioned as follows:—

The poacher cuts from a hazel or elm bough a small crotch similar to those used by boys for catapults; holding his line between the thumb and first finger, he passes it round the back of his two first fingers, between the second and third, round the front of third and fourth, through the second and third, round the front of the first and second, and so on till he has the requisite length of running line neatly folded in a skein, which is then placed in the crotch. One end of the line is

fastened to the stick, the other is wound round the inside of the
fork to hold the skein in its place, and finally fastened by
being drawn through a split in the end of one of the two
forks ; and it is to this end of the line that the poacher attaches
his baited hook.   It is clear that if the crotched stick be suspended pointing downwards, a pull ever so slight will draw
the line from the slit, and thus release the skein of running
line so that the fish is not checked while he gorges the bait,
and is only pulled up on attempting to move away.   Armed
with one or more of these ingenious devices, the poacher goes
to the water at dusk, and attaches them to boughs lying
just under the surface, if possible, or, at anyrate, in unnotice-
able places; but the submerged boughs, of course, afford the
best security, as, even after a fish has been caught, nothing
can be seen from above of what is transpiring below the
surface.   Modifications of this favourite trick are numerous,
and are suited to the peculiarities of the stream or lake.
Most keepers are up to the old plan of fastening night-lines
to dead boughs or pieces of wood, and leaving them to drift
about, the poacher taking the chance of being able to get them
out again ; while many a good fish falls a victim to a dead
bait thrown in and left to sink to the bottom, especially in
flood time, when they feed close to the bottom and congregate
in quiet corners.

Snaring also is much in vogue in Broadland, and if a
native happens to have the good luck to see a fish lying in an
accessible spot he has it out in no time.   A pole of some sort,
or a bough of a tree, is sure to be handy, whilst he soon
adapts his boot-laces to a workable snare, and the rest is
quickly accomplished.

Spearing fish by night has quite died out and is not likely
to be revived, whilst the nature of the district hardly per-
mits the use of lime, dynamite or chemical compounds.

With regard to legitimate angling, the number of fish
taken per annum since 1890 in Broadland is large.   On one
private water, for example, the owner has constantly landed
over thirty fish in a day to his own rod.   On the Waveney

near Beccles one boat landed seventy-four in three days. On
the Yare, near Buckenham, thirty-one fish were landed in
one day; whilst often it happens that an angler takes more
fish in weight than he can comfortably carry home. It is
rarely that a season passes without a long list of fish scaling
over twenty pounds each in weight being recorded, and a fish
of thirty-five pounds is by no means a record. The best centres
to make are Oulton Broad, Wroxham and Potter Heigham.

The local stories of pike and their ways are endless, and
visitors to Broadland will hear many, some of them real
startlers, if they take the trouble to inquire, when in the
neighbourhood. One which has been before recorded is
worthy of repetition.

It concerns a gander and a pike. The former developed a
nasty habit of wandering, so to cure it the owner tied to its
leg a big fish-hook with half a frog attached. The bait took
the fancy of a pike, who swallowed it, thereby arresting the
progress of the gander, and causing it to perform a number of
somersaults on the surface of the water. For some time the
struggle was most amusing, the fish pulling and the bird
screaming, each with all its might; the one attempting to fly,
and the other attempting to swim from the invisible enemy;
the gander at one moment losing, and the next moment re-
gaining, his centre of gravity. At length victory was with
the gander, who, bearing away for the shore of the pond,
landed on the green grass one of the finest pike ever caught
in the neighbourhood.

Professor Day, or "Josser" as he is dubbed by those who
know him intimately, is one of the characters of Broadland.
History does not record whether he earned the distinguished
title for his prowess at "the noble art of self-defence," or at
the more peaceful "art of angling," but it is a well-known
fact that he is equally proficient at either, and further, that
his skill and local knowledge regarding the latter sport is,
and has been, unequalled during the present century. The
Professor can tell before he starts out for the day whether
sport will be obtained or whether it would not be better to

seek some other more profitable pastime. How he works
when the fish are shy and almost unobtainable is a secret he
shares with very few, but his results are invariably the same,
and one cannot but be envious of his takes, nor withhold a
wondering admiration of the masterly manner in which he
handles his simple and almost primitive rods and appurtenants
of the fisherman's outfit. To give a history of our old friend
"Josser," his experiences, adventures and doings, would fill

another volume as bulky as
the present one, and probably a great deal more
interesting; therefore we
must rest content with but
a passing reference to this
veteran angler and hero of a
thousand thrilling episodes.

The legitimate fishing
as practised in Broadland
is confined almost entirely
to three methods—snap-
tackle, spinning and trolling. Paternostering is by
no means fashionable,
although visitors may occasionally try it, and the
same may be said of gorge-
bait and the other methods
of pike fishing.

PROFESSOR DAY.

In spinning, or, as it is often called, "casting," the Broadland
angler coils his line on the thwart,* or on the bottom of the
boat, in preference to throwing from the reel in the Notting-
ham style. Dace and roach are mostly used, and large bait
are chosen in preference to small; occasionally goldfish and
gudgeon are taken out, and all kinds of artificial bait are used
for trolling. But a dead roach is mostly in favour.

Some anglers revive their bait with a drop of brandy or

* A seat running from one side of a boat to another—generally amidships.

whisky, but the majority of anglers take plenty of bait with them so they need not be used with a sparing hand.

Large landing-nets and gaffs are employed to extract the fish from the water, but the natives use only their fingers and haul them out by the eyes.

To give some idea of a day's pike fishing in Broadland we will take another extract from our diary of bygone days and recount the proceedings of an excusion we made to a small private broad during the first Jubilee year. Although it was by no means remarkable for the weight of the bag, that particular day will in the memory long survive.

## A Day's Pike Fishing

It was a sharp, crisp morning, with an overcast sky and a gentle breeze stirring the naked tree-tops, that saw us rattling along at a good ten an hour over the frost-bound road *en route* for the fishing waters. Hubert, our companion on this occasion, was in exuberant spirits; he had never caught a pike in his life and was as keen to get there as any schoolboy bound home for the holidays. Gaily he chattered about baits, tackle and rods, not giving anyone else a chance to get in a word edgeways, much less to answer the hundred and one questions he incessantly raised. Twice he insisted on stopping whilst he dismounted from the cart to refreshen the bait by a change of water from a convenient stream which flowed under the roadway.

After he had for about the tenth time inquired if we were not nearly there, we turned down an avenue or short lane (called loake in Broadland) and reached an old-fashioned farmhouse.

There was no keeper to the estate, but an old marshman, who looked after the watermill, tended to our wants and stabled the horse. He had been forewarned of our coming and had accordingly laid a few liggers (planks) over the dykes to facilitate foot passage to the broad; he had also baled out the boats ready for use and occupation.

In picking a way along the swampy glades of the low-lying alder carr our spirits rose in anticipation of the forth-coming sport, and we pictured in the imagination a record bag.

The nearer we approached the water, the more convinced were we of the favourable auspices of the day. The sun was vainly endeavouring to break the cloudy barrier which obscured its face, whilst a gentle breeze was bending the tree-tops and blowing the fluff from the reed-heads across the open water, upon which the wavelets rippled and danced in the most inviting manner.

Yes, it was an ideal day for the sport and we had every intention of taking full advantage of it.

On turning a corner of the thick fell we were brought to within twenty yards of the boathouse, a primitive thatched shed of picturesque attractions and built upon a small well-chosen promontory of firm land which jutted into the broad. Here a halt was called in order to fit the rods, prepare tackle, refresh the bait kettle and partake of a final nip to luck and prosperity before parting with our attendant and commencing the business of the day in real earnestness.

The broad covered several acres, whilst its shores were deeply studded with an impassable reed swamp, in which otters loved to dwell, and being only three and a half feet to five feet deep it was a wonder so many pike were to be found there.

Surrounded by a thick belt of trees and bounded on all sides by marshes, it looked like an oasis on the flat level ; but when the shades of evening fell and the heron winged its way thither over the thick marsh mists, the broad became as weird and uncanny a place as it now looked pleasant and inviting.

Hubert manned a large cumbersome boat known there-abouts as a reed-flat, and steered a course, before the wind, towards a watcher's house which nestled amongst the Scotch fir trees on the northermost bank, as he had been told that a deep hole existed some thirty yards to the south of it and he was eager to try his luck therein whilst we preferred spinning round the bays.

Knowing there were two boats upon the broad we had brought a couple of bait cans so the dace and roach could be divided between us, and we could fish at our pleasure without disturbing one another by constant calls for requisites.

The first bay we tried had been disturbed by a bunch of mallard and teal, numbering twenty-six in all, which rose at our approach, and although we tried a cast or two we could hardly expect to get a rise.

In the next bay we were not more fortunate, a large dog otter disappearing before us on our rounding the point of the reeds, and we knew from former experience that it was little use fishing in his wake. So we turned the bow of the punt and rowed towards the northern shore, passing Hubert on the way, sitting contentedly over the hole which he had successfully managed to locate and in which a lively roach, deftly suspended from a patent invisible trace, was now vainly endeavouring to free itself.

Away to the right lay a quiet, secluded bay with trees and rushes growing round its shores in wild profusion. It was out of the wind and the foliage was reflected on its surface with mirror-like exactness. It looked just the place for a small Jack, and without disturbing the water we carefully curled our line upon the bottom boards, and casting the bait well into the edge of the rushes, so that it alighted upon the water with little splash, commenced to work it gently inwards. Before two yards of the line had been recovered there was a mighty swirl in the placid waters and the reel hummed in a manner which did the heart good.

We looked round to see whether our luck had attracted Hubert's attention, and were only too delighted to see him standing up in his boat giving the butt of his rod to a fish which bent it almost double.

Although our Jack had gone off with such a rush it was

soon played out, and ten minutes later we pulled it into the boat. It was a healthy, good-conditioned fish, scaling about six pounds, lightly hooked, and as game as fish of that size usually are. On the other hand, Hubert's fish was by no means so easily landed. Three times he reeled it to the boat after he had played it for a good fifteen minutes, and three times it rushed from him, taking out ten or fifteen yards of line on each occasion. We were watching him with the greatest interest when he frantically signalled to us to come to his assistance. Thinking that he would hardly do this unless he had hooked something extraordinary we made all haste to obey, and a few moments later had punted up behind him and boarded the flat. He was so excited he could hardly speak. When he did so he gasped, " For heaven's sake gaff him—I can't. Don't lose him whatever you do. Isn't he a shark and no mistake ? "

Again he reeled in the fish, but just as we were about to plant the gaff in its side it gave a turn of its tail and as nearly as possible broke the trace.

We rebuked Hubert forcibly but he immediately retaliated in a similar train, for he was so over anxious to successfully land the fish that we all but lost it.

For the fifth time he reeled it in, and on this occasion no mistake was made. A well-directed jerk, a splash, and a beautiful pike of about eleven or twelve pounds in weight was jumping on the bottom of the boat.

It was Hubert's first fish and his joy knew no bounds. So enchanted was he with his catch that he simply sat gloating over the prize for nearly an hour before he would attempt to try for another. Sitting thus we left him and worked our way all round the water, spinning every bay, hole and corner that was thought at all likely to hold a fish.

At midday we repaired to the before-mentioned watch-house to lunch and while away a couple of hours sketching.

From two-thirty to five we fished assiduously—spinning, trolling and with snap-tackle.

Of runs we had many, but the fish seemed loth to bite firmly and after a few seconds' play we lost them. Several peculiar incidents happened which more particularly caused us to remember that day from many others. For instance, after some considerable sport we drew a nice fish of about nine pounds to the side of the punt, and as we were reaching down for our gaff it freed itself from the tackle and made off. We again had recourse to rebukes self-merited, but fortunately we were at that time fishing with snap-tackle and had two rods out, one on each side of the boat. Imagine our astonishment on turning round to follow the course the lost fish had taken in the clear shallow water, to perceive it most distinctly make for the other bait and take it. Quickly catching up this rod we struck the fish and eventually landed it.

On another occasion we were quietly punting through some rushes to stir the fish up a bit when we saw one strike in a bay ahead, and casting a live bait well out we soon had a run and secured the fish. It was not a large one, but quite big enough to kill. This fish we took out by the eyes, and no sooner had we got a firm hold of it than it spat out the bait and tackle, so we really picked the fish out of the broad with our fingers only. Throwing it into the boat we turned round to the bait can and proceeded to put on another dace, when to our annoyance the fish, which seemed to have vindictive intentions, jumped up and inserted its teeth into a very tender part of the anatomy which politeness forbids us to mention, although we may perhaps go so far as to say that we did not sit down in comfort for some time afterwards.

It is not uncommon to hear of fish that have attacked persons when in the water either whilst bathing or searching for aquatic plants, etc. One story concerns a boy bathing in a pond at Inglemere, near Ascot, who had to fight almost for his life with a pike of upwards of thirty pounds. The story has the impress of truth as the boy had the impress of its teeth on his hands and arms, which he will carry to his grave. It is by no means infrequent in Broadland to hear of instances where pike have made a rush at people's fingers when they have been dabbling them in the water over the side of a boat, which stories may have given rise to Mr Pennall's pleasantry, that these fish are "piscivorous, carnivorous, hominivorous and omnivorous."

When we had reached the boathouse and given up for the day, one of our rods had been left lying in the boat with a dead roach upon the spinning trace, which was not in the water but dangling over the gunwale of the boat. A pike of about two and a half to three pounds in weight actually jumped from the water and took the bait. We played and landed it, but threw it in again on account of its size.

This ended the sport for the day, so, stringing the fish together, we loaded up the old marshman until he could scarcely stagger under the weight, and carrying the gear and other paraphernalia ourselves we turned our backs upon the broad, leaving it in a peaceful solitude, which was only likely to be broken by wildfowl and otter.

THE FISHING BOX AT BUCKENHAM BROAD.

# CHAPTER XXV

## PHEASANTS FROM SHELL TO SHOT

DURING a long stay in Broadland, the doings on one
particular day, perhaps to us the most enjoyable of the many
whiled away in that delightful district, stand prominent in
mind. The exact *locus in quo* shall remain undivulged in
spite of the fact that the honest old English gamekeeper,
in whose company the fleeting hours were passed, has since
gone to his well-earned rest.

Good old Balls! he was one of the best and as true a soul
as ever spiked the humble daisy, yet he was a queer customer
to tackle by anyone who did not know him or who attempted
to sail under his weather—as is said when racing on the
river.

The day in question was a lovely one, and luncheon had
been served in a manner that made a walk imperative to
well-being. Whilst lounging on the deck of the craft that

made a temporary home, and lying at length upon the hatchways in the shade, a wreath of blue smoke, curling heavenwards above the dense foliage on the borders of the uplands, called to mind the fact that an old friend, John Balls, resided close by. What more natural than that an afternoon walk should resolve itself into a visit to his cosy yet picturesque abode.

## A RAMBLE ROUND THE COVERTS.

" Morning, Balls! going for a walk round? Well, we'll come too if we may and listen to your idea of what covert management ought to be "—and good old Balls opens his wicket gate, crosses the rustic bridge which spans the brook rippling past his cottage, and we foot it together down the central glade.

Now John Balls, head keeper to ——, was a typical specimen of what a head keeper ought to be. He knew " what was what," yet never refused to listen to the views of others, nor condemned a suggested improvement in his calling without giving it a fair trial, *because it was new*. Like Cato (where time was no object) he would reason with anyone, because it could do him no harm and he might learn something.

" Well you see, sir, now the season's over, I want my beats to lie as quiet and snug as possible, and I give orders to my men to leave their guns and dogs at home. If a chap ain't cute enough to get along with his traps, he ain't much use to me. A gun is useful at times, and a good dog is serviceable in finding nests, but I don't like 'em even then. No! traps! traps! traps! them's the boys for me. I can't explain to you now, sir, all I know about traps; I could talk for a week and then I should want to go on for another—but let us just walk through here. This is my idea of a covert, not too thick, but just thick enough, allowing the sun to get in, with some nice open places for the birds to play and dry themselves after rain and avoid the constant drip in foggy weather. Notice

how nicely the firs are scattered about. On that light-landed
bank over yonder are what the master calls Douglas firs—
they grow quicker there than any I ever saw, and silver firs
are just the same, while lower down, where the ground is
boggy, you will notice what master says are the black spruce;
they are slower growing but stand a long time. We find the
common spruce does not last above thirty years, and are often
blown down just as they begin to be large enough for the birds
to use. In the little covert we are coming to shortly we had
an experiment. The undergrowth was all raspberry canes
and alder poles, with giant ash trees above. Well, master
had most of the big trees cut down and the place well cleared
out to let the sun in, then we planted a lot of firs at intervals,
about three in a group, and now that place is one of the
favourite haunts, where ten years ago you'd hardly ever find
a bird. In another place we planted rhododendrons among
the undergrowth; they provide good cover and the rabbits
won't touch them. Again, you know the ten-acre piece on
old Chunkey Brown's farm? Well, that heavy land ain't
favourable for firs and such like, so we got some common yew
trees and put them in, three in a group, and they did wonders."

"What are those strips dug for?"

"Oh! you see we plant sunflowers, brank, garden peas,
and such like, because then the birds have attractions and
stay at home. By-the-bye, they are very fond of peas, and
we always give them the best of everything. Then you see
we tie up bunches of barley and hang them on the bushes, so
the birds must jump up to get at them, which takes up their
time, amuses them at home, and so prevents straying.

"I've heard of many ways of feeding them, and tried them
all almost, and, in my opinion, there is none to equal the old
rustic feeding-house principle. I've got one down here, and
if you've a mind, we'll just have a look at it," and turning the
corner of a nut walk, a picturesque little shed catches the
view. It was an oblong building supported by six unpeeled
rough poles sunk well into the ground, with others attached
at the top for rafter plates, on to which the skeleton of the

Y

roof was fixed; this in turn was thatched with reeds (litter or boughs would answer equally well); an open trellis floor of poles was fixed a couple of feet from the ground, and on this barley in the ear was laid. Underneath it was quite dry, and as we approached an old cock rose from the dust and sneaked out, causing a couple of hen birds, who were pulling down barley from above, to notice us and accompany him.

"You'll find in the little water-meadow, near Bloodmoor

A RUSTIC FEEDING HOUSE.

Hills, our fourth beat, a similar feeder for partridges, which a foreign gentleman told me to try. It's got a trellis-work floor like this, but is round instead of oblong, and the supports do not rise above the flooring. In the middle it has a post seven feet high, on the top of which a strong circular trap for hawks can be set; but as I've handled 'bout most of the breed round these parts, there is little use for that.

"Down the bottom ride there's some work going on I must see, sir, and maybe you'll also be interested—it's a pheasant-catcher.

" Speaking of that, there's many ways nowadays to take
birds alive, and I've tried 'em, but always gone back to my
old plan. Some keepers set up a coop with a stick and a
string on the old brick-trap principle, some use a kind of clap
nets, and some the round drop hoop, netted over, but I always
think netting when it is brought in contact with the birds
does not do them any good. My plan is simple and sure
without hurting them. I take some hurdles, well interwoven
with heather or straw, and set them about near the regular
feed ground, gradually getting them nearer and nearer. First
I get one side up, then the
other, next put an end on,
then the top netted over
with loose twine netting.
The birds soon get used to
it and pay no attention to
it whatever, feeding on quite
confidently; and one fine
morning when it's full I
drop a net across the en-
trance, and there they all

A COVERED WEASEL TRAP.

are, like fowl in the pocket of a decoy pipe, when I just pick
out what I want and let the others go.

" Having caught them," continued Mr Balls, " they are carefully taken to the mew; you must see my mew, sir, it's the
outcome of years' experimenting although apparently so very
simple. Ah, they've got the two sides of the catcher up.
Now, we'll go to the mew. Over this stile, sir, and across the
meadows to the Home Wood.'

Fifteen minutes later we enter the netted door of the
mew. It was a big structure, divided into several compart-
ments and very simple. A suitable position in the wood had
been selected and posts erected, around which was stretched
wire netting forming the sides to the enclosure. Rat-proof
netting was added all round to the height of two feet, being
interwoven with fir boughs. On the outside more rat-proof
netting had been laid flat upon the ground and covered over

with soil to intercept the vermin, which, endeavouring to enter, scrape down to the netting, then give it up as hopeless. In one corner artificial runs with cover traps were set ; in one of these a rat had paid the penalty of venturesomeness. The top of the mew was open, allowing a visitation to the harem of outside admirers. Mr. Balls also explained that he always kept one cock in the mew, as an extra precaution, for if not, many of his eggs turned out badly, besides which it had the effect of attracting cocks to enter to fight his pinioned or clipped one for the ladies' favours.

The inside was freely decorated with cut larch and fir boughs, forming an excellent cover for the birds to hide or lay in. The whole can be well described as the essence of rustic simplicity.

"And now, sir, the birds are drawing up to perk and the sooner we turn homewards the better ; and if I may make so bold, perhaps you'll come in and have a bowl of tea and see the Squire's new Irish water spaniel and my old missus." Our further conversation was adjourned in favour of Mrs Balls' hereditary rheumatism and the spaniel pup.

.　　.　　.　　.　　.　　.　　.　　.

After we had agreed with the venerable Mrs Balls that the weather was very very trying indeed, to say nothing of dear John, who, by the way, was now luxuriating in the fumes of a good cigar, we were able to again lead round the conversation to the topic so ardently desired, namely, pheasants and the shooting of them.

### POACHERS, AND THE HANDLING OF THEM.

Yea, verily, sir, the man who wears velveteens may well sigh. He has many enemies to malign his character in those who love to handle their neighbour's property, and he cannot well fulfil his calling without raising their animosity.

Recourse to the law is often resorted to, and sometimes with good effect, but, Lor' bless you, sir, I know a game far better than that, and, as you know, there are few with coverts better stocked with game, easier of access, and yet at the same time less annoyed by poachers than ours.

As I have before remarked, for all four or two-footed vermin my motto is " Traps ! traps ! traps ! "  And before leaving that evening we were more than ever convinced that throughout the whole countryside a more artful old cuss, and a more faithful, honest servant than Mr John Balls was not to be found.

This is how he went to work :—He was not a great reader, nevertheless, he knew the ins and outs of the Game Laws, at least, whenever he did get a conviction the evidence was undeniable and the sentence heavy.  It was rarely he " pulled a man," as he expressed it, for day poaching. " What's a quid to a chap ?  No, give him a lay-in job and sureties to find when he comes out, if you beak him at all."

A mysterious man to some was Mr Balls ; indeed, if an unfortunate patronised his acres he was freely allowed to do so at first, until, confidence gained, his nice little practices were suddenly nipped in the bud by being taken red-handed *past the first hour after sunset,* and more probably together with several companions.

But Mr Balls derived no satisfaction from the law ; he preferred to meet his foes on even terms, and if he could best a poacher he'd chuckle to himself over it for the remainder of the season.  When Mr Balls first came to that part of the country, and before his reputation had gone forth, his beats were particularly favoured by the mouching fraternity, and as egging time drew round so assuredly did they.  One instance in particular showed his cleverness.  It was as follows :— He had somehow obtained an inkling that his whole place would be visited at a certain time and he acted accordingly. Every man living near to the nesting-grounds that he knew was privately warned by him, and an old gun or pistol supplied to each for emergency.  The eventful morn soon arrived ; when the worthy Mr Balls was as usual jaunting up a green lane about daylight, he met a portion of the gang.  He stopped and discussed the weather and matters of interest generally, but did not forget to fire his gun thrice in succession ; within

half-an-hour of his so doing every one of his *pro tem.*
watchers were out, the word having been passed over the
whole estate. It was lucky the preparation had been so complete, for the number of the would-be eggers was considerable,
and in every covert they entered they found a son of the
plough with a musket on his shoulder ready to accompany
them whithersoever they listed. In disgust they adjourned to
a distant alehouse, where the following sentiment was given
vent to:—"'Tain't no blimey use a coming to this 'ere ——
—— place, every —— covert has a great hairy —— with a
—--- great gun on his shoulder —— 'im and that there ——
Balls too."

Another gentleman of the same class, not to be led into
committing himself, was however compelled to dive pretty
deeply into his pocket. This youth was fond of trespassing,
until he one day climbed over a rail fencing *(doctored by Mr
Balls)*, and the amount of the trespass, damages and costs
created an impression upon his memory which caused him in
future to favour other "fields and pastures new."

Following the same principle, he successfully caught an
egger near a low-lying alder carr on the marshes. He was
seen hanging about in the neighbourhood and preparations
for his welfare were accordingly made. A plank was doctored
by sawing it half through and filling up the incision. It was
then laid in place of the sound one, which it resembled, and a
short time afterwards it deposited its victim into three feet of
water and four of soft black highly-scented sediment.

Stretched wire he advocated as a splendid and favourite
adoption as a preventive against the intrusion of both man
and dog. It should be just high enough to allow a hare or
rabbit to pass under, but low enough to catch a dog. But
what a poacher most dreads are pitfalls. These are more often
associated with the wooden dummy pheasants, and act when
the poacher, having his eye on the dummies, is walking round
preparatory to his attempts to secure them. All keepers who
have large woods under their surveillance should also bear in
mind that poachers often slip into them before it is daylight,

securing the pheasants round and about the feeding grounds ; they remain in the wood till darkness again sets in, when they leave with their ill-gotten gains.

Last, but not least, never resort to lawyers until a really good case has been obtained and the evidence is strong, otherwise you will do no good, and have to pay pretty dearly for the amusement (?).

THE WATCH HOUSE.

## Hatching and Rearing.

In springtime we keepers complain as much as farmer Turniptops at the persistent cussedness of our eccentric English climate—it is the period when cares weigh heavy on our souls ; outlying nests give constant anxiety ; our hands are full to overflowing with home hatchings, and last, but not least, the partridges are enough to consign us to an early grave.

But faint heart never reared fat pheasant, and persever-ance with care will work wonders. Let us take a cursory glance at the work. Why does our keeper so persistently search the boundary beat and the rough marshes next the river ? Ah! as he comes home the answer is plainly seen, for does he not bring with him a goodly supply of early eggs, gathered from the first nests ; some of these he places under hens at home ; with others he possibly fills up nests on the inside beats, which may from various causes lack their full complement. He has reasons for collecting early eggs. The birds, in all probability, will lay a second time, and the second batch is more likely to thrive than the former, as the weather will be warmer when the poults are brought off.

From the mew many eggs are taken, each hen generally averaging a score, often more, but here a point must not be forgotten ; if the cock shows a partiality to chip or peck the eggs he must instantly be removed, otherwise he will teach the hens to do the same.

As these eggs are gathered they are set under hens, each of which is entered on the keeper's register with full details.

Silky fowls are, perhaps, the best mothers, and cross-bred game are strongly recommended, but any hen will do if she is known to be quiet and good-tempered. Brahma-Dorkings are spoken of as free from vice or disease, perfect sitters and devoted mothers ; being sociable and not active, they are easily kept within bounds, but are wide rangers when free.

Hens should not be set in a close, stuffy shed, but where they can obtain as much air as possible, an open door not being sufficient. We know one keeper who places his coops on the ground, setting his hens under them ; an improvement upon this principle are the hatching and nest boxes with netted bottoms.

The hens are trained to come off for food and exercise at regular times, when the eggs are sprinkled with water and turned. A dust bath, with black sulphur in it, is a capital antidote for vermin, and very healthy for the old birds. Whilst sitting they should further be dusted with "insect" powder, and the same freely used in their laying boxes ; this will be found successful in driving away any remaining vermin, which otherwise tend to make them irritable and bad-tempered.

The incubation period progressing, the eggs are tested by looking at them before a strong light; the bad being rejected and their places filled up by others set on the same date.

As the twenty-fourth and last day of sitting draws near, the nests set the same date should be thoroughly examined, and the most forward eggs placed under the same hen. The hens must also be watched to see that they do not kill their poults as fast as they are hatched, and if they are restless and uneasy when some of their birds are off, must be put out at once, and the unhatched eggs transferred to another hen. It is the wisest course to knock all bad mothers on the head.

The mother and poults are now transferred for a day or so to a coop, when, the weather being dry, they are conveyed to the field where they are to be reared, prior to being turned into the woods.

The site of a rearing-ground is always a debatable one. Mr Balls was in favour of rough layers or a light-landed park, with an acclivity if possible. Paths should be cut, dividing off the standing grass into squares like a chess-board, thereby affording the youngsters a cool retreat from the glare of the midday sun. Here they are under constant surveillance, each coop packed up at eventide, opened again early in the morning, and moved twice daily. They must be fed frequently, and at first it will be found an advantage to lay a thin board near to each coop to scatter the food upon, as the poults are not strong enough to search amongst the herbage for it.

Their food now is an all-important item; it must be of the very best, and expense must not be spared. Chopped eggs, boiled rice (each grain separate), curds, greaves, bread crumbs, custards, bruised hemp seed, and finely-chopped green food, etc. A little good artificial food will be found invaluable, as, when mingled with other foods, it adds an irresistible relish, warding off that deplorable sight of fine healthy birds pining and wasting away in the midst of plenty because their diet is unnatural to them. Ants' eggs are valuable, but care must be used in giving gentles, and on no account do so unless they are perfectly white in colour. But on this point of food two persons rarely hold the same views, each clinging to his own despite the arguments of others, reminding one of Butler's lines—

> " He that complies against his will
> Is of the same opinion still."

This diversity of opinion may be accounted for by the fact that the birds require different diet according to the climate, situation and surroundings in which they are being reared.

It is always as well, however, to hear the experience of others. We move with the times. The rearing of young pheasants has become a science, and it has been proved by the best authorities that the judicious mingling of artificial food with their natural diet is not only beneficial, but, to hand-reared birds, an indispensable necessity.

Mr Balls' motto was—" Try everything and decide by results."

Water is another equally debatable subject; some give much, many little, and others none at all. An unlimited supply of pure spring water is correct. If it is stagnant, or open to the excrement of the birds, they will be liable to gapes. Moral —change it as often as possible. A remedy for this is dilution with camphor, or giving the birds camphor pills.

The old and well-known cure for gapes is, of course, spirits of turpentine, which is administered down the windpipe by the assistance of a feather tip, but Mr. W. B. Tegetmeier, in his most excellent book on pheasants, gives the result of an experiment with the fumes of carbolic acid as highly successful, and the authority of one so experienced is well worthy of re-petition. " It can easily be accomplished by putting three or four drops of the carbolic acid in a spoon, holding the latter over the flame of a lamp, and placing the head of the affected bird in a cloud of rising vapour." In this case each bird is separately treated, which means work where many are affected, and, therefore, it would seem that the present methods of fumigating are more easily manipulated and equally effective.

Finally, the birds which are to be turned out should be fed for a long period after they have left the hen, for they are not so capable of providing for themselves as their wilder brethren, yet they will by degrees take to the roving life free and unhampered by human yoke, until the eventful day of the year arrives when, let us hope, they will only succumb to a shot worthy of the endless trouble and anxiety they have given to him who has watched and tended them from their earliest youth upwards.

Thus did Balls ramble on unceasingly whilst we nodded our acquiescence and made mental notes of what was new to us.

A casual remark upon the oft-arising controversy in leading sporting journals regarding battue *versus* the old fashioned style of shooting, caused the veteran keeper's eyes to twinkle, and he raised himself on his elbow for a fresh outburst of sporting lore.

### PHEASANT SHOOTING.

Some there are who condemn pheasant shooting as slaughter, others positively affirm that there can be no sport in it.

"Who couldn't hit a bird as big as a diminutive haystack and as tame as the common garden hen? They are reared like chickens, coming at your beck or whistle, and the day before the shoot turned off in the woods. Even then they have to be probed with sticks before they will rise, and when they do get up they offer the easiest of shots."

Now, this is all very well to state, but how many places are there in the United Kingdom where such cowardly and unsportsmanlike proceedings take place.

Not one! Persons who make such statements, are piteously ignorant of the details, and unduly prejudiced Pheasant shooting, when properly conducted, is veritable sport ; indeed, it is the sport of princes.

Where is the man who, having enjoyed a well-organised

day at these birds, can condemn it? If such there be, he would either eclipse the immortal Ananias or he could have no love for the gun or its usual surroundings; his soul could never have been roused by the sport of shooting, and he could not realise one spark of that overpowering fascination and enjoyable excitement which takes possession of the true sportsman's every sense and nerve.

Yet, however good the sport may be, it is a very difficult task to evenly distribute it or bring it about in such a manner as to please all who participate therein, unless the whole party is comprised of real genuine sportsmen, for they alone remain fully satisfied with whatever their position or luck may bring, and realise almost as much pleasure in observing their neighbours' success as though they were similarly situated.

In partridge shooting this is a much easier matter, for there one can either walk the birds up, drive them, or intermingle the two. Positions can be drawn for, allotted by the host, or placed in the hands of a head keeper. They can be reversed or changed each beat, or once only, after lunch. And, as a rule, with these provisions, each gun comes in for his fair share of the shooting, although, of course, "luck," in this as in everything else, will occasionally have its sway.

But in pheasant shooting it is totally different. The birds almost invariably favour certain corners, where they will break, no matter who or what is there to prevent them. Then there are other places where they now and again break according to the atmospherical effect or fancy, so the chances of the guns occupying more or less desirable positions are, to say the least, uncertain and precarious. Nevertheless, guns must be placed there, otherwise, with the invariable perverseness of nature, the birds would be sure to break on the first occasion of the omission.

The guns who walk with the beaters have few opportunities at the genuine rocketer, except an occasional shot at a bird which either from lack of courage or sly cunning endeavours to steal back over the tree-tops. These joys are few and far between; nevertheless, they are made up for in a way, as the guns who walk have all they can manage in looking after ground game ; so, taking one consideration with another, this is a berth, if anything, to be desired rather than avoided.

The wing guns who perambulate the outskirts of the cover do not always occupy an enviable time or position, unless the boundaries are very rough and irregular, in which case ground game and birds are constantly breaking.

Now all these—to the outside guest—trivial details must be carefully taken into consideration and provided for by the host, who should find out and remember after each drive what shooting the guns have had, and on the next occasion replace them with a view to divide the sport to the best of his ability, also according to how and where he desires the game killed.

There is yet another difficulty to be contended against. The birds will run forward and congregate, instead of rising by degrees, as desired. Many are the stratagems, methods and plans resorted to in endeavours to reverse this state of affairs. Sometimes nets are placed at intervals, rags on strings, small hoardings, stops, etc., all of which more or less tend to interfere with the ground game. But, of course, if this objection is immaterial, they probably may be utilised with success.

To exemplify the above, an instance is quoted which took place on Balls' home beat. On that occasion, whilst shooting the big wood, where the bag amounted to upwards of 400, until an hour previous to knocking off two solitary pheasants only were killed, which, having risen far ahead of the beaters, were stopped whilst endeavouring to break back. The entire body ran for one corner, which was surrounded, with the before-mentioned result.

Another trouble to be surmounted is, to so work the birds that, besides moving in the direction desired, they at the same time *offer to the shooters the most difficult shots possible.* And this, as a rule, is the hardest task to successfully achieve.

There are always some birds which work the exact reverse
in every respect to what is desired ; others lie so close that
they never rise until fairly kicked up ; some sneak up drains,
overgrown ditches, and anywhere rather than fly, all of
which, if the guns are close to covert, are killed by an easy
shot at twenty or thirty yards' range.

Furthermore, unless the stands are considerately chosen,
the birds will be on to the
top of the guns before they
have gathered any idea of
their exact whereabouts.

This must be avoided, as,
if such is permitted, the birds
will present themselves with
outstretched wings, skimming
along at a leisure pace, which
is not wanted.

The target most desirable
is a bird flying high, strong
and speedy, in all the glory
of vigorous health and
grandeur, with a full sense of
the danger by which he is
surrounded, so that it is a case
of pitting your skill and cunning against his. A bird thus
killed gives to the sportsman

" SIC TRANSIT GLORIA.'

a sip from the cup of true happiness. How sweet to him
to stop an old cock in all his glory as he sails majestically
along, sweeter still to hear his lifeless form crashing through
the tree-tops and underwood, with the echoing thud when
finally brought in contact with Mother Earth.

" And all his hopes and fears lie with him in the dust."

Not a bird stiff and cramped from long hours in a hamper
during conveyance from some rearing-farm, or tame, as our
biassed friend describes, which runs along before one, and

only rises, or, rather, flutters up when actually poked with a stick or trodden upon.

Yet, on the other hand, the stands must not be so exposed as to turn the birds back or enable them to sheer off. They must be placed, according to locality and circumstances, so that they bring about the results desired.

In some parts it is next to impossible to situate the guns where they can secure rocketing shots, in which case one must act for the best and remain satisfied, for, as the old proverb has it, "Contentment is more than a kingdom."

Beaters, too, cause great anxiety. Although the keepers may muster them and see to their punctuality, organisation and all connected with them, it is always advisable to have someone in authority constantly in their midst — at least, so long as they are in covert. If this is not provided for, when they go into the underwood, where they cannot be seen, they wander about in all directions except the way they should go, following each other like a flock of sheep. Before a start is effected it should be seen that they are all equi-distant apart, and, most essential requirement of all, *in line*. Do not allow them to shout and yell like maniacs, but to keep continuously tapping the underwood with their sticks. Advance steadily and regularly, always in a line, and never permit four or five to get together in a cluster, as they have a great partiality for doing. On coming to a ditch or other stoppage the whole line should halt until all are over and occupying their regular places, *in line*, before the advance is signalled.

Now, although this may read to many as quite superfluous, it is really a very serious matter, and greater care should be taken in marshalling the beaters than is generally done.

In many large preserves, where the beaters are numbered and drilled like a volunteer corps, they know from constant practice precisely what is required. But in others, where they are frequently changed, there is chaos.

The actual methods of shooting the game are various, and worked according to the temperament of the happy possessor. To deal with them at all comprehensively would fill a big volume, but perhaps the following paragraph will imply far more than could otherwise be expressed in a long-detailed argument.

*A "shooter" is one thing, a "sportsman" another, who have nothing in common beyond the handling of a gun.*

It is *overdone* battues for shooters which work the mischief and thoughtlessly unpopularise the Game Laws.

For sport the birds are reared, and in a fair and sports-manlike manner they should be killed, not giving our neighbours on the Continent the opportunity of saying, with a shrug of the shoulders, " Ah, ze Engelsk fésant battue is no sport, it is von grand representation of skill vitt de gun."

On extensive grounds, where the beats are large and numerous, real business rarely commences before 1st November, nor, indeed, is a bird killed—except an occasional brace for presents and the table, or extra wilful birds which persist in fancying a neighbour's acres in preference to their own comfortable and well-preserved home ; and that aforesaid neighbour is known to be one of those objectionable gentlemen who sneak about at all hours of the day, or gloaming, gathering as his own " all that may come to his net."

But when this business does commence, when these large tracts of wood, pasture and moorland, dell and dale, wherein the echoing report of the death-dealing fire-iron has sounded only to knell the decease of some arch enemy, when those sacred precincts are at last invaded by that small and mirthful army of guns, loaders, keepers and beaters, yea, even the all-inspiring petticoat at luncheon, then indeed 'tis a day to be ever remembered and looked back to with pleasurable sensations. 'Tis for ever deeply written on the happy pages of our retrospective past, never to be eradicated until—

" Death surprises us in the midst of our hopes."

There are many who consider woods and coverts a *sine quâ non* to pheasant shooting and that one cannot have pheasants without them. It is not only possible but very simple for pheasants to be kept, and good sport shown with them, on almost any estate (of fair size), provided, of course, a certain amount of attention and a little trouble is given. "A ramble round any properly-laid-out coverts" should tell that the secret lies in the utilisation of the waste grounds to make temporary holding places for the birds.

When the enthusiastic Mr Balls at last stopped for a breather we chimed in that the time was getting away and the rising mists might make the return journey over the marshes difficult, not to say dangerous. Poor old Balls was all apologies for having chattered so much, but on hearing that it had delighted us beyond measure to listen, and that we should not visit him again if he talked less, he conducted the way to his rustic porch beaming over with good-nature, and he would have gone further and seen us safely along the marsh dam had we not almost forcibly insisted upon his remaining by his own comfortable fireside.

The stars were bright overhead when the cottage door creaked on its hinges, and the mists were rising.

"Good-night, sir, I shall look forward to your next visit. Good-night, sir!" The door is put to, the flood of flickering firelight shut in which, as Gray expresses it,—

"Leaves the world to darkness and to me."

"BRAT."

Z

# CHAPTER XXVI

## OTTER HUNTING EXTRAORDINARY

OTTER hunting is a branch of sport not in very strong favour in Broadland, probably because of the inconvenient nature of the ground rather than the scarcity of the quarry. Throughout the whole district otters are plentiful—more so, perhaps, than in any other part of England—but in their home in the vast expanse of reed, rush and swamp they defy both hounds and hunters, and can only be taken in traps, or shot in the twilight of early morn or eve.

In parts of East Anglia where landsprings run from the uplands to the marshland, or where trout streams wind from one lake to another, otters are taken unawares, and if the services of a pack of hounds can be secured a good hunt may be organised. Occasionally a pack visits certain districts where hunting is possible, but the sport obtained is not so good as that shown in more suitable otter-hunting districts.

During the winter, when King Frost has covered everything with his white mantle, and made the water, mere and swamp accessible to all, otter hunts can be successfully carried out, although the sport in most cases is reduced to slaughter, and the fun and merriment which usually marks an otter hunt in one's memory is replaced by a seriousness hardly appropriate to such an event.

Or at times a scratch pack of dogs (they cannot be called hounds) is collected, and a hunt organised in a district that is

354

thought accessible and suitable, although many of those who make up the party entertain grave reasons for doubting it before the day's proceedings are brought to a close. A search in an old sporting diary unearthed the recollections of such a day, which may be considered worth repeating.

It was one of the most amusing and exciting ever attended, and it was only by luck that the date of it happened to be brought to notice, cramped away as the announcement of the meet was in the "wanted" columns, and sandwiched in with a variety of other peculiar advertisements which the rustics of East Anglia are wont to send to their local papers. Some of these advertisements are often well worthy of perusal from an amusing point of view. This one ran somewhat as follows :—

"GRAND CO-OPERATIVE OTTER HUNT.

"As of late several otters have been observed in the upper reaches of the North River, a hunt will be organised on Thursday, the —th day of ——— 189—, starting from ——— at 10.30 a.m. sharp. *Everyone is invited to bring a dog.*"

Possibly, if the result of this invitation could have been foreseen, it would have been omitted from the advertisement altogether. Now, the traces of otters in the locality named had frequently come under our notice when pike fishing—many a fat half-eaten fish testifying to the presence of these amphibious epicures. Indeed, when fishing in the twilight, they had often been seen swimming from one bank to the other, and when bobbing for eels one, unconscious of or undisturbed by our silent visit, landed in the rushes within a yard or two of the boat. Even had this *prima facie* evidence been wanting, there was circumstantial evidence of the existence of otters in this part of the river by the frantic drives our dogs would make into the dense undergrowth of reeds and rushes when out at exercise; but so thick is the vegetation of Broadland that it is almost always impossible to verify by ocular proof what is actually the cause of all the excitement that "Spot" (one of the terriers in question) works himself into on so many occasions, his bearings being alone indicated by nodding reeds and the music of his tongue.

A hunt, on the upper reaches of the North River, where it flows through undulating meadows and pretty wooded landscapes, was quite feasible. The banks, although swampy and overgrown in places, are usually firm enough to walk upon for miles, whereas lower down the river, in the heart of the broads, a wide margin of treacherous swamp, hardly negotiable to a water spaniel, is the only apology for a foothold.

This advertisement was attractive. The writer cut it out of the paper, and on arrival home the excitable "Spot" (his favourite fox-terrier) was informed that he had been personally invited, and the eventful day, the prospects of which were doubtless discussed every evening in the bar-parlours and tap-rooms of the village inns for miles around, was looked forward to with considerable anticipation.

The morning of the meet broke beautifully fine. Arriving at the appointed rendezvous it was evident the invitation had been most cordially and unconditionally responded to. Some brought one dog, some two, others three, and some as many as six. Such a collection of the canine race, it may be safely asserted, has never before been seen in the field, and probably never will be again. Dogs of every description, and every dog of no description, had come from many miles of country round to swell the throng.

As Mark Twain would say, " There they were, black dogs, white dogs, yellow dogs, red dogs, variegated dogs, flea-bitten dogs, dogs with tails, dogs without tails, rat-terriers, bull-pups, poodles, fox-hounds, spaniels, setters, Newfoundlands, mixed breeds, pointers, retrievers, Airedales, collies, cross-breeds, Scotch-terriers, Irish-terriers, Welsh-terriers, English-terriers, and a multitude of other varieties, all growling, yelping, barking, snapping and jumping about, while the noise was like a menagerie at meal time." The crowd was as motley as the pack. Well-dressed men in faultless sporting toggery, with well-dressed dogs of high degree, mingled with the evil-looking loafer with his still more evil-looking lurcher snarling at his heels; whilst poachers (man and beast), on the lookout for anything that would turn up, jostled with absolute indifference against the velvet-coated keepers of the neighbouring coverts.

Some of the light-hearted members of the community sang vociferously

" We'll all go a-hunting to-day,
  All nature looks smiling and gay,"

followed by other chorus songs which however were muchly interrupted by recurring dissensions and disputes arising in the yelping canine crowd which occasioned a good deal of forcible language and strong application of the ash plant to maintain even an armed neutrality amongst the seventy-five hounds which comprised this heterogeneous pack. At length a start was made working up the stream. Sometimes it was necessary to cross wide and ugly ditches, and then the scrimmage at the boats was most entertaining. Some succeeded in jumping far enough to toe the gunwale, and then, to the delight of the crowd, would miss their footing and fall backwards into the water in a sitting posture, sinking over head and ears into slimy ooze.

At other times, when a covert was being looked, part of the hungry pack would get on the scent of a hare and make such a noise that they would lead everyone to think an otter had been started ; or a poaching lurcher would pounce upon a squatting pheasant, and the owner of the dog would try to annex it unobserved—quite an impossibility under the circumstances. Again, endless diversions were forthcoming from rat-hunts. Not finding an otter, the hunters seemed determined on sport.of some kind—nothing came amiss to them so long as it could move. In the excitement of the moment some of the ratters would hit a dog when aiming at a rat, the dog would resent the injury by fastening its teeth in a tender part of his assailant's anatomy, the crowd would laugh, and a fight was often the outcome.

. At one point in the chase a village wiseacre, who sat upon a railing overhanging a partly grown-up but extremely muddy-looking dyke, was holding forth to a gaping crowd, and pointing out to them " where he'd seed the ortters,"— when he was unceremoniously capsized into the dyke by a well-known poacher, who told him to "hold his slarver * and let other folks pass."

The fun for a time was fast and furious. Leaping the smaller ditches and ferrying over the larger ones provided endless diversion, but minutes shaped themselves into hours, which in turn slipped by with never a sign of an otter.

Otters there were in the locality beyond doubt, but whether a " find " would be made seemed a vanishing probability. Two keepers said they had only recently despatched an otter by the unique method of one holding it down with a spade while the other slit up its windpipe with a knife, which, considering the chances of the victim wriggling from under the spade, must have been rather a ticklish operation.

After two hours of skirmishing through swampy thickets and drawing all the most likely spots absolutely blank, a depression seemed to settle on the crowd, and one and all began to feel that their mighty hunt, which started so gaily, would end in miserable failure. Anxious eyes began to scan the horizon for the nearest " pub," when a furious barking in some thick undergrowth of long dry grass brought the hunters together and confusion reigned. A moment after a magnificent otter tumbled headlong out of his lair, towing the irrepressible " Spot " and another terrier, whose teeth were firmly fixed in his quarters, over the banks of the river into the depths below.

All three, otter and dogs, disappeared together. "Spot" soon reappeared, sneezing and panting for wind, but continued to paddle about, raising himself in the stream, and peering with most comical sidelong glances into the water below to ascertain what had become of his mysterious foe.

* Idle talk.

His comrade, a plucky little Skye terrier, rose to the surface some seconds later thoroughly exhausted, and the poor little chap was barely rescued from being torn to pieces by the swarm of dogs which, urged on by the excitable crowd on the bank, mistook him for the otter in his sodden and altered appearance.

The banks were now lined with eager hunters, and when the water had cleared from the first commotion, which had stirred up the muddy bottom, the quarry was viewed, and a most uncanny object he looked swimming for dear life close to the bottom, going at a tremendous pace down stream. The crowd followed shouting, hooting and gesticulating.

Having gone sixty or a hundred yards the otter was compelled to rise to the surface for air, when the crowd, how excited almost to madness, again hooted and threw every missile that they could lay their hands on at its head as it showed just above the surface of the water. For a second it was seen taking in a breath of air through its twitching, dilated nostrils, its eyes glaring with indescribable ferocity at its tormentors, and its fierce moustaches glistening in the sunlight; then the pack of blood and mongrel dogs of every variety of breed went for it *en masse*. Raising its head and showing its formidable teeth, it dived again, swimming with marvellous celerity. This was repeated three or four times, but at length, unable to hold out any longer, it was brought to bay and floated at the surface, filling its lungs for the final struggle, its nose puckering with rage, and its long white teeth showing sharp as needles.

An Irish terrier was the first up. Instantly the dog was seized and dragged by the otter under water. When they reappeared two other dogs rushed in to join the fray, the long, brown, sinuous body of the hunted animal writhing and twisting in the water with snake-like motions as it attempted to drown its assailants by forcing them below the water. It was a splendid conflict. The terrier, gamest of the game in spite of the powerful plunges of the otter, held on like grim death, fixing its fangs more firmly at every opportunity.

But alas! this splendid combat was soon ended. The otter, amidst the plaudits of the crowd, was seized by as many dogs as could find holding room, and dragged bodily ashore, dying game and fighting desperately to the last.

It turned out to be a dog otter, and the scale registered twenty-five pounds. Its remains now repose in a glass case in a position of honour in one of the old country Halls, but its features have lost little of their ferocity in the preservation, as it still seems to snarl and glare from behind the crystal frontage of this last resting-place.

At the death everyone turned up, wet or dry, and the amount of (what in Broadland is commonly called) "jaw," "slarver" and "know" was something to be heard to be realised. Everyone seemed to want to talk at once and to tell everybody else "what ought to have been done; how the otter ought to have been killed; what his dog had done, and his dog before that," etc., and so on, without cessation. Babel was let loose. Then there was a dog fight or so, which resulted in the owners fighting between themselves, until a friend tripped them into a dyke to cool their ardour, and finally an adjournment was made to the nearest public-house, which was soon drank out of everything except water. Then the company broke up and wended their respective ways homewards, accompanied by their four - footed companions.

This narrative must not of course be taken as characteristic of otter hunting proper in East Anglia, as a good pack of hounds exists which is ably hunted on the very upper reaches of the rivers and at times shows excellent sport; but these meets can hardly be said to take place in Broadland proper.

# APPENDIX

## THE ORIGIN OF FISH PRESERVATION IN BROADLAND

MANY years ago fish were netted in the waterways of Broadland by the ton, and old yachtsmen remember the days when large heaps were to be seen rotting on the banks of the North River, from Horning to St Bennet's Abbey, left there by the netters because they were not large enough to send to market and because they did not trouble themselves to return them to the water, although occasionally they would sell them to a farmer for manure. It was also a disastrous custom in those days to net the spawning fish when they congregated in the shallows on the backwaters and broads, and to such an extent was this practice carried on that in the year 1857 the indignation of Norwich anglers was aroused, and a memorial was sent to the Norwich Corporation praying that the existing Charter might be put in force, and pointing out that the Corporation should take steps to protect the rivers against wholesale netting. For the furtherance of this object a private meeting was held at the old Library Room, St Andrew's Hall, when the "NORFOLK AND NORWICH ANGLERS' SOCIETY" sprang into existence, with the late Mr James Skippon as Secretary. The subscription was only five shillings per annum, yet out of this a paid watcher was appointed at a salary of ten shillings per week. The Society did good work, but were much handicapped for want of special powers to deal with offenders.

In 1870 Mr Skippon resigned the secretaryship in favour of Mr Charles Jeremiah Green.

In 1874 a meeting was held by the Society at the Maid's Head Hotel for the purpose of considering a proposal to apply for an Act of Parliament to regulate fishing in the Wensum, Yare and Bure, Mr I. O. Howard Taylor, the President of the Society, being in the chair; but had it not been for Mr J. B. Pearce legislative preservation would probably have been delayed for many years. That veteran angler spoke very forcibly in favour of a general Act, finishing his speech by throwing a five-pound note on to the table and appealing to those present to follow his example. In a few minutes Mr Pearce's original five-pound note had swollen to seventy pounds. This lead was followed by Mr W. S. Everitt of Oulton Broad, who was more particularly interested in the Waveney, and who, through the assistance of Mr Josiah Poyser and others, raised a substantial fund for the purpose of including that river and district within the Act.

In June 1875 a meeting was held at the Guildhall, Norwich, for the purpose of conferring with Mr Frank Buckland, the Commissioner inquiring into the fisheries of the Norfolk coast. Mr Buckland expressed sympathy with the object of the meeting and promised his assistance. On November 1st of the same year a further meeting was held at the Norfolk Hotel, Norwich, for the purpose of receiving Mr Buckland's report, and on February 5th, 1876, a deputation from the YARE PRESERVATION SOCIETY (the new name for the old Norfolk and Norwich Anglers' Society) and riparian owners visited the Home Secretary for furthering the objects they had in view.

In January 1877 successful meetings were held at the Town Hall, Great Yarmouth, and in February of the same year at the Guildhall, Norwich, whilst a public subscription list was opened at Messrs Gurney's Bank and a petition was got up, to which many thousands appended their signatures. Thus by degrees the small and ever-energetic committee of enthusiastic anglers gradually worked upon public feeling until it culminated in March of the same year at a meeting at the Royal Hotel, when support was promised from most influential quarters in both counties, and the Bill became looked upon as a certainty, whilst the greatest enthusiasm was manifested.

On the 12th July 1877 the Norfolk and Suffolk Fisheries Act was placed upon the statute books, and at the annual dinner of the Yare Preservation Society Mr J. J. Colman, M.P., President, remarked that "had the Bill been introduced as a political measure it would never have become law, but because it was supported by members on both sides of the House opposition was disarmed and the Bill was now operative."

Under this Act a Board of Conservators was appointed by the Magistrates of Norfolk, Suffolk, Norwich, King's Lynn and Sudbury, who met at periodical intervals and framed the excellent bye-laws which are set out hereafter. Meanwhile the Yare Preservation Society, which worked hand-in-hand with the various angling clubs of the district, continued to do good work—acting as a kind of watch-dog to the Conservators and reporting to them from time to time anything which they thought would further the preservation of fishing and improve angling generally on the waterways.

The first general meeting of the Board of Conservators was held at the Shirehall, Norwich, on the 10th October 1877, at which it was reported that the following gentlemen had been appointed under the Act as follows :—

## BY THE JUSTICES OF NORFOLK

| NAME. | RESIDENCE. |
| --- | --- |
| The Earl of Leicester (Lord-Lieutenant of the County) | Holkham Park |
| The Earl of Kimberley | Kimberley Park |
| Sir H. J. Stracey, Bart. | Rackheath Park |
| Sir Reginald Proctor Beauchamp, Bt. | Langley Park |
| Sir W. H. B. ffolkes, Bart. | Hillington Hall, Lynn |
| Sir Willoughby Jones, Bart. | Cranmer Hall |
| Sir R. J. Buxton, Bart. | Shadwell Court |
| R. Thornhaugh Gurdon, Esq. | Eccles Hall |
| Edward Birkbeck, Esq. | Horstead, Norwich |
| T. C. Blofield, Esq. | Hoveton House |
| R. H. Blake Humfrey, Esq. | Heggett Hall |
| C. Louis Buxton, Esq. | Bolwick, Marsham |
| Lieutenant-Colonel Duff, M.P. | Westwick |
| Lieutenant-Colonel H. Fitz Roy | The Close, Norwich |
| Anthony Hammond, Esq. | Westacre |
| John J. L. Lubbock, Esq. | Catfield Hall, Norwich |
| W. H. Jary, Esq. | Burlingham, Norwich |
| The Mayor of Great Yarmouth | Great Yarmouth |
| The Mayor of Thetford | Thetford |
| H. R. Harmer, Esq. | Great Yarmouth |

## BY THE JUSTICES OF SUFFOLK

| NAME. | RESIDENCE. |
| --- | --- |
| The Duke of Grafton | Euston Hall, Thetford |
| The Marquis of Bristol | Ickworth, Bury St Edmunds |
| The Lord Henniker | Thornham, Eye |
| The Lord Waveney | Flixton Hall, Bungay |
| The Lord Rendlesham, M.P. | Rendlesham, Woodbridge |
| Sir Edward C. Kerrison, Bart. | Oakley Park, Scole |
| Sir C. J. Fox Bunbury, Bart. | Barton Hall, Bury St Edmunds |
| The Mayor of Ipswich | Ipswich |
| H. Spencer Waddington, Esq. | Leavenham Hall, Soham |
| J. Thelluson Rowley, Esq. | Tendring Hall, Stoke; by Nayland |

## BY THE JUSTICES OF SUFFOLK (*continued*)

| NAME. | RESIDENCE. |
|---|---|
| Lieutenant-Colonel H. M. Leathes | Herringfleet Hall, Lowestoft |
| Thomas Thornhill, Esq., M.P. | Pakenham, Bury St Edmunds |
| William Angerstein, Esq. | Weeting Hall, Brandon |
| Edward P. Mackenzie, Esq. | Downham, Brandon |
| Dr Aldred | Dene House, Gt. Yarmouth |
| J. E. Crisp, Esq. | Beccles |
| W. Spencer Everitt, Esq. | Oulton Broad, Lowestoft |
| Alfred Cobbold, Esq. | Ipswich |
| The Rev. Robert Gwilt | Icklingham, Soham |
| The Rev. E. R. Benyon | Culford, Bury St Edmunds |

## BY THE JUSTICES OF THE CITY AND COUNTY OF THE CITY OF NORWICH

| NAME. | RESIDENCE. |
|---|---|
| The Mayor of Norwich | Norwich |
| J. J. Colman, Esq., M.P. | Carrow Abbey, Norwich |
| Samuel Gurney Buxton, Esq. | Catton Park |
| I. Odin Howard Taylor, Esq. | Norwich |
| R. E. Burroughes, Esq. | Norwich |
| Edward Field, Esq. | Norwich |
| John Barwell, Esq. | Norwich |
| A. J. N. Chamberlin, Esq. | Wroxham |
| Harry Bullard, Esq. | Norwich |
| J. B. Pearce, Esq. | Norwich |

## BY THE CORPORATION OF KING'S LYNN

| NAME. | RESIDENCE. |
|---|---|
| The Mayor of Lynn | King's Lynn |
| G. Holditch, Esq. | King's Lynn |
| R. Bagge, Esq. | Gaywood Hall |
| F. J. Cresswell, Esq. | King's Lynn |
| F. Brittain Archer, Esq. | King's Lynn |

## BY THE CORPORATION OF SUDBURY

| Name. | Residence. |
| --- | --- |
| Samuel Higgs, Esq. | Sudbury |
| J. Francis Hills, Esq. | Sudbury |
| A. H. White, Esq. | Sudbury |
| G. Lancelot Andrews, Esq. | Sudbury |
| Alfred Smith, Esq. | Sudbury |

At a meeting of the Board of Conservators held at the Shire-hall, Norwich, the 27th April 1878, on the proposition of Lieut.-Col. Duff, M.P., an association was formed, called "THE NORFOLK FISHERIES PRESERVATION ASSOCIATION," for the purposes of collecting funds for and carrying into effect in the county of Norfolk the Norfolk and Suffolk Fisheries Act, 1877, of which Association the Conservators for Norfolk, Norwich, Yarmouth, Thetford and Lynn were appointed the committee.

This Association was a success, its principal regulations being the appointment, from time to time, of keepers, watchers, boatmen and others employed by landowners to be water-bailiffs, with power to act in certain defined districts and localities under the Norfolk and Suffolk Fisheries Act, 1877, and the institution and conduct of prosecutions in Courts of Summary Jurisdiction in the name of the Board of Conservators, the costs of such prosecutions being defrayed out of the funds of the Association.

In 1879 no less than forty-two water-bailiffs for the preservation of fishing had been appointed by the Norfolk Fisheries Association, 242 members had been enrolled in the Yare and Bure Preservation Society's books, and many cases of poaching were detected and vigorously prosecuted; whilst extra water-bailiffs were appointed every year following.

From the time that Mr Buckland first took interest in East Anglian waters he was always found to be of great help and assistance, and in 1879 he promised Mr W. S. Everitt that if a meeting was called to discuss the advisability of introducing foreign fish to Broadland he would attend and deliver an address. The meeting was summoned at Lowestoft, under the auspices of the Waveney and Oulton Fish Protection Society and its President, the Rev. Sir Charles Clarke. It was presided over by Lord Waveney. After Mr Buckland had addressed the meeting, an interesting debate arose, from which originated what was then termed THE NATIONAL FISH ACCLIMATIZATION SOCIETY, of which the Marquis of Bristol was appointed Chairman and W. Oldham Chambers, Secretary. The first business of this Society was a decision to hold a fishing exhibition at Lowestoft, Sir Edward Birkbeck agreeing to become Chairman of the committee formed for such purpose. The support of His Royal Highness the Prince of Wales was solicited, who favoured the project, after which the venue of the exhibition was removed from Lowestoft to Norwich, where it was eventually held in the year following (1880) with great success. Following this exhibition was another fishery exhibition in Edinburgh in 1881, and in London at South Kensington almost immediately afterwards. The London Fishery Exhibition, it will be remembered, was the fore-runner of the London summer exhibitions.

In 1883 netting was totally abolished, except for the purpose of obtaining bait.

In 1885 the question of angling rights on Wroxham Broad was tried, but the defendant was fined one shilling and £1, 1s. 6d. costs.

In 1888 twenty-one angling clubs were subscribing to the Yare Preservation Society by way of appreciation of their efforts concerning river fishing and for the improvement of the sport of angling. Several meetings seem to have been called to discuss the question of a close-time for rods, but this appears to have been thought unnecessary, one of the strongest reasons urged being that such would deprive the poor of reasonable recreation during the best time of the year.

In 1888 the city members commenced to subscribe £25 each for prizes to the various angling clubs, provided the clubs registered themselves as supporters of the Society.

In 1889 the Society for the Preservation of the Bure began to sadly feel the want of funds, as also did the Waveney Protection Society, in consequence of which watchers were withdrawn, and without doubt the fishing suffered in consequence.

During the year following the Bure Society became merged in the Yare, but the latter Society did not feel they were sufficiently financially strong to take over the responsibilities of the Waveney and Oulton Broad Preservation Society, so the latter Institution, owing to want of support, has practically ceased to exist; but the Yare and Bure continues to flourish, in spite of the many difficulties that beset its path, although, if the support was accorded to it that it deserves, anglers and angling would be the more benefited thereby.

## PRESIDENTS OF THE YARE AND BURE PRESERVATION SOCIETY

| | | | |
|---|---|---|---|
| 1857—1866 | ... | ... ... | R. N. Bacon, Esq. |
| 1866—1868 | ... | ... ... | J. Barwell, Esq. |
| 1868—1869 | ... | .. ... | E. Field, Esq. |
| 1869—1870 | ... | ... ... | R. E. Burroughes, Esq. |

| | | | |
|---|---|---|---|
| 1870—1871 | ... | ... | ... G. S. Hutchinson, Esq. |
| 1871—1873 | ... | ... | ... Major Micklethwait |
| 1873—1875 | ... | . . | ... I. O. Howard Taylor, Esq. |
| 1875—1876 | ... | ... | ... Sir Harry Bullard, M.P. |
| 1876—1877 | ... | ... | ... Sir Reginald Beauchamp, Bart. |
| 1877—1878 | ... | ... | ... S. G. Buxton, Esq. |
| 1878—1879 | ... | ... | ... J. J. Colman, Esq., M.P. |
| 1879—1880 | ... | ... | ... S. Grimmer, Esq. |
| 1880—1881 | ... | ... | ... G. F. Buxton, Esq. |
| 1881—1882 | ... | ... | ... Sir Edward Birkbeck, Bart. |
| 1882—1883 | ... | ... | ... C. L. Buxton, Esq. |
| 1883—1884 | ... | ... | ... Sir R. J. Buxton, Bart. |
| 1884—1885 | ... | ... | ... Sir W. Vincent, Bart. |
| 1885—1886 | ... | ... | ... Sir S. Hoare, Bart , M.P. |
| 1886—1887 | ... | ... | ... Sir William ffolkes, Bart. |
| 1887—1888 | ... | ... | ... Rt. Hon. Lord Walsingham |
| 1888—1889 | ... | ... | ... F. Oddin Taylor, Esq. |
| 1889—1890 | ... | ... | ... Hon. Ailwyn Fellowes, M.P. |
| 1890—1891 | ... | ... | ... J. Cator, Esq. |
| 1891—1892 | ... | ... | ... H. R. Burroughes, Esq. |
| 1892—1893 | ... | ... | ... Fred Bullard, Esq. |
| 1893—1894 | ... | ... | ... Sir E. Birkbeck, Bart. |
| 1894—1895 | ... | ... | ... G. M. Chamberlin, Esq. |
| 1895—1896 | ... | ... | ... E. S. Trafford, Esq. |
| 1896—1897 | ... | ... | ... G. C. Davies, Esq. |
| 1897—1898 | ... | ... | ... W. Hackblock, Esq. |
| 1898—1899 | ... | ... | ... Russell J. Colman, Esq. |
| 1899—1900 | ... | ... | ... Major Jary |
| 1900—1901 | ... | ... | ... Sir C. R. Gilman |
| 1901—1902 | ... | ... | ... J. T. Hotblack, Esq. |

Those who come from a distance to visit Norfolk waters for the purpose of fishing should take into their consideration the fact that no sport can be conducted nor maintained without expense, and before they depart, it is to be hoped, leave a sum in accordance with their means in gratitude for the sport they have obtained and to assist these worthy Societies to continue in their good work. If the *Angling Press* may be believed, London fishermen have a grand time of it in Broadland waters ; but how much do they contribute towards their protection? A few, it is true, give a subscription, feeling perhaps that they could not conscientiously enjoy their sport without doing so, but the vast majority, as the riverside boxes too truly prove, care only for themselves or perhaps the money that the fish they catch will bring to them in the shape of prizes from their London clubs.

For over thirty years Mr C. J. Green continued to act as Secretary to the Society, but in 1901 he was compelled, by reason of his increasing years, to resign in favour of Mr A. J. Rudd. The members of the Society at present number 257 ; it has an income of about £150 per annum, of which at least £25 is contributed by the Great Eastern Railway Company, £15, 15s. is subscribed by way of fees from local angling clubs (of which there are over seventy in the city of Norwich alone), whilst under £2 is taken from the many collection boxes which are scattered all over Broadland.

---

## NORFOLK AND SUFFOLK FISHERIES ACT, 1877.

### (40 *and* 41 *Vict., c. XCVIII.*)

An Act to preserve the Fisheries in the Navigable Rivers and Broads of the Counties of Norfolk and Suffolk and of the County of the City of Norwich (12th July 1877).

Whereas the Fisheries in the Navigable Rivers of the Counties of Norfolk and Suffolk and the County of the City of Norwich and in the Broads connected with such Rivers have of late years been greatly injured and it is expedient that better provision be made for preserving and increasing the same but that object cannot be accomplished without the authority of Parliament. May it therefore please Your Majesty that it be enacted by the Queen's Most Excellent Majesty by and with the advice and consent of the Lords Spiritual and Temporal and Commons in this present Parliament assembled and by the authority of the same as follows :—

1. This Act may be cited for all purposes as the Norfolk and Suffolk Fisheries Act 1877.

2. This Act shall extend and apply only to the navigable rivers in the Counties of Norfolk and Suffolk and the County of the City of Norwich and to the Broads connected with such and shall not include the sea or sea-coast.

3. The Justices of the Peace of the Counties of Norfolk and Suffolk and of the City and County of the City of Norwich at any Court of Quarter Sessions held in and for their respective counties after the passing of this Act (due notice having been previously given according to the practice of such Sessions) and the Mayor Aldermen and Burgesses of the Boroughs of King's Lynn and Sudbury (hereinafter called the Corporation) shall have power to appoint Conservators as follows (that is to say) the Justices of the County of Norfolk twenty Conservators, the Justices of the County of

Suffolk twenty Conservators, the Justices of the City and County of the City of Norwich ten Conservators and the Corporation five Conservators each, which Conservators shall be a Board of Conservators (hereinafter called the Board) for the preservation and regulation of the fisheries within the limits of this Act.

4. Whenever any vacancy in the office of Conservator appointed by the before-mentioned respective Justices shall occur, the same may at any time be filled up by any Justices assembled at General or Quarter Sessions as follows viz. :—If the vacancy be caused by a Conservator of the County of Norfolk by the Justices of Norfolk assembled at Norwich, if the vacancy be caused by a Conservator for the County of Suffolk by the Justices for Suffolk assembled at Ipswich and if the vacancy be caused by a Conservator for Norwich then by the Justices of Norwich, and if any vacancy shall occur in the number of conservators to be appointed by the Corporation the same shall be filled up by the Corporation of King's Lynn or Sudbury as the case may be.

5. The Board shall be a body corporate having perpetual succession and a common seal with power to make contracts and to sue and be sued by the name or style of "The Conservators of the Norfolk and Suffolk Fisheries."

6. No act or proceeding of the Board shall be questioned on account of any vacancy or vacancies in their body and no defect in the appointment of any person or persons acting as member or members of such Board shall be deemed to vitiate any proceedings of such Board in which he or they have taken part.

7. The Board shall meet for the dispatch of business and shall from time to time make such regulations with repect to the election of a Chairman of their meetings, the summoning, notice, place, management and adjournment of their meetings and generally with respect to the transaction and management of business including the quorum of meetings as they think fit subject to the following conditions.

(a) The first meeting after the formation of the Board shall be held at the Shire Hall in the County of Norfolk within three months after the passing of this Act and all subsequent meetings at such place or places as the Board may from time to time direct.

(b) An extraordinary meeting may be summoned at any time and place on the requisition of three members of the Board.

(c) The quorum to be fixed by the Board shall consist of not less than three members.

(d) Every question shall be decided by a majority of votes of the members voting on that question and in the event of equality of votes the Chairman for the time being shall have a second or casting vote.

2A

8. The Board may appoint committees of their members, may fix a quorum for each committee and may lay down rules for its guidance.    Every question before a committee shall be decided by a majority of votes of the members voting on that question and in the event of an equality of votes the Chairman for the time being shall have a second or casting vote.

9. Any minute made of proceeding at a meeting of the Board if signed by the Chairman of that meeting either at the meeting of the Board at which such proceeding took place or at the next ensuing meeting of the Board at which such person may be present shall be receivable in evidence in all legal proceedings without further proof and until the contrary is proved every meeting of the Board in respect of the proceedings of which the minutes have been so made shall be deemed to have been duly convened and held and all members thereof to have been qualified.

10. The Board shall have power within the limits of this Act to do the following things or such of them as they may in their discretion think expedient (*i.e.*).

(1) From time to time by writing under the seal of the Board to appoint a sufficient number of water bailiffs and other officers to assign to them their salaries and duties and to remove any water bailiff or officer so appointed.

Provided always that nothing herein contained shall prevent the Board from obtaining the services of additional constables under the Act third and fourth Victoria Chapter 88 section 19 for the purpose of carrying out the provisions of this Act ; such constables when appointed to have all the powers and privileges of water bailiffs and to be paid for their services by the said Board.

(2) To take legal proceedings against persons violating the provisions of the Act.

(3) Generally to execute such works do such acts and incur such expenses as they may deem expedient to be executed done or incurred for carrying out the purposes of this Act but so that it shall not be lawful for the Board to pay to any member of the Board any salary fees or other remuneration for his acting in any way as a member of or under the Board. Provided that this section shall not authorise the construction of any works below high water mark or anything which may injuriously affect any navigable river, cut or inland navigation.

11. The Board shall have power to make and similarly from *time to time vary or rescind* byelaws for any or all of the purposes following (*i.e.*)

(1) To determine the time in each year during which it shall be illegal to fish for take or kill or attempt to take or kill otherwise than by rod or line all or any of the different kinds of fresh-water fish found within the limits of this Act.

(2) To determine the mesh size and description of nets and to regulate the use of nets engines trimmers liggers or instruments of any kind for the purpose of taking fish within the limits of this Act. The Board may take any byelaw to apply to the whole or to any part or parts of the said navigable rivers and broads.

12. Any byelaws made in pursuance of this Act shall come into force only when the following conditions have been complied with

(1) They shall have been advertised as proposed byelaws in one or more newspapers generally circulating in each of the Counties of Norfolk and Suffolk.

(2) They shall after the expiration of one month after such advertisement have been approved by one of Her Majesty's Principal Secretaries of State.

Provided always that all byelaws made in pursuance of this Act shall be advertised as approved byelaws in one or more newspapers generally circulating in each of the Counties of Norfolk and Suffolk and shall be further published in such manner as the Board shall think fit and the production of a written or printed copy of any byelaws purporting to have been made by the Board and approved by a Secretary of State shall in any legal proceedings be taken to be proof of the due making allowing publication and existence of such byelaws until the contrary be shewn.

13. Any person acting or attempting to act in contravention of any byelaw made in pursuance of this Act for each such offence shall incur a penalty of *not exceeding ten pounds* in addition to the forfeiture of nets or instruments used in contravention of such byelaw.

14. Any Officer of the Conservators or any Police Constable or other Officer may within the limits of this Act stop and search any wherry or boat in which he shall have *reasonable grounds* for believing there are any fish taken or any *nets engines trimmers liggers* or other instruments used or intended to be used for the taking of fish within such limits in contravention of any such byelaw and if he shall find any person using or attempting to use or having used any such nets *or other things* within such limits in contravention of any such byelaw he may seize and detain the same and he shall in such case forthwith apply to some Justice of the Peace for a Summons citing the person in charge of such wherry or boat or in possession or use of any such fish nets or other things to appear before two Justices who shall inquire and determine whether such person has incurred any penalty under this Act *and in the event of the Justices* finding that he has *incurred any such penalty* they may determine *in addition to such* penalty that all or any such fish nets and other *things shall be forfeited.*

15. Any person refusing to allow any such wherry or boat to be stopped and searched as in the last preceding section provided or

resisting or obstructing such search shall for every such offence be liable to a penalty not exceeding *five pounds.*

16. All penalties imposed by this Act and all costs and expenses may be recovered in a summary manner within six calendar months of the commission of the offence before two Justices as in manner directed by an Act passed in the 11th and 12th years of the reign of Her present Majesty Queen Victoria Chapter 43 entitled " An Act to facilitate the performance of the duties of Justices of the Peace out of Sessions within England and Wales with respect to Summary convictions and orders " or of any Act amending the same and all monies received in respect of such penalties shall be paid to the Board to be applied by them to the purposes of this Act unless the Justices for some special reason shall otherwise order and all forfeiture shall be disposed of as the Justices may direct and the proceeds (if any) shall be applied in manner in which the monies received in respect of penalties for offences under this Act are hereby directed to be applied.

17. Where any offence under this Act is committed in or upon any waters forming the boundary between the Counties of Norfolk and Suffolk such offence may be prosecuted before any Justices of the Peace in either of such Counties.

18. Provided always that nothing in this Act contained shall prejudice or interfere with the rights or privileges of the body corporate of the Mayor Aldermen and citizens of the City of Norwich or of Great Yarmouth Port and Haven Commissioners in or over the rivers and broads within the limits of this Act.

---

## NORFOLK AND SUFFOLK FISHERIES ACT, 1877.

### (40 *and* 41 *Vict., c. XCVIII.*)

### FISHERY BYE-LAWS.

The following Bye-laws have been made by the Board of Conservators appointed under the Norfolk and Suffolk Fisheries Act, 1877, and approved :—

### CLOSE TIME—ALL WATERS.

1. No person shall fish for, catch, take, or kill, or attempt to catch, take, or kill, otherwise than by rod and line, within the limits of the above Act, any Trout, between the 10th day of September and the 25th day of January, both days inclusive, or any other kind of fish, between the 1st day of March and the 30th day of

June, both days inclusive, except Smelts, Bait, and Eels, as herein-after provided.

## Nets Generally.

2. No person shall, for the purpose of taking Fish within the limits of the above Act, do any of the following things :—

(1) Use or attempt to use any Net between one hour after sunset and one hour before sunrise, except in the River Ouse below Denver Sluice, and in the River Nene below Wisbech Bridge.

(2) Use or attempt to use for the purpose of taking Fish, other than Tench, Smelts, Bait, and Eels, any net having a mesh of less dimensions when wet than three inches from knot to knot, measured on each side of the square, or twelve inches all round.

(3) Use or attempt to use any Net having a wall or facing, with a mesh of less dimensions when wet than seven inches from knot to knot, measured on each side of the square, or twenty-eight inches all round.

(4) Use or attempt to use, in any navigable river, any Bow Net.

(5) Use or attempt to use, in any navigable river, any Drag Net having a poke or pocket.

(6) Use or attempt to use a Drag Net of any kind in the under-mentioned waters :—

(a) The River Yare or Wensum—

(b) The River Waveney—

(c) The River Bure below the lower entrance into Wroxham Broad—

(d) The River Ant below the lower entrance into Barton Broad—

(e) The River Thurne below the entrance into Somerton Broad—

except with the previous permission in writing of the Board of Conservators, under their Common Seal.

3. No person shall, within the limits of the above Act, use or attempt to use, any Net for taking Fish, unless it is sufficiently weighted to sink vertically in the water, or take or attempt to take Fish by placing two or more Nets behind or near to each other, or use any other device or artifices so as practically to diminish the size of the mesh of any Net allowed to be used by these Bye-laws, or to evade this provision.

## Prohibiting Use of Trimmers, &c., in Navigable Rivers.

4. No person shall use, or attempt to use, any Trimmer, Ligger, Dead Line, or Snare, or any like Instrument or Engine, for the purpose of taking Fish in any navigable river within the limits of

the above Act, except Lines for taking Eels as hereinafter provided.

### Taking Smelts—Rivers Yare and Wensum.

5. No person shall, within the limits of the above Act, use, or attempt to use, any Net in the River Yare or Wensum for the purpose of taking Smelts, except a Cast Net or Drop Net, between the 10th day of March and 12th day of May, both days inclusive, and then only between the New Mills, in the Parish of St Swithin, in the City of Norwich, or Trowse Bridge, in Trowse, or Trowse Newton, and the junction of the Rivers Yare and Wensum at a place known as Trowse Hythe, and between Hardley Cross and the junction of the Rivers Yare and Waveney.

6. No person shall use, or attempt to use, a Cast Net or Drop Net exceeding 16 feet in diameter, in the River Yare or Wensum, within the limits of the above Act.

### Taking Smelts—River Waveney.

7. No person shall, within the limits of the above Act, use, or attempt to use in the River Waveney, above the Borough Cement Works, any Net for the purpose of taking Smelts, except between the 10th day of March and the 12th day of May, both days inclusive, and then only at the places and by the means hereinafter mentioned, viz., between Rose Hall Fleet and the Boathouse Hill, near Beccles, and in the Pen of Shipmeadow Lock, by a Cast Net or Drop Net not exceeding sixteen feet in diameter, and if any such Net be used between one hour after sunset and one hour before sunrise, the same shall be used with a light or flare, and not otherwise.

### Taking Smelts—Rivers Ouse, Nar, and Nene.

8. No person shall, within the limits of the above Act, take or kill or attempt to take or kill Smelts in the Rivers Ouse, Nar, or Nene, between the 1st day of April and the 31st day of August, both days inclusive.

9. No person shall, within the limits of the above Act, use, or attempt to use in the Rivers Ouse, Nar, or Nene, for the purpose of taking Smelts, any net having a mesh of less dimensions, when wet, than five-eighths of an inch from knot to knot, measured on each side of the square.

### Taking Smelts—Breydon Water.

10. No person shall, within the limits of the above Act, use, or attempt to use, in the water known as Breydon Water, for the purpose of taking Smelts, any Net in the months of May, June, July, and

August, or any Net between the 1st day of September and the 30th day of April, both days inclusive, having a mesh of less dimensions, when wet, than five-eighths of an inch from knot to knot, measured on each side of the square.

### Taking Bait—Navigable Rivers.

11. No person shall, for the purpose of taking Bait in any navigable river within the limits of the above Act (except in the River Ouse below Denver Sluice, and in the River Nene below Wisbech Bridge), use any Net other than a Cast Net, or any Cast Net having a mesh of less dimensions, when wet, than five-eighths of an inch from knot to knot, measured on each side of the square.

### Taking Bait—All Waters.

12. No person shall, within the limits of the above Act, use, or attempt to use, any Cast Net exceeding eight yards in circumference,* or having a sack or purse exceeding fourteen inches in depth, when extended, for the purpose of taking Fish for Bait, and the word "Bait" shall mean Roach, Rudd or Roud, Bream, Dace, Ruff or Pope, Gudgeons, and Minnows, measuring less than eight inches from the nose to the fork of the tail.

13. No person shall, within the limits of the above Act, Net for Bait at any time on a Sunday, and no person shall, within such limits, Net for Bait at any time on a week-day except between one hour before sunrise and one hour after sunset, nor unless such Bait is for use in angling, or trolling, or taking Eels within the limits of the above Act.

### Taking Eels—Rivers Yare and Wensum Above Hardley Cross.

14. No person shall, for the purpose of taking Eels in the Rivers Yare and Wensum, above Hardley Cross, do any of the following things :—

    (1) Use or attempt to use, in the months of April, May, and June, a line with a hook or hooks, except in connection with a rod used for the purpose of Angling.

    (2) Use or attempt to use any Net in the months of April, May, and June.

    (3) Use or attempt to use, at any other time of the year, a Line, whether fixed or not, with more than one hook, except in connection with a rod used for the purpose of Angling.

    (4) Use or attempt to use any Net other than a Skim or Skein Net.

* By a Resolution passed by the Board of Conservators on the 4th February 1888, and duly confirmed by the Board of Trade, it was enacted that Cast Nets be allowed up to TWELVE yards in circumference from 11th October till the 1st April in each year.

### Taking Eels—All Other Waters.

15. In all other waters within the limits of the above Act, Lines with one hook only, whether fixed or not, and fixed Nets, but no others, may be used at any time for taking Eels only.

16. No person shall use, or attempt to use, in any water within the limits of the above Act, a Dag or Spear, for the purpose of taking Fish other than Eels.

### All Waters.

17. Any person, within the limits of the above Act, taking any Fish except Smelts, Eels, or Bait, in any Net allowed by these Bye-laws to be used for taking Smelts, Eels, or Bait respectively, shall immediately return such first-mentioned Fish to the water without avoidable injury.

18. The foregoing Bye-laws shall not apply to any other than fresh-water fish, or to the water known as Breydon Water, except as to Smelts, as hereinbefore provided.

By Section 13 of the Norfolk and Suffolk Fisheries Act, it is enacted that any person acting or attempting to act in contravention of any Bye-laws made in pursuance of that Act shall for each such offence incur a penalty of not exceeding £10, in addition to the forfeiture of the Nets or Instruments used in contravention of such Bye-law.

And by Section 14, any Officer of the Conservators, or any Police-constable or other Police Officer is authorised within the limits of the Act, to stop and search any wherry or boat in which he shall have reasonable ground for believing there are any Fish taken, or any Nets, Engines, Trimmers, Liggers, or other instruments used or intended to be used for the taking of Fish within such limits, in contravention of any Bye-law, and to seize and detain such Nets or other things, and to proceed in the matter in the mode prescribed by the said Act. And any person refusing to allow such wherry or boat to be so stopped and searched, or resisting or obstructing such search, will for every such offence be liable to a penalty of not exceeding £5.

## SALMON AND FRESH-WATER FISHERIES ACTS, 1861 TO 1886.

### Norfolk and Suffolk Fishery District.

Notice is Hereby Given, that on the 9th day of August, 1890, a Certificate was granted by the Board of Trade (by virtue of the power conferred upon them by the Provisions of the Salmon and Fresh-water Fisheries Acts, 1861 to 1886), confirming the following Bye-law made by the Conservators of the Norfolk and Suffolk Fisheries :—

Within the Counties of Norfolk and Suffolk no person shall use any snare, snatch wire, ligger, gun, spear (except an eel spear), or any net (except a fixed net for taking eels, or a landing net used as auxiliary to angling with rod and line), for the purpose of taking fresh-water fish in any dyke communicating with any navigable river within the Counties of Norfolk and Suffolk, within a distance of a quarter of a mile from such river, or in that portion of the River Waveney which lies below Bungay Bridge.

PENALTY CLAUSE.—Any person offending against these Bye-laws shall be liable to a penalty not exceeding five pounds for each such offence, and all nets, instruments, and devices used in contravention thereof, all fish found in the possession of a person contravening the same, and all fish caught by any such means, or in any such manner as is contrary thereto, shall be seized and may be forfeited on the summary conviction of the offender.

GEOFFREY FOWELL BUXTON,
*Honorary Secretary.*

## TABLES OF DISTANCES.

### COPY OF GOVERNMENT SURVEY.

#### THE YARE—FROM CARROW BRIDGE.

|  | MLS. | FUR. | YDS. |
|---|---|---|---|
| To Trowse Eye | 0 | 4 | 80 |
| ,, Thorpe Second Bridge | 1 | 4 | 180 |
| ,, Whitlingham Ferry | 2 | 0 | 110 |
| ,, Corby's Dyke | 2 | 2 | 0 |
| ,, Postwick Grove | 3 | 1 | 40 |
| ,, Postwick Hall | 3 | 6 | 0 |
| ,, Wood's End | 4 | 1 | 40 |
| ,, Wilde's Cottage | 4 | 4 | 0 |
| ,, Surlingham Ferry | 5 | 6 | 0 |
| ,, Coldham Hall | 7 | 5 | 44 |
| ,, Walpole's Reed Bush | 9 | 0 | 0 |
| ,, Buckenham Ferry | 10 | 1 | 0 |
| ,, Hasingham Dyke | 10 | 6 | 0 |
| ,, Langley Dyke | 11 | 7 | 0 |
| ,, Cantley Red House | 12 | 6 | 0 |

| | | MLS. | FUR. | YDS. |
|---|---|---|---|---|
| To | Devil's House | 13 | 2 | 0 |
| ,, | Hardley Mill | 14 | 0 | 0 |
| ,, | Hardley Dyke | 14 | 2 | 0 |
| ,, | Hardley Cross | 15 | 2 | 0 |
| ,, | Norton's Staithe | 15 | 3 | 0 |
| ,, | Reedham Ferry | 15 | 5 | 0 |
| ,, | Reedham End of New Cut | 17 | 0 | 0 |
| ,, | Upper Seven Mile House | 18 | 4 | 0 |
| ,, | Berney Arms | 20 | 6 | 0 |
| ,, | Burgh Flats | 21 | 0 | 0 |
| ,, | Yarmouth Drawbridge | 25 | 3 | 0 |
| ,, | Gorleston Pierhead | 27 | 2 | 0 |

### THE WAVENEY—FROM REEDHAM BRIDGE.

| | | MLS. | FUR. | YDS. |
|---|---|---|---|---|
| To | Herringfleet Bridge | 3 | 0 | 0 |
| ,, | Somerleyton Bridge | 4 | 5 | 0 |
| ,, | Oulton Dyke | 7 | 3 | 110 |
| ,, | Oulton Broad | 8 | 7 | 0 |
| ,, | Mutford Lock | 9 | 6 | 0 |
| ,, | Lowestoft Bridge | 11 | 4 | 0 |
| ,, | Lowestoft Pierhead | 11 | 6 | 0 |

### TABLE OF TIDES.

| High Water | Lowestoft * | 0 h. 43 m. later than Yarmouth Bar. | | |
|---|---|---|---|---|
| ,, | Reedham | 2 h. 30 m. | ,, | ,, |
| ,, | Harwich | 2 h. 50 m. | ,, | ,, |
| ,, | Cantley | 3 h. | ,, | ,, |
| ,, | Ipswich | 3 h. 15 m. | ,, | ,, |
| ,, | Acle Bridge | 3 h. 30 m. | ,, | ,, |
| ,, | Buckenham | 3 h. 30 m. | ,, | ,, |
| ,, | Coldham Hall | 4 h. | ,, | ,, |
| ,, | Oulton Broad | 4 h. | ,, | ,, |
| ,, | Horning | 4 h. | ,, | ,, |

The tide flows and ebbs in the Bure one hour later than at Yarmouth Bridge.

| | | | Springs | | Neaps | |
|---|---|---|---|---|---|---|
| The rise at | Oulton | is 2 | feet | | $1\frac{1}{4}$ | feet |
| ,, | Cantley | $2\frac{1}{2}$ | ,, | | $1\frac{1}{2}$ | ,, |
| ,, | Yarmouth | 6 | ,, | | $4\frac{1}{2}$ | ,, |
| ,, | Lowestoft | $6\frac{1}{2}$ | ,, | | $5\frac{1}{4}$ | ,, |
| ,, | Harwich | $11\frac{1}{2}$ | ,, | | $9\frac{3}{4}$ | ,, |

* The tide continues to run in the offing one hour later than in shore.

## EXTRACT FROM THE GREAT YARMOUTH PORT AND HAVEN ORDER, 1891.

### RIVER TOLLS ON VESSELS.

For every Vessel using the Rivers Yare, Bure and Waveney, or any of them, or any part thereof, for carrying goods, &c., or for Gift, Pay or Hire :

|  | s. | d. |
|---|---|---|
| If propelled by Steam or other mechanical power, per ton | 2 | 0 |
| If propelled in any other way, per ton | 1 | 0 |

For every Vessel, except Rowing Boats, used for pleasure only and not for Pay or Hire :

|  | s. | d. |
|---|---|---|
| Under 5 tons, per annum | 5 | 0 |
| Of 5 and under 10 tons, per annum | 10 | 0 |
| Of 10 tons and upwards, per annum | 15 | 0 |

The above Rates are payable for every year commencing on the 25th day of March, and are due on the day in each year on which the Vessel shall first float or be navigated.

The following is an extract from the Great Yarmouth Port and Haven Order, 1891 :—

SEC. 5. The Owner or Master of every vessel upon which any Rate or Toll is leviable under the second Schedule to this Order shall forthwith, upon this Order coming into operation, and thereafter once in every year, namely, on the 25th day of March, or on the day in every year commencing on the 25th day of March, on which every such vessel shall for the first time be used or navigated on any part of the rivers, cause every such vessel to be registered with the Commissioners, and for that purpose shall at the same time fill up and furnish to the Commissioners, or to the Collector of Rates, particulars for the registration of every such vessel in the form contained in the third Schedule to this Order, or in such other form as the Commissioners may from time to time require, and if any Owner or Master fail to supply the Commissioners with such particulars or give any false particular, he shall for every such offence forfeit not exceeding Ten Pounds.

SEC. 6. The tonnage or measurement of every vessel to be registered under the last preceding section shall, if so required by the Commissioners, be ascertained previously to such vessel being registered, and the mode of ascertaining the same shall be according to the following rule (that is to say)—

The length shall be taken in a straight line from the fore end to the after end of the loadwater line, and the breadth shall be taken from the outside of the outside plank in the broadest part of the vessel whether that shall be above or below the main wales inclusive of all manner of doubling planks (except the usual mouldings), then adding such breadth to the length and multiplying the sum thus obtained by itself and the product by the breadth and dividing the final product by 1730 the quotient shall be˙ deemed to be the tonnage. Provided always that fractions of a ton shall be reckoned as one ton.

## THE GREAT YARMOUTH PORT AND HAVEN ACTS, 1866 & 1900.

BYE-LAWS for the Registration, Numbering, Regulation, and Control of Pleasure Vessels used on the River Yare and for other purposes thereunder.*

*By virtue and in exercise of the Great Yarmouth Port and Haven Acts, 1866 and 1900, and the Acts incorporated therewith,*

*We, the Great Yarmouth Port and Haven Commissioners, do make the following Bye-laws for the Registration, Numbering, Regulation and Control of Pleasure Vessels used on the Rivers Yare, Bure and Waveney, and for other purposes, that is to say—*

1. These Bye-laws may be cited as " The Yare," " The Bure," and " The Waveney " Bye-laws, 1901, and shall come into operation immediately on the same being confirmed by the Board of Trade.

2. In these Bye-laws the words and expressions hereinafter mentioned shall have the meanings hereby assigned to them respectively unless there be something in the subject or context repugnant thereto, viz. :—

> The expression " The Commissioners " shall mean the Norwich Commissioners.
>
> The expression " The Yare " or " river " shall mean and include all such parts of the Rivers Yare and Wensum or Wenson, otherwise Yare, and the navigable branches thereof, and of the Shores and Banks of the same rivers and branches as are within the Port and are not within the Haven.
>
> The expression " The Bure " or " river " shall mean and include all such parts of the River Bure and the navigable branches thereof, and of the Shores and Banks of the same

* These Bye-laws were framed and came into force some years after the body of this book was written. This note more particularly refers to Bye-law No. 12, sub-section 4.—*The Author.*

river and branches as are within the Port and are not within the Haven, as defined by the Haven Act, 1866.

The expression " The Waveney " or " river " shall mean and include all such parts of the River Waveney and branches thereof, and of the Breydon and Burgh Flats and of the Shores and Banks of the same river, branches and flats as are within the Port and are not within the Haven, as defined by the Haven Act, 1866, but shall not mean or include Oulton Dyke or Oulton Broad, or any of the shores or banks of Oulton Dyke or Oulton Broad.

The word " Master " when used in relation to any vessel shall be understood to mean the person having the command or charge of the vessel for the time being.

The expression " pleasure boat " includes any boat, pleasure wherry, house boat, skiff, dinghy, punt, canoe or yacht, and craft of every kind, whether propelled by sails, steam, electricity, or any other motive power, and not being used exclusively for rowing, or solely as a tug, or for the cartage of goods.

## REGISTRATION.

3. These Bye-laws shall not apply to any pleasure boat visiting the said rivers from another river, not being the Yare, Bure or Waveney, and used upon the said rivers for not more than 14 days in any year, or excused from Registration by the Commissioners by a resolution in writing.

4. Every pleasure boat except as aforesaid used or intended to be used upon the said rivers, shall be registered and marked as in these Bye-laws provided.

5. No person shall use or assist or be concerned in using or cause or suffer to be used upon any part of the said rivers any pleasure boat, unless such boat shall be registered and marked as in these Bye-laws provided.

6. No person shall hire or let for hire, or hold out or offer for hire, or suffer or permit to be let for hire, any pleasure boat to be used upon the said rivers, or to ply for hire with any pleasure boat upon the said rivers unless the same shall be registered and marked as in these Bye-laws provided.

7. Every person applying to the Commissioners for registration of a pleasure boat shall furnish to the Commissioners in writing upon a form to be obtained at the Tonnage Office of the Commissioners at Carrow Bridge, Norwich, or at the office for the time being of the Commissioners, or from such of the officers or servants of the Commissioners as may be from time to time supplied with such form correct information as to the particulars following, that is to say :—

(a) The true name and usual residence of the owner thereof.

(b) The number of such pleasure boats belonging to such owner.

(c) The class to which each of such pleasure boats belongs, as for example, skiff, wherry, yacht, dinghy, punt or otherwise, as the case may be.

(1) At the time of making such application for registration, the applicant shall pay to the Commissioners the sum of two shillings and sixpence for every boat to be registered.

(2) The Commissioners may, if they shall think fit, before complying with any application for registration of a pleasure boat, require such pleasure boat to be measured by such person in the employment of the Commissioners as they shall think fit, such measurement to be ascertained in accordance with the provisions of Section 30 of the Haven Act, 1900.

(3) Upon registration, there shall be appropriated by the Commissioners to the owner of every such pleasure boat a number to be called the "boat's number," and such number shall be entered in the register together with the full name and address of the owner and the date of registration, and shall be appropriated to such person in respect of such boat.

(4) Upon registration of every such boat there shall be furnished to the person registering the same, a certificate containing the name in full and residence of the registered owner and the boat's number and the date of such registration, and such other particulars as the Commissioners shall think fit.

(5) Every such boat shall have fixed in a conspicuous position on such boat the boat's number, which number shall be plainly legible black figures on a white ground, on a plate of an oval shape, and not less than four inches by three inches. The plate shall be provided by the Commissioners at the time of registration, and shall be placed by the owner on the tabernacle, or not more than three feet above the deck line, or in the case of an open boat shall be placed on the mast thwart. The boat shall not be used after such registration until the plate has been so fixed, nor except whilst such plate is plainly visible thereon. If the boat be not navigated on the river in any year commencing on 25th March, the plate shall be returned to the Commissioners by the owner of the pleasure boat immediately after the following 25th March, and the registration shall be cancelled.

8. Every person applying to the Commissioners for renewal of

the registration of or certificate or plate for a pleasure boat, shall furnish the same information and make the same payment as is hereinbefore prescribed with reference to the first registration or certificate, and every such renewed registration and certificate shall have effect from the date thereof.

9. Upon every transfer of the ownership of a pleasure boat registered under these Bye-laws, the transferor shall, and the transferee may forthwith give to the Commissioners notice in writing of such transfer, and the Commissioners shall in either case upon payment of the prescribed fee, cause the transferee's name and address to be inserted in the register in the place of the name of the transferor, and until such notice shall have been given the transferor shall for all the purposes of the Great Yarmouth Port and Haven Acts, 1866 and 1900, and of these Bye-laws and of all other Bye-laws, rules, orders and regulations of the Commissioners for the time being in force, be deemed to be the owner of such pleasure boat.

(1) Upon every such transfer of ownership, the person previously registered as the owner of such pleasure boat, shall return to the Commissioners at the Office of the Commissioners, the certificate for the time being in force in respect of such boat.

(2) Immediately upon the granting of a fresh certificate, the certificate previously in force in respect of the same boat shall become void.

10. Notwithstanding anything contained in the preceding Bye-laws relating to registration, the Commissioners may, if in the case of any particular pleasure boat they shall think fit by writing under the hand of their Clerk or other officer, duly appointed for that purpose by the Commissioners, require or sanction the marking of any such boat in some manner different from that required under the foregoing Bye-laws, and in such case such boat shall be marked according to such writing.

11. Any name, number or other distinctive mark or thing by these Bye-laws required to be placed or kept, in, upon or about any pleasure boat, shall be placed in a conspicuous position, and if outside the boat above the water-line, and shall be kept and maintained by the owner of every such boat in a cleanly and plainly distinguishable condition, and to the satisfaction of the Commissioners.

(1) No person shall knowingly conceal or cause or suffer to be concealed, any name, number, or other distinctive mark or thing by these Bye-laws required to be kept, in, upon or about any pleasure boat.

(2) Every certificate of registration when issued, shall be subject to the condition that the owner or other person in charge of the vessel to which the same relates, shall, on demand, either produce the certificate, or show the registration

plate or boat's number, to any officer of the Commissioners, and to any officer or constable of the Norwich City Police force, and to any Police officer or constable acting for any of the Counties of Norfolk and Suffolk, or any borough the police jurisdiction of which extends to any place upon the river.

12. No person shall, while using, or while in, upon or about the River Yare, Bure or Waveney or the banks or shore thereof, or any land of the Commissioners, do or cause, or incite any other person to do any of the acts specified in the following sub-sections of this Bye-law.

    (1) Commit any offence against decency or be otherwise disorderly, or bathe without proper bathing dress or drawers.

    (2) Use obscene, scandalous, abusive, indecent or improper language to the annoyance of any person who shall lawfully be using, or who shall lawfully be in or about the River Yare or the banks or shores thereof.

    (3) Do any act which may cause damage to any person or property, or occasion a nuisance, obstruction or annoyance to the public or to any person.

    (4) Use any fire-arm or air-gun. Provided always that this sub-section shall not affect the rights of the riparian owners of land on either side of the river.

    (5) Do any act injuriously affecting the safety or amenity of the river.

13. Any person acting in contravention of any of these Bye-laws, shall for every such breach be liable to a penalty not exceeding £5, which said penalty shall be recoverable, enforced and applied according to the provisions of the Great Yarmouth Port and Haven Acts, 1866 and 1900, and the Harbours, Docks and Piers Clauses Act, 1847.

*Given under the Common Seal of the Great Yarmouth Port and Haven Commissioners, this seventeenth day of January, 1901.*

HARRY BULLARD, *Chairman.*
J. TOLVER WATERS, *Clerk.*

*The Board of Trade hereby confirm the foregoing Bye-laws.*

T. H. W. PELHAM,
*Assistant Secretary.*

BOARD OF TRADE, *7th June,* 1901.

# INDEX